# Common Core, PECL and DCFR: could they change shipping and transport law?

Editors:
Wouter Verheyen
Frank G.M. Smeele
Marian A.I.H. Hoeks

# Common Core, PECL and DCFR: could they change shipping and transport law?

intersentia

METRO

Ius Commune Europaeum

Wouter Verheyen, Frank G.M. Smeele and Marian A.I.H. Hoeks (eds.)

Common Core, PECL and DCFR: could they change shipping and transport law?

Intersentia Publishing Ltd
Sheraton House | Castle Park
Cambridge | CB3 0AX | United Kingdom
Tel.: +44 1223 370 170 | Email: mail@intersentia.co.uk

ISBN 978-1-78068-332-4
D/2015/7849/84
NUR 822



British Library Cataloguing in Publication Data. A catalogue record for this book is available from the British Library.

Wouter Verheyen

## PREFACE

Common core, PECL and DCFR, could they change shipping and transport law? This question was included in the call for papers for the 8th European Colloquium on Maritime Law Research (ECMLR) that was hosted by the Rotterdam Institute for Shipping & Transport Law of the Erasmus University Rotterdam. Even though this question goes beyond traditional transport law research, 23 scholars from 18 Universities went outside their comfort zone and answered it, all from their own field of expertise. With this, this conference created a unique cross fertilization of sometimes very specialist areas of shipping and transport law and general contract law. As we are convinced that this fruitful conference can contribute to the debate on future harmonisation of shipping law, but also on general contract law harmonization instruments, speakers were invited to submit an article for this book.

The great response to the call suggests that even though harmonization of shipping and transport law has a much greater tradition than harmonization of general private law, still shipping and transport law could be impacted by and even benefit from the harmonization instruments. This should come as no surprise. First of all, if these harmonisation instruments would *de lege ferenda*, result in an (optional) European instrument, this can also have a great impact on harmonisation of shipping and transport law. Secondly, these harmonisation instruments could possibly bring solutions to fragmentation that still exists in many fields of shipping and transport law.

However, there is also a possible indirect impact, as (inter)national rules could get 'contaminated' by the rules underlying such European instrument.

A great number of contributions allow to assess the possible impact of such optional instruments, as answers to specific questions are compared under (national) shipping and transport law on the one hand, and the harmonisation instruments on the other. For example the contribution of professor TETTENBORN specifically investigates the potential impact on English shipping law of the introduction of a universal idea of good faith through the medium of possible European contract harmonisation. Similarly the possible impact on third party rights under shipping documents under English law is investigated by professor LAMONT-BLACK. Finally professor THOMAS investigates agreed damages clauses in charterparties under both regimes. While professor TETTENBORN is rather pessimistic about the possible impact of the harmonisation instruments, professor LAMONT-BLACK comes to the conclusion that implementation of the DCFR third party rules throughout, including the whole of shipping and transport law, would have potential for welcome simplification of English law. These diverging opinions can also be found in dr. ORRÙ's contribution on unexpected circumstances in shipping contracts, professor PELLEGRINO's contribution on general principals and dr. GARCÍA ALVAREZ's contribution on liability for other persons with a focus on the differences between (inter) national law and the harmonisation instruments on these specific points. Dr. OSANTE introduces the Principles of European Insurance Law and investigates whether they can impact marine insurance. Finally mr. CONSTENLA argues that the EU should not (ab)use harmonisation instruments to navigate around international conventions.

A second possible impact lies in the fact that despite the long standing tradition, unification of shipping and transport law didn't go as far as would be desirable from a trade perspective as on many points there are cracks in uniformity. Further unification of private law aspects of shipping and transport law seems therefore highly desirable. Nevertheless, some legislative fatigue has crept into unification of private law aspects of shipping and transport law. To remedy these shortcomings, a two-fold role can come to the harmonisation instruments. First of all from a methodological point of view, the grassroots perspective taken by harmonisation instruments could offer an example for shipping and transport law. Second, the provisions of the harmonisation instruments could be useful when developing future European shipping and transport law instruments, but could also be very beneficial as a tool for gap-filling. Thus, contractual incorporation of one of these instruments could for example create a neutral gap-filling mechanism. In this book it is examined, for three prominent causes of fragmentation in shipping and transport law, whether the harmonisation instruments could contribute to uniform shipping and transport law.

A first cause of fragmentation is that some important areas of transport law are still excluded from uniform law. The lack of such uniform rules in these fields is often also detrimental for uniformity in unified fields of law. For example, the lack of uniform rules on transport intermediaries impacts the qualification by national courts of a service provider as a carrier or rather as a transport intermediary and creates therefore also a crack in uniform carriage law. The possible impact of the harmonisation instruments on the law of transport intermediaries is addressed by dr. KOZUBOVSKAYA PELLÉ and dr. VERHEYEN. While these authors are relatively sceptical about the possible role for the harmonisation instruments in this field, dr. MAGKLASI's contribution illustrates how the harmonisation instruments could be a useful help in the interpretation of volume contracts under the Rotterdam Rules. Finally dr. INGRATOCI's contribution investigates the impact of the rules on non-contractual liability on the classification societies extra-contractual liability, a matter that is likewise not governed by uniform legislation.

Secondly, even in fields that are unified, there is often only a partial unification, addressing only specific questions. Consequently other questions are left outside the unification. Again, fields that are left outside unification can strongly impact the uniformity of decisions in cases subject to uniform law. For example, the lack of uniform rules on contract interpretation and validity of the contract will obviously impact the interpretation of contracts subject to uniform law in different member states, and will can also lead to diverging court decisions in these member states.

Finally, even for subjects falling within the scope of uniform law, uniform rules are often nonetheless interpreted in a different way by national courts, as these courts read their national law concepts into the uniform rules. This prevents these uniform legislations from resulting in uniform law. Therefore professor LEGROS examines whether the harmonisation instruments could be useful to interpret shipping law.

Even though the future and eventual impact on shipping and transport law of the harmonisation instruments is uncertain, after reading this book, the reader should be able to answer the research question himself: Common core, PECL and DCFR, could they change shipping and transport law?

CONTENTS

Cécile Legros*

# COMMON CORE, PECL AND DCFR: COULD THEY BE USED TO INTERPRET SHIPPING LAW?

## I. Introduction

1. For some years now, European institutions have launched several working groups focused on the development of a harmonized European contract law. This resulted in several works, especially The Principles of European Contract Law – PECL[1], and The Draft Common Frame of Reference – DCFR[2], both aimed to constitute the basis for a future European Civil code. The Principles of European Contract Law are a set of model rules drawn up by leading contract law academics in Europe.[3] They attempt to elucidate basic rules of contract law and more generally the law of obligations which most legal systems of the Member States of the European Union hold in common. The PECL are based on the concept of a uniform European contract law system. The DCFR adopts a wider approach which is not confined to contract law. It provides first general "Principles" considered as universally applicable to European legal systems, and further "model rules" to be used as models for drafting contracts or even law making, like for instance UNCITRAL Model laws. These rules can also govern contracts if voluntarily incorporated by the contracting parties.

2. Currently, such texts do not constitute hard law, as they have not been incorporated into normative Acts. One of the legal proposal issued from these works, the recent Commission Proposal for a 'Regulation on a Common European Sales Law (CESL)'[4], is still pending. However, these works, even if remaining at the stage of soft law, may be useful to solve some issues raised by international contracts. Indeed, as announced by

* Professor at the University of Rouen- Normandy University Institute of International Transport Law (IDIT).

1 Original version (Part I) in 1995 (revised in 1998); Part II in 1999; Parts I and II revised in 2002; Part III issued in 2002.

2 Ch. Von Bar, E. Clive and H. Schulte-Nolke, *Principles, Definitions, Model Rules of European Private Law – Draft Common Frame of reference (DCFR)* (Sellier. European Law publ. 2009).

3 Works were carried out by the Commission on European Contract Law (an independent organization) and started in 1982 under the chairmanship of Ole Lando, a Danish professor.

4 Brussels, 11.10.2011 COM (2011) 635 final – 2011/0284 (COD).

Chapter one itself of the PECL entitled 'General Provisions': 'These Principles are intended to be applied as general rules of contract law in the European Communities'. The relevance of these works lies in the fact that they propose rules, acceptable and compatible with both Civil and Common Law systems, and beyond, with all domestic contract law of the 28 European Member States. Such Principles could constitute a 29$^{th}$ regime for international contracts, as the Commission's proposal for a Regulation on a Common European Sales Law.

**3.** But in the field of shipping law, the question arising is the following: are they of any use for operators dealing with shipping law? If the answer is yes, or why not, it raises many issues to be dealt with. This paper focuses on one aspect which is interpretation. A general definition of this term can be found in the Cambridge dictionary as an explanation or opinion of what something means. A more legal definition could be the following: 'The art or process of discovering and expounding the intended signification of the language used in a statute, will, contract, or any other written document, that is, the meaning which the author designed it to convey to others[5]'. Applied to interpreting a law, a statute or a contract, it consists in explaining the meaning and scope of an obscure or ambiguous text. This question is critical in international relations, and obviously as for the uniformisation of international transport. Among the great variety of international sources governing transports in general, the place of international conventions is prominent. But one of the limits of the harmonization process is the lack of *supra*-national Court empowered to rule on such cases.[6] Thus, international conventions are implemented by national Courts. But when they face questions of interpretation, they are often likely adopting interpretations based upon domestic concepts, forgetting the international character of the interpreted text or contract. Many works have been carried on the different ways to improve uniform interpretation of international uniform law. The concern here is to discuss whether European Common Core developed in the past decades in the EU could settle the issue of interpretation discrepancies.

**4.** Two main types of sources are concerned with legal interpretation: legal sources (International Conventions, domestic laws, Statutes, European Regulations) and contracts. However, rules governing interpretation of international instruments are different from those governing interpretation of contracts. The first falls within the competence of international public law, while contract law governs the following. The idea of interpreting those sources with European soft law instruments is relevant as both PECL and DCFR contain specific provisions on interpretation of contracts.[7] Thus, PECL provisions or general guidelines of DCFR seem to be likely to provide satisfactory solutions to current interpretation issues related to international contacts. But are they

5 *The Law Dictionary Featuring Black's Law Dictionary*, Free Online Legal Dictionary (2nd Ed.).

6 The CMR Convention however contains a provisions giving jurisdiction to the International Court of Justice to settle dispute between Contracting Parties relating to the interpretation or application of this Convention (Art. 47). But this provision has never been used so far.

7 PECL – Chapter 5: Interpretation; DCFR – Book II – Chapter 8: Interpretation.

relevant for shipping law? To try to answer these questions, we will take a two-phase approach. First considering the scope of application of these texts (I). Indeed, it seems necessary to check whether shipping issues are covered or not by these instruments. Then, the content of these interpretation provisions will be analysed (II). Both questions will be dealt with regarding relevance towards shipping law.

## II. Scope of Application of PECL & DCFR

5. Both PECL and DCFR define their scope of application. As regards shipping law, it seems necessary to analyse whether these scopes cover or not such domain. The material scope of these instruments (1.), their geographical scope (2.) and finally their recipients (3.) will be successively analysed.

### *2.1. Material scope*

6. Both PECL and DCFR specifically address contract law, thus DCFR scope of application is wider.[8] As they constitute a common body of law governing contracts, these texts have been designed to apply to all types of contracts. As a consequence, they should be relevant for shipping contracts, and therefore interpretation of such contracts.[9] The delicate issue with regards interpretation is interpretation of Law in the narrow sense of the word, ie legal instruments.

7. ***Interpretation of contracts.*** As regards general contract Law applied to shipping contracts, both PECL and DCFR aim to constitute a common core for international contracts. PECL provisions are very general and contain basic rules governing contracts. What is called in France 'le droit commun des contrats'. DCFR are more developed as they deal first with general contract rules, and later Book IV addresses specific contracts. But shipping contracts are not mentioned amongst these. It infers that the drafters of these principles did not consider such contracts needed to be addressed specifically and could satisfy with general contract law provisions. These contracts are even excluded from the section dedicated to service contracts.[10] We must come to the conclusion that shipping contracts are only governed by general contract rules under these instruments.

8 PECL: Article 1:101 (1): 'Application of the Principles'. The scope of application of DCFR is wider: Book I – Article I. – 1:101: 'Intended field of application': '(1) These rules are intended to be used primarily in relation to contracts and other juridical acts, contractual and non-contractual rights and obligations and related property matters'.

9 Negotiable instruments are however excluded from the scope of application of DCFR Article 1:101 (2 d). Such exclusions only have a warning function, aiming at noting that the rules have not been drafted taking these excluded specific matters in mind. But they do not forbid the use of these rules for such matters, provided that the users make adaptation.

10 IV. C. – 1:102: 'Exclusions': This Part does not apply to contracts in so far as they are for transport, insurance, the provision of a security or the supply of a financial product or a financial service.

**8.** ***Interpretation of legal instruments.*** As for interpretation of Law, it must be noted that both PECL and DCFR provisions on interpretation do not address Law interpretation but only interpretation of contracts. This raises the following question: Would it be possible to use these instruments to interpret Law and in particular shipping Law, that is international conventions, domestic law, or even European regulations? Such a proposal is sensible as, like Unidroit Principles[11], PECL and DCFR contain provisions related to their own interpretation which could possibly be used to interpret legal instruments.[12] But, if we stick to the words employed in these texts, PECL and DCFR seem however irrelevant to interpret shipping Law. Indeed, these provisions concern the interpretation of the instrument itself. For obvious reasons, domestic laws, and EU Regulations should not be interpreted with soft law instruments drafted for contracts. The conclusion could be different as for interpretation of international conventions.[13] Indeed, current methods of interpretation of international conventions are not so different than those designed for contracts as international convention are also agreements between parties. The analysis of Article 31 of the Vienna Convention on Treaties[14] shows various provisions very similar to those drafted for contracts. In this sense, using PECL and DCFR interpretation provisions could be considered when interpreting conventional instruments. But we must admit that such a proposal is quite artificial. First, it is incompatible with public international law principles, especially hierarchy of norms. Besides, the European origin of these works clearly prevents them from being used to interpret non-EU instruments.

**9.** As a consequence, we must come to the conclusion that PECL and DCFR scope of application should limit to interpretation of shipping contracts, thus excluding interpretation of international conventions. Such instruments prove to be useless to solve interpretation discrepancies of shipping conventions.

## *2.2. Geographical scope*

**10.** PECL and DCFR are European texts applicable to contracts. Should they apply only to European contracts or could they apply more broadly?

***European contracts.*** PECL and DCFR have been drafted at the initiative of European institutions, by European scholars. The aim of these works is to provide European institutions and operators with a set of common rules forming the basis of a harmonized European contract law. In the introduction of DCFR and especially in the paragraph entitled 'Purposes of DCFR', several references are made to EU Law, though in the article dedicated to the scope of application of these model rules, no geographical reference appears.[15] By contrast, according to Article 1:101, paragraph 1 of PECL, these principles

[11] Chapter I: General provision: Art. 1.6.

[12] See under page 6.

[13] F. Latty et S. Touzé (dir.), 'Les techniques interprétatives de la norme internationale', *Revue générale de droit international public* 2011/2.

[14] Vienna Convention on the Law of Treaties (1969).

[15] DCFR- Book I – General Provisions – Article I-1:101: 'Intended Field of Application.'

apply in the European Communities. So far, they are certainly likely to rule European contracts, provided that such contracts could be defined. The 2nd paragraph of Article 1:101 precises that PECL only apply on a voluntary basis, through incorporation into a contract. But paragraph 3 goes further as PECL are declared to be applicable when parties have 'agreed that their contract is to be governed by "general principles of law", the "lex mercatoria"' (a), or, 'not chosen any system or rules of law to govern their contract' (b)[16], meaning they may be declared applicable by Courts, or more likely by arbitrators even if not chosen by the contracting parties. As a result, even if these principles have a European origin, they may be applicable to any international contract if chosen by the parties according to paragraph 1. But, when not designated by the parties, my opinion is that only arbitrators could apply such Principles on the grounds of paragraph 3. As for European Member States' Courts, as PECL is soft law, judges cannot apply them under Rome I regulation[17], in the absence of specific reference in the contract itself. However, although the PECL preamble declares them to be part of *Lex mercatoria*, it is doubtful that such principles could be considered as equivalent to "general principles of law", the "lex mercatoria" or the like, for several reasons all related to their origin. First, their European origin limits their universality. Besides, their academic origin stands in contradiction with such assimilation. *Lex mercatoria* is precisely a set of rules founding its sources in professional practice and it would be rather paradoxal to consider an academic work as equivalent. Of course, it is undeniable that such principles intend partly to codify trade practices[18], but the very nature of these rules are fundamentally opposed. At least such principles could eventually become part of *Lex mercatoria* if used by courts or arbitrators.[19] Obviously however, arbitrators to 'European' contracts could possibly apply these rules. But what is a European shipping contract? Is it a contract concluded between parties established in the EU? A contract performed in the UE? A contract governed by a European domestic Law, even subsidiarily? In the absence of an official definition, arbitrators using such principles should justify the application of these sources from a geographical point of view.

**11.** Assuming that PECL and DCFR can be applied to European shipping contracts, could they also apply to non-European contracts?

***Non-European contracts.*** Could the examined provisions be applied to contracts outside the EU, on a domestic or international scale? This interrogation is particularly

16 See Unidroit Principles – PREAMBLE (Purpose of the Principles §3) stating in the same way '*They may be applied when the parties have agreed that their contract be governed by general principles of law, the lex mercatoria or the like.*'

17 Recital 13 of the Preamble of REGULATION (EC) No 593/2008 OF THE EUROPEAN PARLIAMENT AND OF THE COUNCIL of 17 June 2008 on the law applicable to contractual obligations (Rome I) authorizes parties to incorporate by into their contract a non-State body of law or an international convention, but under French interpretation, designation of a soft maw set of rules cannot be considered as a choice of Law under article 3.

18 Indeed, The PECL were inspired by the United Nations Convention on Contracts for the International Sale of Goods (CISG) from 1980, which is considered somehow as a codification of lex mercatoria regarding international sales' Law.

19 E. Loquin, 'Les rapports entre le droit modelisé et la lex mercatoria', [2003] *Petites affiches* 63.

relevant as regards to shipping law which extent is rather global than regional. If chosen by the parties to govern a shipping contract, the answer is certainly yes. Nothing prohibits it. But on the grounds of paragraph 3 of *Article 1:101* of PECL, it is unlikely that court or arbitrators would consider such rules as part of *Lex mercatoria*, or apply them when no choice of law has been made as regards contracts outside the scope of EU. Indeed, such principles may be regarded as reflecting European Common Law but it is questionable whether their application could be extended outside Europe. However, it must be noted that they are on many points very similar to Unidroit Principles, and could be thus taken as general principles of contract law by arbitrators.

### *2.3. Recipients*

**12.** Finally, must be considered the recipients of such soft Law. According to these texts, the potential users are contracting parties, courts and arbitrators, and finally legislators. As regards to interpretation, the first recipient of these rules should be the contracting parties or their legal advisers confronted to a different interpretation from the parties to an agreement. But more likely, interpretation issues arise when there is a dispute. Thus, recipients of these instruments are judges in a broad sense. Provided that these rules apply on a voluntary basis, through incorporation into a contract, courts (ECJ, Domestic courts) are bound by them, as well as arbitrators. But, if the parties have made no specific reference to me, only arbitrators could apply such rules if the contract is considered as European. One of the other possible uses of DCFR is to serve as model-law for European legislators, both EU institutions and Member States. Thus, interpretations provisions, like all provisions of this common core, could be used by legislators when drafting legal texts on international contracts, like for instance a possible regulation on multimodal transport.[20] From now on, we will consider that PECL or DCFR may govern shipping contracts. Thus, it is now time to analyse the specific provisions related to interpretation to ensure their relevancy for this type of contracts.

## III. PECL & DCFR Interpretation Provisions

**13.** First will be analysed the content of the specific provisions on interpretation, and then their relevancy for shipping contracts.

### *3.1. Content of the provisions*

**14.** Both texts contain general and specific provisions related to interpretation.[21] General references to good faith and fair dealing, uniformity of application, legal

[20] See: *"European Multimodal Sustainable Transport: Quo Vadis?"*, Colloquium held in September 2014, Institute of International Economic Law, University of Helsinki. Also See: InterTran project: www.helsinki.fi/katti/english/InterTran-project.htm.

[21] PECL – Chap. 1: General Provisions – Section 1; Scope of the Principles – Section 2; General Obligations -Article 1:201 ff.; DCFR – Book I – General Provisions Article I-1:102.

certainty can be found. Such general principles are frequently used when dealing with interpretation.

15. ***General provisions on interpretation*** relate to the interpretation of the instrument itself.

> *PECL*CHAPTER 1: GENERAL PROVISIONS
> **Section 1: Scope of the Principles**
> *Article 1:106: Interpretation and Supplementation*
> (1) These Principles should be interpreted and developed in accordance with their purposes. In particular, regard should be had to the need to promote good faith and fair dealing, certainty in contractual relationships and uniformity of application.
> (2) Issues within the scope of these Principles but not expressly settled by them are so far as possible to be settled in accordance with the ideas underlying the Principles. Failing this, the legal system applicable by virtue of the rules of private international law is to be applied.
>
> **Section 2: General Obligations** -*Article 1:201 (ex art. 1.106): Good Faith and Fair Dealing*

> *DCFR*
> **Book I** – ***General Provisions***
> *Article I-1:102: INTERPRETATION AND DEVELOPMENT*
> (1) These rules are to be interpreted and developed autonomously and in accordance with their objectives and the principles underlying them.
> (2) They are to be read in the light of any applicable instruments guaranteeing human rights and fundamental freedoms and any applicable constitutional laws.
> (3) In their interpretation and development regard should be had to the need to promote:
> (a) uniformity of application;
> (b) good faith and fair dealing; and
> (c) legal certainty.

16. These general provision focuses on overall consistency of the interpretation, taking into account the purpose of the instrument and the 'underlying principles'.[22] The first paragraph of both texts refers to the interpretation of the instrument itself. These provisions intend to provide guidance on an appropriate interpretative approach for legislative drafters, judges, arbitrators, or even searchers. The second paragraph of *Article 1:106 of PECL* contemplates the issues not expressly settled by the Principles. In

22 DCFR 'Underlying principles' (Introduction, §15) are freedom, security, justice and efficiency.

such case, the interpreter is encouraged to follow nevertheless the 'underlying principles', or, to apply the relevant legal determined by conflict of law rules.

17. The reference to uniformity of application though autonomous interpretation is significant at it is precisely one of the major goals of these instruments. The reference to good faith and fair dealing also constitute a fundamental guideline of these provisions. Such guidelines however may give Courts too much power which justifies them to be balanced by legal certainty. These interpretation principles are common to several legal systems. Indeed, these works are supposed to reflect a common legal European approach on several questions. In a certain way, they can certainly be considered as "general principles of European law", and thus applied to European shipping contracts.

18. ***Specific provisions related to interpretation.*** As regards interpretation, these instruments also contain specific provisions precisely dedicated to contracts which are essentially identical, as DCFR is indeed inspired of PECL. As a consequence, only DCFR provisions, which are the more recent and the more developed will be commented, except when PECL provides for significant differences.

*PECL*
**CHAPTER 5: INTERPRETATION (Article 5:101 and following).**

*Article 5:101 (Ex art. 7.101/ 101A): General Rules of Interpretation*
(1) A contract is to be interpreted according to the common intention of the parties even if this differs from the literal meaning of the words. (2) If it is established that one party intended the contract to have a particular meaning, and at the time of the conclusion of the contract the other party could not have been unaware of the first party's intention, the contract is to be interpreted in the way intended by the first party. (3) If an intention cannot be established according to (1) or (2), the contract is to be interpreted according to the meaning that reasonable persons of the same kind as the parties would give to it in the same circumstances.
*Article 5:102 (ex art. 7.102): Relevant Circumstances*
In interpreting the contract, regard shall be had, in particular, to:(a) the circumstances in which it was concluded, including the preliminary negotiations;(b) the conduct of the parties, even subsequent to the conclusion of the contract;(c) the nature and purpose of the contract;(d) the interpretation which has already been given to similar clauses by the parties and the practices they have established between themselves;(e) the meaning commonly given to terms and expressions in the branch of activity concerned and the interpretation similar clauses may already have received;(f) usages; and(g) good faith and fair dealing
*Article 5.103 (ex art. 7.103): Contra Proferentem Rule*
Where there is doubt about the meaning of a contract term not individually negotiated, an interpretation of the term against the party who supplied it is to be preferred.

*Article 5:104 (ex art. 7.104): Preference to Negotiated Terms*
Terms which have been individually negotiated take preference over those which are not.
*Article 5:105 (ex art. 7.105): Reference to Contract as a Whole*
Terms are interpreted in the light of the whole contract in which they appear.
*Article 5:106 (ex art. 7.106): Terms to Be Given (Full) Effect*
An interpretation which renders the terms of the contract lawful, or effective, is to be preferred to one which would not.
*Article 5:107 (ex art. 7.107): Linguistic Discrepancies*
Where a contract is drawn up in two or more language versions none of which is stated to be authoritative, there is, in case of discrepancy between the versions, a preference for the interpretation according to the version in which the contract was originally drawn up.

*DCFR*
**Book II** – ***Contracts and other judicial Acts***
**CHAPTER 8: INTERPRETATION**
**Section 1: Interpretation of contracts**
*II. – 8:101: General rules*
(1) A contract is to be interpreted according to the common intention of the parties even if this differs from the literal meaning of the words.
(2) If one party intended the contract, or a term or expression used in it, to have a particular meaning, and at the time of the conclusion of the contract the other party was aware, or could reasonably be expected to have been aware, of the first party's intention, the contract is to be interpreted in the way intended by the first party.
(3) The contract is, however, to be interpreted according to the meaning which a reasonable person would give to it:
  (a) if an intention cannot be established under the preceding paragraphs; or
  (b) if the question arises with a person, not being a party to the contract or a person who by law has no better rights than such a party, who has reasonably and in good faith relied on the contract's apparent meaning.

*II. – 8:102: Relevant matters*
(1) In interpreting the contract, regard may be had, in particular, to:
  (a) the circumstances in which it was concluded, including the preliminary negotiations;
  (b) the conduct of the parties, even subsequent to the conclusion of the contract;
  (c) the interpretation which has already been given by the parties to terms or expressions which are the same as, or similar to, those used in the contract and the practices they have established between themselves;

(d) the meaning commonly given to such terms or expressions in the branch of activity concerned and the interpretation such terms or expressions may already have received;
(e) the nature and purpose of the contract;
(f) usages; and
(g) good faith and fair dealing.

(2) In a question with a person, not being a party to the contract or a person such as an assignee who by law has no better rights than such a party, who has reasonably and in good faith relied on the contract's apparent meaning, regard may be had to the circumstances mentioned in sub-paragraphs (a) to (c) above only to the extent that those circumstances were known to, or could reasonably be expected to have been known to, that person.

*II. – 8:103: Interpretation against supplier of term or dominant party*

(1) Where there is doubt about the meaning of a term not individually negotiated, an interpretation of the term against the party who supplied it is to be preferred.
(2) Where there is doubt about the meaning of any other term, and that term has been established under the dominant influence of one party, an interpretation of the term against that party is to be preferred.

*II. – 8:104: Preference for negotiated terms*

Terms which have been individually negotiated take preference over those which have not.

*II. – 8:105: Reference to contract as a whole*

Terms and expressions are to be interpreted in the light of the whole contract in which they appear.

*II. – 8:106: Preference for interpretation which gives terms effect*

An interpretation which renders the terms of the contract lawful, or effective, is to be preferred to one which would not.

*II. – 8:107: Linguistic discrepancies*

Where a contract document is in two or more language versions none of which is stated to be authoritative, there is, in case of discrepancy between the versions, a preference for the interpretation according to the version in which the contract was originally drawn up.

**19.** *Article II: 8:101* (1) *DCFR 'General Rules of Interpretation'*[23], provides for a subjective method of interpretation, based upon primacy of the common intention of the parties. Such method exists in both Common Law and Civil Law, even if EU domestic Courts may combine differently subjective and objective approach. When a common intention cannot be discerned, paragraph 2 recommends taking account of the knowledge of the other party's intention. Subsidiarily, paragraph 3, encourages to employ an objective method of interpretation, by taking an external view. Recourse to the understanding of

[23] Identical to Article 5:101 PECL.

a reasonable person does not explicitly exist under French Law, but using objective criteria like good faith for example, leads to the same result.

20. *Article II: 8:102 'Relevant Circumstances'*[24] lays down a list of circumstances that should be taken into account. This list addresses interpreters using both subjective and objective method. This provision is quite identical to Article 5:102 of PECL, but some differences exist. Paragraph 2 'Particular case of a third party' of Article II 8:102 contains indeed a specific provision related to interpretation towards third parties (for instance an assignee). In such case the only acceptable method is the objective one. Indeed, preliminary negotiations or conduct of the parties cannot obviously been taken into account.

21. *Article II: 8:103 'Contra Proferentem Rule'*[25] indicates that interpretation of a term should be made against the party who supplied it. This provision refers to a rule widely recognized in European law or case law, and even in international law. It rests on the idea that the party (or third party) who drafted the contract should bear the risk of interpretation. This rule is relevant as regards shipping contracts as many pre-drafted contracts exist in this field of activity. Standard contracts generally contain standard terms draw up unilaterally by carriers or professional associations of carriers. Thus, shipper and consignee need to be protected in case of ambiguity.

22. *Article II:8:104 'Preference to Negotiated Terms'*[26] ensures that terms specifically negotiated by contracting parties prevails over terms of standard contracts. Such a provision is also quite relevant for shipping contracts that often are standardized. For instance, if the parties have agreed a specific jurisdictional clause, it will set aside the standard clause mentioned on a bill of lading.

*Article II:8:105 'Reference to Contract as a Whole'*[27] ensures the overall coherence and consistency of the contract.

*Article II:8:106 'Terms to Be Given (Full) Effect'*[28] rejects an interpretation which renders the terms of the contract lawful, or effective.

*Article II:8:107 'Linguistic Discrepancies'*.[29] When an international contract has been drafted in several languages, and the parties have not provided an authoritative version, this article gives preference for the interpretation according to the version in which the contract was originally drawn up.

23. From reading these articles, we can easily recognize familiar principles of interpretation of contracts for European lawyers. Thus, there should be no problem to apply them to shipping contracts.

24 Identical to Article 5:102 PECL.
25 Identical to Article 5:103 PECL.
26 Identical to Article 5:104 PECL.
27 Identical to Article 5:105 PECL.
28 Identical to Article 5:106 PECL.
29 Identical to Article 5:107 PECL.

### 3.2. *Application to shipping contracts*

**24.** As regards shipping contracts, provisions related to interpretation appears to be applicable and even quite relevant on many points. Such a use of these principles could moreover contribute to improve a harmonized interpretation providing a common basis to domestic courts and arbitrators. Thus, shipping operators should be encouraged to designate such texts along with the choice of an international convention or a domestic law, as their are compatible with these latter sources. And in fact they contain rules currently applied by EU State Courts, even if, according to the legal culture of each Member State, one method may be preferred to another.

**25.** French cases related to interpretation of transport contracts show that in practice the search for common intention is the predominant method of interpretation. This tendency is reflected in the two following cases. The first case of 2010[30] dealt with air transport but the solution can be transposed to all means of transport. The issue related to the identification of the consignee. The Court interpreted the contract according to the common intention of the parties, noting that the *Société Régionale CAE* was mentioned in the consignee box on the air waybill, and came to the conclusion that this company was the actual consignee. The decision specifically refers to interpretation of the common intention of the parties. But it must be noted that in France, interpretation rules are considered as guidelines and are therefore not biding. Moreover, interpretation is a question of fact which is not reviewed by the Cour de Cassation, as evidenced by the frequent usage of the expression 'interprétation souveraine' by the Court of Appeal (sovereign interpretation). As a consequence, affairs dealing with interpretation are quite rare before the Cour de Cassation. The second case[31] concerned the signing of a bill of lading and the identification of the ship owner. A maritime company had signed the bill specifying 'signed on behalf captain and ship owner'. The Court considered that such a formulation could have two meanings: the first one was that this company was the ship owner, and the second possible interpretation was that the company had signed on behalf of the ship owner. Finally, the Court interpreted the contract according to the evidence submitted and concluded that the company who had signed was not the actual ship owner. These few examples show that even if the above methods of interpretation are not clearly mentioned by French Courts, these follow an interpretation process which is in accordance with European principles.

**26.** Besides, the provisions contained in these instruments are very close to those of Unidroit Principles on International Commercial Contracts. Several provisions of Unidroit Principles refers to interpretation: In chapter I – 'General provisions' and in

[30] Cass com 8 July 2014, N° 12-29383, unpublished. www.legifrance.gouv.fr/affichJuriJudi.do?oldAction=rechJuriJudi&idTexte=JURITEXT000029247019&fastReqId=860492351&fastPos=1.

[31] Cass com 30 November 2010, N° 09-14892, unpublished. www.legifrance.gouv.fr/affichJuriJudi.do?oldAction=rechJuriJudi&idTexte=JURITEXT000023168560&fastReqId=897147087&fastPos=1.

chapter IV – 'Interpretation'. A single non-significant difference may be noted. In chapter IV, Article 4.8 'Supplying an omitted term' has no equivalent in European instruments. But I believe Courts and arbitrators usually correct any defect or supply any omission with regards consistency of the contract, even when such a provision is lacking. Thus, discrepancy related to interpretation seems to be unlikely. In the light of the foregoing considerations, it is now time to conclude to the original question.

## IV. Conclusion: May Common Core, PECL and DCFR be Useful to Interpret Shipping Law

27. At this study's conclusion, it is likely to conclude that PECL and DCFR may be useful to interpret shipping contracts and could even contribute to improve harmonization. But however some reservations still exist. First, these provisions provide for common contract rules that may not prove to be really relevant to solve specific difficulties arising from shipping contracts. A single example can evidence this doubt. A very frequent issue in shipping litigations is the applicability of the bill of lading's provisions to the consignee. And yet, PECL or DCFR provisions on interpretation do not contain any relevant solution to these problems.

28. Another reservation concerns the scope of application of these texts. Such texts cannot be considered as codification of *Lex Mercatoria,* and even less of *Lex Maritima.* As a consequence, they cannot apply when not specifically addressed by contracting parties, except possibly by arbitrators. And yet we know that the success of Unidroit Principles is not so effective, although they spread on a wider scale.[32] The success of appropriation of these works by European shipping operators somewhat appears to be jeopardized. Besides, from a geographical point of view, these works addresses mostly European relations. Their applicability on a global level could be acceptable, as their content on interpretation is finally quite similar to Unidroit Principles, which were specially designed for all international contracts. Talking about European legislation on transports however, the concern is always the same: is the regional level an appropriate level to rule on Transports Law? In certain areas, like road transport, or passengers' transport, EU may be the appropriate level. But it is much less likely when it comes to Maritime Law.

32 E. Jolivet, 'Les Principes UNIDROIT dans l'arbitrage CCI', [2005] *ICC ICA* 01/10/2005, 71; 'La jurisprudence arbitrale de la CCI et la lex mercatoria', [2001] *La Gazette du Palais*, 36; Ch. Seraglini, 'Du bon usage des principes UNIDROIT dans l'arbitrage international', [2001] *Rev. arb.*, 1101.

Francesca
Pellegrino*

# PRINCIPLES AND RULES OF EUROPEAN CONTRACT LAW BETWEEN THE PECL AND THE DCFR

## I. Introduction

1. General Principles play a fundamental role in any legal system, and in particular in European Union law, which is a specific legal system having independent sources and principles. In the past, the use of fundamental principles reflecting human rights was limited to the field of constitutional and administrative law. More recently, private law principles or 'general principles of civil law' have been recognised by the European Court of Justice. In fact, the European Court of Justice has recognised private law norms and values contained in the EU Treaties as "general (common) principles" (the principles of subsidiarity, supremacy or primacy of European Union Law and loyal cooperation).[1]

2. Finally, very important instruments make explicit reference to the principles of European contract law.[2] In particular, the 'General Principles' have played an important role in the projects aimed at promoting harmonization of national contract law in Europe[3] such as the PECL ('Principles of European Contract Law')[4] and the DCFR

* VIII ECMLR Colloquium, Rotterdam, 11–12 September 2014.

1 B. de Witte, 'Institutional Principles: a special category of General Principles of EC Law', in U. Bernitz – J. Nergelius (eds.), *General Principles of European Community Law*, The Hague, 2000, 143; X. Groussot, *General Principles of Community Law*, Groningen 2006, 56 ff.; M.E. Storme, 'Une question de principe(s)?', in A. Fuchs (ed), *European Contract Law – ERA Forum Special*, Issue 2008, in *ERA Forum scripta iuris europei*, Heidelberg, Springer, 2008, 72; A. Hartkamp, 'Principles of Contract Law, in A. Hartkamp et al (eds.), *Towards a European Private Law. Draft Common Frame of Reference (DCFR)*, Munich, 2009, 9; A. Hartkamp, 'The General Principles of EU Law and Private Law', in *Rabels Zeitschrift für ausländisches und Internationales Privatrecht*, 2011, 75, 241, 255 ff.

2 M. Herdegen, 'The Origins and Development of the General Principles of Community Law', in U. Bernitz – J. Nergelius, above mentioned, 17 f.

3 See M. Meli – M.R. Maugeri (eds.), *L'armonizzazione del diritto privato europeo. Il Piano d'azione 2003*, Milan, 2004.

4 In French PDEC (Principes du droit européen du contrat).

('Draft Common Frame of Reference').[5] In addition, the proposed CESL ('Common European Sales Law')[6] also contains a chapter dedicated to 'General Principles'.[7]

3. Several questions naturally arise. This is the first question:

## II. What are the PECL and the DCFR?

4. As it is well known, the PECL are a set of basic rules of contract law which most legal systems of the Member States of the European Union hold in common. They are the first body of private law which exist in parallel with national law. Because there are often considerable differences with regard to certain regulations, the differing national law in question was merged to form a *common core*. In particular, the PECL created a mixed legal system between civil and common law (as well as Non-European Law). In other words, these Principles are those core norms of private law which are shared by the legal traditions of the Member States (*ius commune Europaeum*).

5. According to the European Commission communications[8], the DCFR is – in turn – a toolbox, of a technical and political nature, containing model rules on private law. This approach is intended to eliminate obstacles to cross-border contracts created by differing national rules of contract law and to complete a common market without frontiers within the EU.

5 C. von Bar – E. Clive – H. Schulte-Nölke et al (eds.), *Principles, Definitions and Model Rules of European Private Law. Draft Common of Reference (DCFR)*, Munich, 2009, 9; C. von Bar, *Non-Contractual Liability Arising out of Damage caused to Another*, Munich, 2009, 243 ff. See also S. Grundmann, 'The Structure of the DCFR – Which Approach for Today's Contract Law?', *European Review of Contract Law*, 2008, 225; A. Somma, *The Politics of the Draft Common Frame of Reference*, Alphen aan den Rijn, Kluwer, 2009; H. Eidenmuller – F. Faust – H. Grigoleit – N. Jansen – G. Wagner – R. Zimmermann, "The Common Frame of Reference for European Private Law – Policy Choices and Codification Problems", 2008, 28, *Oxford Journal of Legal Studies*; A. Somma, 'Towards a European private law? The Common Frame of Reference in the Conflict between EC law and national laws', in *Yearbook of European Law*, 2010, 28, 3 ss.; U. Breccia, 'Principles, Definitions and Model Rules', in *Comune quadro di riferimento europeo (Draft Common Frame of Reference), I contratti*, 2010, 95; K.P. Purnhagen, 'Principles of European Private or Civil Law? A Reminder of the Symbiotic Relationship Between the ECJ and the DCFR in a Pluralistic European Private Law', in *Centre for Study of European Contract Law Working Paper*, Series No 2011–04.

6 In 2011 the European Commission proposed a Common European Sales Law to help break down barriers between the Member States.

7 See M. Heidemann, 'European Private Law at the Crossroads: The Proposed European Sales Law', *European Review of Private Law*, 2012, 20, 1128 ff.; S. Whittaker, 'General Principles and Underlying Principles in the Proposed Common European Sales Law and their Role in its interpretation', in *Osservatorio di diritto civile e commerciale*, 2 dicembre 2013, 361 ff.; Y. Adar – P. Sirena, 'Principles and Rules in the Emerging European Contract Law: From the PECL to the CESL, and Beyond', *European Review of Contract Law*, 2013, 9 (1), 1–37.

8 See the Action Plan (COM [2003] 68 final), that proposed to develop 'Common Principles of European Contract Law' (CoPECL). See also the European Commission Communication COM(2004)651 final on European Contract Law and the 2010 Green Paper, mentioned *infra*.

## III. What is the Legal Nature of these Texts?

6. Despite the fact that both the PECL and the DCFR provide assistance to judges[9] in national and European courts and arbitrators deciding cross-border issues, they do not represent a legally enforceable regulation. In fact, they are so-called soft law (or non-binding law) documents.[10] "The term 'soft law' is a blanket term for all sorts of rules, which are not enforced on behalf of the state, but are seen, for example, as goals to be achieved.".[11] Nevertheless, this difference between soft and hard law, traditionally based on legally binding force, vanishes when the parties to a contract expressly refer to the rules contained in the PECL or in the DCFR. In this case those rules become clauses of the contract.

7. In fact, according to Article 1:101, these Principles must be applied – as general rules of contract law – when the parties have agreed to incorporate them into their contract or that their contract is to be governed by them. Instead, these Principles may be applied in two different cases: a) when the parties have agreed that their contract is to be governed by 'general principles of law' or the '*lex mercatoria*' and b) when they have not chosen any system or rules of law to govern their contract. In turn, as the DCFR explains, the adjective "model" connected to the rules indicates that the rules are not put forward as having any normative force, but are soft law rules of the kind contained in the PECL and similar publications.[12]

## IV. When was the Project for a European Private Law Launched?

8. This subject can best be understood if one understands the long evolution of the project for a European Private Law. Initially, the creation of a 'European private law' was conceptually difficult for jurists who traditionally understand private law as those provisions enclosed in continental civil codes to regulate contracts. Since the early 1990s things have changed radically. For the first time, the Treaty of Maastricht gave the Community the power to harmonise national laws only if this contributed to the establishment and functioning of the internal market (Article 95 EC).

9. This provision gave the European Community a relatively broad power to issue directives to harmonise specific private law rules: for example, the Directives 85/374/EEC (Product Liability)[13], 85/577/EEC (Contracts Negotiated Away from Business

9 In fact, they received the attention of many Higher Courts in Europe.

10 But it is not certain if the PECL may be also considered part of the *lex mercatoria* (merchant law) or the new *lex mercatoria*, an autonomous body of rules, with different origin and contents, emerging mainly from the practice, created by the community of merchants and dedicated to serve the needs of international trade. Instead, the PECL also contain specific rules for consumers.

11 See the following website: *ivr-enc.info/index.php?title=Rules_and_Principles.*

12 So, they might be used as a model for the improvement of legislation.

13 Council Directive 85/374/EEC of 25 July 1985 on the approximation of the laws, regulations and administrative provisions of the Member States concerning liability for defective products (OJ L 210,

Premises)[14], 86/653/EEC (Self-Employed Commercial Agents)[15], 87/102/EEC (Consumer Credit)[16], 90/314/EEC (Package Tours)[17] and 93/13/EEC (Unfair Terms in Consumer Contracts).[18] In the field of transport, in particular, harmonisation was considered the legal instrument for transport development of goods and passengers in the EU.[19]

**10.** Similarly, Article 114 of the new Treaty on the Functioning of the European Union[20] gives the EU the power to harmonise national law, even in those areas which have always seemed to fall within the exclusive competence of the Member States, such as private law. The European Court of Justice (ECJ) undertook the interpretation of European directives on contract and tort law, thus creating a quasi-federal common law for Europe. For many commentators, through the adoption of the principles of supremacy of EC law and direct effect, the Court became an important instrument for market integration. But these directives have harmonized only specific sectors of European private law. The impetus for the work on the Principles of European Contract Law were two resolutions of the European Parliament of 1989 and 1994[21], which expressed the desire to establish a common European civil law and to bring the private law of the Member States into line.

07/08/1985, p. 29). See C. Baldassarre, 'Responsabilità del produttore: danno risarcibile, onere della prova e logica giuridica', in Danno e responsabilità, 2014, 502 ff.

14 Council Directive 85/577/EEC of 20 December 1985 to protect the consumer in respect of contracts negotiated away from business premises (OJ L 372, 31/12/1985, p. 31). See G. Alpa, 'Direttiva Cee 85/577 e recesso del consumatore', in *Contratti*, 1994, 597.

15 Council Directive 86/653/EEC of 18 December 1986 on the coordination of the laws of the Member States relating to self-employed commercial agents (OJ L 382, 31/12/1986, p. 17). See A. Baldassare (ed.), *Il rapporto di agenzia. Diretttiva CEE n. 86/653 del 18 dicembre 1986 e D.Lg. 10 settembre 1991, n. 303*, Torino, 1995.

16 Council Directive 87/102/EEC of 22 December 1986 for the approximation of the laws, regulations and administrative provisions of the Member States concerning consumer credit (OJ L 278, 11/10/1988, p. 33) See M. Dukic Mijatovic – S. Gongeta, 'Consumer credit in European Union', *European Scientific Journal*, February 2014, I, 410 ff.

17 Council Directive 90/314/EEC of 13 June 1990 on package travel, package holidays and package tours (OJ L 158, 23/06/1990, 59 ff.). See M. Demarchi, 'La direttiva sui viaggi tutto compreso', in *Responsabilità civile e previdenza*, 1992, 518 ss.; S. Zunarelli, 'La Direttiva CEE n. 90/314 del 13 giugno 1990 concernente i viaggi, le vacanze ed i circuiti tutto compreso', in *La tutela del turista* (a cura di G. Silingardi e V. Zeno Zencovich), Napoli, 1993, 27 ff.

18 Council Directive 93/13/EEC of 5 April 1993 on unfair terms in consumer contracts (OJ L 95, 21/04/1993, 29 ff.). See G. De Geest, 'The Signing-without-reading Problem: An Analysis of the European Directive on Unfair Contract Terms', in H.-B. Schäfer – H.-J. Lwowski (eds.), *Konsequenzen wirstschaftsrechtlicher Normen*, Wiesbaden, 2002, 213–35.

19 S. Grundmann – W. Kerber, "European System of Contract Laws: A Map for Combining the Advantages of Centralised and Decentralised Rule-making", in S. Grundmann – J. Stuyck (eds.), *An Academic Green Paper on European Contract Law*, The Hague, 2003, 295.

20 The Treaty on the Function of the EU in combination with the Treaty of the European Union, as amended by the Lisbon Treaty, represents the constitutional basis of the European legal order.

21 Dated 26 May 1989 (OJ C 158, 28/06/1989, 400) and 6 May 1994 (OJ C 205, 25/07/1994, 518 on the harmonisation of certain sectors of the private law of the Member States), in which Parliament asked that a start be made on the necessary preparatory work for the drawing up of a Common European Code of Private Law. See G. Alpa, 'European Community Resolutions and the Codification of Private Law', *European Review of Private Law*, 2000, 2:321–332.

## V. Who Created the PECL and the DCFR and How did They Do It?

11. The PECL were created by the Commission on European Contract Law (the so-called "Lando Commission")[22], a group of comparative lawyers representing many European jurisdictions. They started in 1982 and published the first part of the PECL in 1995; since 1999 the second part has been available and the third part was completed in 2002.Therefore, these Principles only constitute the first phase of a project for a European Civil Code which the parties could choose as the law applicable to their contract. The work of the "Lando Commission" was continued by the Study Group on a European Civil Code.[23]

12. According to the EU Commission's Action Plan[24] that proposed to develop 'Common Principles of European Contract Law' (CoPECL), an interim version of the Draft CFR 'Common Frame of Reference' (DCFR) was published by this Group[25] in 2008. A second revised edition was elaborated in 2009.[26] The DCFR is a draft for the codification of the whole European contract law, in which both the acquis principles[27] and the PECL have been integrated. Another ambitious 'projet de cadre commune de reference' has been elaborated by the Association Henri Capitant and by the Société de Législation Comparée in 2008.[28] Nowadays, European private law comprises a variety of legal rules, which derive from legislative, judicial and scholarly formants, operating at different levels.[29]

## VI. But What are the Differences between the PECL and the DCFR?

13. The DCFR incorporates a revised and updated version of the PECL, but it also includes a lot of new material and general modifications. In fact, the "Lando Principles" are solely focused on uniform contract law in Europe, while the DCFR is not limited to the law of contract, but also includes many articles on tort law. In particular, the whole

22 This Commission, headed by Professor Ole Lando from University of Copenhagen, consisted of 22 members from all Member States of the European Union.

23 A Group founded in 2005 and managed by Christian von Bar, a German law professor.

24 European Communication's Action Plan on a More Coherent European Contract Law of February 2003 (COM [2003] 68 final).

25 Without comments and notes.

26 Among other things, this is a possible model for an actual or political 'Common Frame of Reference' (CFR).

27 Acquis Principles (ACQP) prepared by the Acquis Group, coordinated by G. Ajani and H. Schulte-Nölke.

28 The 'Principes directeurs du droit Européen du contrat'. See B. Fauvarque-Cosson – D. Mazeaud – G. Wicker – J.B. Racine – L. Sautonie-Laguionie – F. Bujoli (eds.), *Principes contractuels commun, Projet de cadre de référence*, Paris, Société de Législation Comparée, 2008.

29 Today, the legal decisions are the result of complex cooperation between institutions operating at different levels (so-called Hart and Sacks' principle). See H.M. Hart – A.M. Sacks, *The Legal Process: Basic Problems in the Making and Application of Law*, New York, Foundation Press, 1958, 1994; R. Sacco, "Legal Formants: a Dynamic Approach to Comparative Law" (part 1, 1–34; part 2, 343–401), 39 in *American Journal of Comparative Law*, 1991, 1, 343; A. Janssen – O. Meyer (eds.), *CISG Methodology*, Munich, 2009, 314.

of PECL has been incorporated in Books I to III of the DCFR, while Book IV contains model rules for particular contracts, contractual relationships, obligations and legal remedies in case of non-performance. In addition, it must be stressed that the EU has implemented only the DCFR by the above mentioned Action Plan[30], by the European Commission Communication on European Contract Law[31] and by the 2010 Green Paper[32] on policy options for progress towards a European Contract Law.

**14.** Now, the most important question is as follows:

## VII. What Sort of Rules do These European Documents Contain?

**15.** These documents contain both general principles and legal rules. In fact, the European internal market not only requires general and abstract principles (for example, the principle of justice)[33], but also legal uniform rules in the field of contract law. According to Article 1:101 of the PECL, these Principles are intended to be applied 'as general rules of contract law in the European Union'. This Article already points out two different meanings of the word principles: as a body or set of rules that do not have legal force on the one hand, and as general rules on the other hand.

**16.** The Preamble of the Unidroit Principles of International Commercial Contracts PICC[34] similarly announces that they 'set forth general rules for international commercial contracts'. In turn, the DCFR includes, among other things, principles and, for this reason, particularly distinguishes 'underlying principles' from 'overriding principles'. The first ones ('underlying principles')[35] are the essence, the *basic general rules* and

30 European Communication's Action Plan on a More Coherent European Contract Law of February 2003 (COM [2003] 68 final), *supra* cit.

31 Communication from the Commission to the European Parliament and the Council, 'European Contract Law and the revision of the Acquis: the way forward' COM(2004)651 final, 11 October 2004. It proposed that the CFR should provide fundamental principles, definitions and model rules. Finally, on May 2011 the Expert Group's feasibility study was published by an expert group on a Common Frame of Reference (CFR) to assist the Commission in making further progress on the development of a possible future European contract instrument.

32 COM(2010)348 final of July 2010.

33 Articles 49 and 56 TFEU.

34 See the first paragraph. The Principles of International Commercial Contracts (PICC) of 2010 is a document drawn up by Unidroit intended to help harmonise international commercial contracts law. The first edition was published in 1994 and the second in 2004. See M.J. Bonell – R. Peleggi, "UNIDROIT Principles of International Commercial Contracts and Draft Common Frame of Reference: a Synoptical Table", *Unif. Law Rev.* 2009, 437 ff.; S. Vogenauer – J. Kleinheisterkamp (eds.), *Commentary on the UNIDROIT Principles of International Commercial Contracts (PICC-Commentary)*, Oxford, University Press, 2009; V. Hetger, 'The Unidroit Principles 2010: Towards a Global Law of International Commercial Contracts', 17–18 February 2012, *European Review of Private Law*, 2012, 20, 889.

35 See M.W. Hesselink, 'If you don't like our principles we have others. On core values and underlying principles in European private law: a critical discussion of the new principles section in the draft CFR', in R. Brownswors – H.W. Micklitz – L. Niglia – S. Weatherhill (eds.), *The foundations of European*

guidelines, upon which more detailed standards are built. They cover both contractual and non-contractual obligations and aspects of property law and help in determining and verifying the valuableness of model rules.

**17.** In the DCFR, this category of principles is composed of the following four principles: freedom, justice, efficiency, security (or legal certainty).[36] They are in line with the EU specific aims to establish an area of freedom, security and justice and promote the free movement of goods, persons, services and capital between Member States. With particular reference to the principle of justice, it is clear that the DCFR does not perceive private/contract law as merely the balancing of private law relations between equally strong natural or legal persons, but it suggests the correction of market failures or contains elements of social justice and protection for weaker parties.

**18.** The second ones ('overriding principles') are principles[37] of a high political nature. For example, the protection of human rights[38], the promotion of welfare and the internal market, the promotion of solidarity and social responsibility, the duty to provide information when concluding a contract with a consumer who is at a particular disadvantage, etc.

**19.** The DCFR itself recognises the overriding nature of these principles. But, what is the difference between principles (or general principles) and legal (or model) rules contained in the DCFR? As well explained in its title, the DCFR contains principles, definitions and model rules of European private law. The notion of "definition" is quite clear, while the notion of 'principles' and 'model rules' requires some explanation. The European Commission's Communications related to the DCFR employ the concept of 'principle', but do not elaborate on it. The word 'principle' is subject to different interpretations and the European Court of Justice contributed to clarify the concept of principles and assess the validity of other, less abstract, legal norms.[39]

*Private Law*, Oxford, 2011, 59 ff. For the jurisprudential interpretation see ECJ, case 13/61, Bosch & van Rijin, in *ECR European Competition Review*, 1962, 45, at 52.

36 The approach taken by the Principes directeurs is different. In fact they recognise three main principles: liberté contractuelle, sécurité contractuelle et loyauté. But loyalty comprises a duty to act in conformity with the requirements of good faith and fair dealing, that are model rules. Efficiency is added because, although this is often an aspect of freedom, it cannot be accommodated under the other principles.

37 But they are also reflected quite strongly in the content of model rules.

38 Article 6 of the EU Treaty expressly refers to general principles derived from the European Convention of 1950 as well as from constitutional traditions common to the Member States. See H.G. Schermers, 'Human Rights as General Principles of Law', in U. Bernitz – J. Nergelius (eds.), above mentioned, 61 ff.

39 ECJ, case 277/05 (Societé thermale d'Eugénie-Les Bains v Ministère de l'Economie, des Finance et de l'industrie), para 24; case 412/06 (Annelore Hamilton v Volksbank Filder eG), para. 24; 16 December 2008, case 47/07P (Masdar v Commissie) para 50; 3 September 2009, case 489/07 (Pia Messner v Firma Stefan Cruger), para 29; case 215/08 (E. Friz GmbHv Carsten von der Heyde), para 48–49. See J. Basedow, 'The Court of Justice and Private Law: Vacillations, General Principles and the Architecture of the European Judiciary', *European Review of Private Law*, 2010, 18, 462 ff.

**20.** In any case, one possible interpretation is that the notion of principles is used following the two meanings used in the PECL, as general rules and as a set of rules that do not have legal force. However, the notion of principles, particularly when they are qualified as 'fundamental', can denote the core objectives and underlying values of the DCFR. The model rules, for instance: 'a party to the contract cannot break the agreement without a valid legal reason' (just cause)[40] are of course based on such fundamental principles (in this case, the principle of justice). But if the word 'principle' is used in the wide sense of rules which are of a more general nature (such as freedom of contract, good faith, etc.), the model rules could be said to include principles. In this sense, they can overlap with each other.

**21.** Therefore, a difference between principles and rules should be made. In fact, following a Dworkinian approach[41], we must recognise the presence in law of general rules which are different from legal rules. They are the fundamental principles. Most legal principles contain normative imperatives and embody moral or social values underpinning the whole society. So, the difference between principles and rules firstly involves their qualification. Therefore, the principles are general rules[42], referred to values of meta-juridical relevance, characterized by a vague connotation and evaluation, while the legal rules are specific and concrete requirements.[43] In addition, the principles justify (or should justify) the rules: for example, the (legal) rule 'a party to the contract cannot break the agreement without a valid legal reason' (or just cause) is justified by the general 'Principle of Justice'.[44]

40 A. Soler Presas, 'Damages for Fundamental Breach of Contract', *Revista Para El Análisis del Derecho (InDret)*, 2009, 3; F. Chirico – P. Larouche (eds.), *Economic Analysis of the DCFR: The work of the Economic Impact Group within the CoPECL network of excellence*, Munich, 2010, 289.

41 R.M. Dworkin, 'Is Law a System of Rules?', *University of Chicago Law Review*, 1967; R.M. Dworkin, 'The Model of Rules', *University of Chicago Law Review*, 1967, 35, 14; R.M. Dworkin, *Taking Rights Seriously*, London, 1978, 22; C. Mak, 'Hedgehogs in Luxemburg? A Dworkinian Reading of the CJEU's Case Law on Principles of Private Law and Some Doubts of the Fox', *European Review of Private Law*, 2012, 20, 323.

42 N. Bobbio, 'Principi generali di diritto', *Novissimo Digesto Italiano*, XXX, Milano, 1966, 887 ff.; A. Falzea, "Relazione introduttiva", in *I principi generali del diritto*, Atti del Convegno dell'Accademia dei Lincei, 27–29 maggio 1991, Roma, 1992, 11 ss.; E. Hondius, 'Principles and the Law', *European Review of Private Law*, 2012, 20, 289.

43 See P. Schlag, 'Rules and Standards', *University of California Los Angeles Law Review*, 1985–86, 33, 379; L. Kaplow, 'Rules versus Standards: An Economic Analysis', *Duke Law Journal*, 1992–1993, 42, 557; K.M. Sullivan, 'Foreword: the Justices of Rules and Standards', *Harvard Law Review*, 1992–1993, 22, 106; E.A. Posner, 'Standards, Rules and Social Norms', *Harvard Journal of Law & Public Policy*, 1997–1998, 21, 101; S. Grundmann – D. Mazeaud (eds), *General Clauses and Standards in European Contract Law: Comparative Law, EC Law and Contract Law Certification*, The Hague, 2006.

44 G. Wagner, 'Vom akademischen zum politischen DCFR', *Zeitschrift für Europäisches Privatrecht*, 2008, 16, 677–78; J. Basedow, 'Kodifikationsrausch und kollidierende Konzepte-Notizen zu Marktbezug, Freiheit und System in Draft Common Frame of Reference', *Zeitschrift für Europäisches Privatrecht*, 2008, 16, 673–76; T. Pfeiffer, 'Von den PECL zum DCFR', *Zeitschrift für Europäisches Privatrecht*, 2008, 16, 679–707; M.W. Hesselink, 'CFR and Social Justice? Munich, 2008; c. Armbrüster, 'Das Versicherungsrecht im Common Frame of Reference', *Zeitschrift für Europäisches Privatrecht*, 2008, 16, 775–812.

22. Consequently, the rules must be made congruent with the principle that justifies them. When principles are in conflict with each other or with legal rules, a balance must be found.[45] For example, one of the basic principles underlying the international law of contracts in general is the Freedom of contracts. According to Article 1:102 of the PECL (Freedom of Contract) 'Parties are free to enter into a contract and to determine its contents' but 'subject to the requirements of good faith and fair dealing, and the mandatory rules[46] established by these Principles'.[47] Therefore, good faith, fair dealing and mandatory rules are three limits[48] to the fundamental principle of freedom of contract, intended to ensure the balance[49] between the interests of the contracting parties.[50]

The next question is:

## VIII. Are Good Faith and Fair Dealing General Principles or Model Rules?

23. They are rather open-ended concepts. The particular vagueness which makes them is not enough to consider them – without a doubt – as principles. In many laws, they are accepted as fundamental principles, as general rules of direct application, but the PECL recognise them as legal rules, in particular as rules of duty under which a certain person is required to act in a certain predetermined way. In fact, Article 1:201 PECL (Good Faith and Fair Dealing) say that: (1) Each party must act in accordance with good faith and fair dealing. (2) The parties may not exclude or limit this duty. It imposes a duty upon each party to observe reasonable standards of fair dealing.[51]

45 M.E. Storme, 'The Foundations of Private Law in a Multilevel Structure: Balancing, Distribution of Lawmaking Power, and Other Constitutional Issues', *European Revue of Private Law*, 2012, 20, 237.

46 Article 1:103 (Mandatory Law) (1) Where the law otherwise applicable so allows, the parties may choose to have their contract governed by the Principles, with the effect that national mandatory rules are not applicable. (2) Effect should nevertheless be given to those mandatory rules of national, supranational and international law which, according to the relevant rules of private international law, are applicable irrespective of the law governing the contract.

47 On the contrary, Article 6 CISG does not contain a similar limitation to the freedom of contract.

48 J. Raz, 'Legal Principles and the Limits of Law', *Yale Law Journal*, 1972, 81, 823 ff., 839 ff.

49 In the case of contractual unbalance and a party's conduct in conflict with the principle of good faith, Article 4:109 PECL (A party may avoid a contract if, at the time of the conclusion of the contract, the other party knew or ought to have known of this and, given the circumstances and purpose of the contract, took advantage of the first party's situation in a way which was grossly unfair or took an excessive benefit) applies as legal remedy 'of new generation'.

50 Article 7.1.6 Unidroit Principles states that 'a clause which limits or excludes one party's liability for non-performance or which permits one party to render performance substantially different from what the other party reasonably expected may not be invoked if it would be grossly unfair to do so, having regard to the purpose of the contract'.

51 See H. Beale, 'General Clauses and Specific Rules in the Principles of European Contract Law: the Good Faith Clause', in S. Grundmann – D. Mazeaud (eds.), above mentioned, 205; O. Lando, 'Is Good Faith an Over-Arching General Clause in the Principles of European Contract Law?', *European Review of Private Law*, 2007, 15, 841.

**24.** In the same way, the role of good faith and fair dealing goes beyond the provision of the fundamental principle of contractual security in the DCFR. The second part of this paper focuses on the role played by PECL/DCFR principles and legal/model rules in the shipping market and shipping law. There is no doubt that the PECL apply to all contracts, in general, including the carriage contracts. The carriage contract also falls within the scope of Books I to III[52] DCFR. But, unlike the PECL, DCFR Book IV includes a huge range of specific contracts: sale and lease of goods, services, mandate, etc.

**25.** Therefore, the contract of carriage should have been included within the category of 'services' contracts, but – on the contrary – it has not been included. In fact, this part of Book IV (on "services") applies in particular to contracts for construction, processing, storage, design information or advice and treatment (Article IV.C-1:101 DCFR). What is the consequence of this exclusion? Considering the confinement of this omission to the specific service contracts rules, the general provisions of the DCFR fully apply to all the contracts, including the carriage contracts.[53]

**26.** In addition, with reference to the discipline for specific contracts (and the rights and obligations arising from them), in some cases, the carriage contract falls within the scope of the contract for the sale of goods.[54] The distance between the places where the goods are located at the time of the sale and the place to which they will have to be moved for the buyer, creates the necessity for the movement of the goods.[55] In fact, in the context of modern transportation (especially by containers) the sale contract of goods defines whether it is the seller or the buyer who will enter into the contract of carriage with the carrier. In particular, a CIF/CIP[56] seller needs to provide a contract of carriage to the final destination to its customer.

**27.** Under Article IV.A-5:202 (Carriage of the goods), when the parties agree that the goods are to be delivered by a carrier or a series of carriers, risk passes at the moment when the goods are handed over to the first carrier, even if the documents representing the goods

[52] Book I (General provisions), Book II (Contracts and other judicial acts), Book III (Obligations within the scope of the DCFR and corresponding rights), Book IV (Specific contract and rights and obligations arising from them), Book V (Benevolent intervention in another's affairs), Book VI (Non-contractual liability arising out of damage caused to another), Book VII (Unjustified enrichment), Book VIII (Acquisition and loss of ownership of goods), Book IX (Proprietary security rights in movable assets), Book X (Trust).

[53] See C. Marchetti (ed.), *Un'introduzione al contract del DCFR: la (necessaria?) bilateralità della formazione del vincolo*, Torino, 2012.

[54] Book IV, Part A of the DCFR is devoted to sale contracts.

[55] See A. von Ziegler, 'Rotterdam Rules and the Underlying Sales Contract', in *CMI Yearbook*, 2013, 275. He said that 'the "raison d'être" of the shipping industry is to overcome this distance'.

[56] CIF (Cost, Insurance and Freight): seller must pay the cost, freight and insurance to bring the goods to the port of destination. However risk is transferred to the buyer once the goods are loaded on the vessel. CIP (Carriage and Insurance Paid): seller pays for carriage and insurance to the named destination point, but risk passes when the goods are handed to the first carrier. This term is used for intermodal deliveries and multimodal container transportation.

(bill of lading) have not yet been delivered, in accordance with Article A-2:201 (Delivery). This Article implies that any damage to the goods during transportation is at the risk of the buyer and it is up to him to try and claim damages from the carrier for improper performance of the transport contract. In other words, where the contract involves carriage of the goods by a carrier or a series of carriers, the seller performs his obligation to deliver by handing the goods over to the first carrier and by transferring the bill of lading to the buyer and any other relevant documents to enable the buyer to take over the goods.

**28.** However, if the contract requires the seller to arrange for carriage of the goods, default rules require that the arranged transportation be reasonable. Therefore, the seller must ensure means of transport appropriate to the circumstances (especially taking into account the nature of the goods) and under terms which are usual for such transportation. If during carriage the goods are damaged due to improper packaging by the seller, the buyer need not pay the price and the seller remains liable for damages resulting from the packaging.[57]

**29.** Article IV.A-202 derogates from the provision described above in the case of a consumer sales contract. In this case, in which the seller is a professional party and the buyer is a consumer ('any natural person who is acting primarily for purposes which are not related to his or her trade, business or profession')[58], *risk does not pass when the goods are delivered to the first carrier, but only when the last carrier hands over the goods to the buyer*, or the buyer fails to take delivery at that time. The legal reasoning behind this provision is clear: according to the general principle of justice, the seller is supposed to be in a better position to calculate the price by integrating the cost of transportation risks in a favourable insurance scheme, while the consumer normally has more problems in pursuing a claim for damages against the carrier.

**30.** Another very important provision applicable to the contract of carriage is contained in Article IV.A.-5:203 referring to the goods sold in transit. It refers to goods that are already travelling from point (or port) of departure to their destination at the moment of contract conclusion. In the case of a 'sale of goods in transit' the risk passes from the time the goods are handed over to the first carrier. This type of sale is based on documents representing the goods, which the buyer may examine before entering into the contract of sale. According to the customary practice in this kind of commercial transaction, the final buyer undertakes the whole transportation risk, usually by taking out insurance. Therefore, the buyer assumes the risk for a time before the conclusion of the sales contract (retrospective effect). It requires the buyer to take out insurance and, in particular, an insurance policy that contains a retrospective clause.[59]

57 I. Schwenzerm – P. Hachem – C. Kee, *Global Sales and Contract Law*, Oxford, 2012.

58 Article I.-1:105 DCFR. See M.M.B. Loos, 'Sales Law in the DCFR', *Law Review*, Volume IV, Issue 1, Jan.-Jun. 2014, 6 ff.

59 'Lost or Not Lost Clause', 'Insurable Interest Clause', 'Claims Made Clause' are the most useful ones. The first one states that the insurer will pay even if the loss insured against has occurred prior to the effecting of the insurance (Section 6 MIA Maritime Insurance Act). According to the "Insurable Interest Clause", the assured shall be entitled to recover for insured loss occurring during the period covered by this

**31.** Nevertheless, if at the time of the conclusion of the contract of sale the seller knew or could reasonably be expected to have known that the goods have been lost or damaged and did not disclose this to the buyer, the loss or damage is at the risk of the seller. This provision refers to the reasonableness principle. According to Article 1:302 PECL 'reasonableness is to be judged by what persons acting in good faith and in the same or similar situation as the parties (reasonable person) would consider to be reasonable'. This principle is the core of the PECL. It is the basic concept and general principle of contract law and combines two other concepts: foreseeability[60] and flexibility. It is not only a principle for the interpretation of contract, but also a norm integrating additional obligations and terms into the contract and restricting the exercise of contractual rights. In fact, the purpose of the reasonableness test is to determine whether a reasonable person would have foreseen and expected particular circumstances or consequences.

**32.** There may be a problem here for the applicability of the DCFR when conflicts of law arise with the national law. Article I.-1:102(5) (Interpretation and Development) of DCFR contains the following prevision: 'Where there is a general rule and a special rule applying to a particular situation within the scope of the general rule, the special rule prevails in any case of conflict' (*lex specialis derogat legi generali*).One could even observe that conflicts cannot arise, because in the DCFR there would be no specific regime covering the contract of carriage of goods, and the general previsions alone would therefore apply.[61]

**33.** But – as has already been mentioned – specific rules relating to the contract of carriage could be applied in the case of sale of goods and of goods sold in transit. Therefore, if the DCFR is the law chosen for a contract of carriage of goods, it would clash with the specific, well-established (national or EU or international) regime applicable in a Member State for this particular type of contract. One possible approach would be to say that the DCFR should be applied in the event of a clash, because that is what the parties have chosen. If the parties to a contract for the carriage of goods by sea chose the DCFR as the governing law, it would deviate from that well-established statutory regime. On the contrary, for those aspects which are exclusively regulated by the national or EU or international law, the special regime shall fully apply.

insurance, notwithstanding that the loss occurred before the contract of insurance was concluded, unless the insured were aware of the loss and the Underwriters were not. See ICC (Institute Cargo Clauses) 11 Claims. The 'Claims Made Clause", applicable to professional liability insurance (business insurance) provide coverage against the insured during the policy period, regardless of when the wrongful act that gave rise to the claim took place. So, coverage reverts back to the policy that was in effect at the time of accident. Claims of professional liability often result many years after an alleged error is committed making it difficult for insurance companies to evaluate their true exposures. On the contrary, the 'Loss Occurrence' policies need to be in effect on the date that an accident causing damage occurs in order to trigger coverage. See A. Boglione, 'Le clausole Loss occurrence e Claims made nell'assicurazione di responsabilità civile (R.C.)' in *Scritti in onore di Francesco Berlingieri, Diritto marittimo*, 2010, 185 ff.

60 See F. Pellegrino, 'Reasonableness, foreseeability and flexibility in the principles of European contract law', *MarIus* 424, January 2014, 7 ff.

61 So, see G. Dannemann, S. Vogenauer (eds.), *The Common European Sales Law in Context: Interactions with English and German Law*, Oxford University, 2013, 514.

Ioanna Magklasi

# CAN PECL HELP WITH VEXING ISSUES OF MARITIME LAW? CRITICAL REFLECTIONS FROM THE EXAMPLE OF THE ROTTERDAM RULES

## I. Introduction

1. This paper studies the trajectory, background and objectives of PECL[1] and identifies the link between contract law and maritime laws (namely carriage of goods by sea and international sale of goods). The author will present the intricacies of these laws, in an attempt to justify why, despite extensive codification and standardisation, maritime law is still in need of legal certainty and occasionally of fairer application of the law to the disputes not only by national courts, but also in the wider European context. After determining the principles of PECL and maritime law, the author reflects upon the benefit that certain provisions of PECL could have on the better integration of the latest harmonising convention in the area of carriage of goods by sea, namely of the Rotterdam Rules[2], by providing interpretational help to volume contracts with derogations in a way that promotes both PECL and maritime law's objectives.

### *1.1. Introduction to PECL*

2. DCFR and PECL have come to harmonise European substantive contract law[3] and they are believed to prove handy in the application interpretation or creation of laws within Europe.[4] They originated from the Commission on European Contract Law, which was a circle of distinguished lawyers from across the European Union. They have both been the product of laborious work and cooperation of European lawyers,[5] experts on private law, comparative law and EU law. They are soft law provisions, and they do not have a normative character, which means that they were not drafted in

1 Principles of European Contract Law.

2 UN Convention on Contracts for the International Carriage of Goods Wholly or Partly by Sea. Hereafter referred to as "The Rotterdam Rules" or "RR".

3 Roy Goode, *Transnational Commercial Law: Texts, cases and materials* (OUP 2007), para 14.02.

4 Ibid, para 14.12.

5 Ole Lando, 'Salient features of the Principles of European Contract Law: A comparison with the UCC' (2001) 13 *Pace International Law Review* 339–340.

order to be automatically legally binding.[6] Thus, they take into account the particular contract law principles of European countries, as they could best foster inter-European Trade.[7]

3. PECL are the product of distilling common principles of contract law among jurisdictions of the Member states of the EU.[8] Through PECL, the Lando Commission has set the plausible goal of achieving a greater uniformity in areas of contract law based on the understanding, which is also a true fact, that the legal systems of European countries have the same historical, philosophical and conceptual underpinnings.[9] Contrary to the UNIDROIT Principles which were the product of another important uniformity project applicable only to international commercial contracts,[10] PECL are designed to apply to inter-European contracts or to a contract governed by the law of one of the EU Member-States.[11]

4. Since they are soft law in nature, one of the primary benefits of PECL is that they will be available to courts and arbitrators for the interpretation of the law, and they may apply by analogy.[12] Parties can expressly incorporate them into their contract. According to article 1(101)(3a) of PECL if parties say that their contract should be governed by principles of international law or *lex mercatoria*, then PECL may apply.[13] But PECL is more flexible than that, as the Principles can be applied if any European Court believes their application is more suitable, either supplementing or deviating from the rules of a certain national law.[14]

### 1.2. *Benefits and objectives of PECL*

5. The formulation of PECL aspires to amalgamate the core principles of European contract law.[15] The principles have been pronounced to lift barriers from the cross-

6 Roy Goode, H Kronke, E McKendrick, *Transnational Commercial Law* (OUP 2007) 509.

7 Ole Lando, 'European Contract Law', in Petar Carcevic (ed) *International Contracts and Conflicts of Laws: A collection of Essays* (Graham & Trotman, London 1990) 1, 5.

8 Ole Lando, 'Salient features of the Principles of European Contract Law: A comparison with the UCC' (2001) 13 *Pace International Law Review* 339, 340.

9 On this see: Nils Jansen, Reinhard Zimmermann, 'A European civil code in all but name: discussing the nature and purposes of the draft common frame of reference' (2010) *CLJ* 98, 103; Ole Lando, 'Some features of the law of contract in the third millennium' (2000) *Scandinavian studies in law*.

10 Roy Goode, H Kronke, E McKendrick *Transnational Commercial Law* (OUP 2007), para 14.16.

11 Roy Goode, 'International Restatements of Contract and English contract law' (1997) II *Unif L Rev* 231, 235–6.

12 Ibid.

13 J Morrissey, J Graves, *International sales law and arbitration: Problems, cases and commentary* (Kluwer Law International 2008) pp. 28–29.

14 Ole Lando, 'Salient Features of the Principles of European Contract Law: A comparison with the UCC', (2001) 13 *Pace International Law Review*, 339.

15 Ole Lando and H Beale(eds.), *Principles of European Contract Law, Part I, Performance and Non-performance and Remedies* (Martinus Nijhoff 1998), p. xv.

border business between European countries.[16] Intra-European trade will gradually be fostered through the familiarisation with the principles, which also have the advantage of not necessarily reflecting a certain legal system.[17] Additionally, PECL help towards the materialisation of the objectives behind the European Union, which are to have a common approach towards regulation in order to enforce the single European market.[18] Clearly, PECL can constitute the model upon which community laws may be based, and take the effort of harmonisation even further.[19] Most importantly, and this is where this paper will elaborate on, PECL stands as a tank of provisions, guidelines and principles for national courts and arbitrators and also for legislators and policy makers.[20] This means that PECL embrace both the consolidation and codification elements underpinning the concept of legal codified regulation. They stand for the consolidation of the law as it exists, but they are enriched in provisions to address issues that currently national laws are either silent on or regulate insufficiently.[21] Moreover, the Principles of European Law will be beneficial in bringing civil and common law together, especially by filling the gaps created by the varied terminology, structure and legal reasoning, policy considerations and diverse approaches on other important legal concepts.[22]

**6.** The purposes of the Principles speak for themselves: They provide a platform for the evolution of European legislation. PECL can serve as a mechanism for the better orientation or coordination of the regulations of the organs of the European Union. Parties could readily incorporate PECL in their contracts, as they form refined, and thus, more suitable solutions offered by European legal systems. The PECL and the DCFR represent not just the collection of common principles of contract law observed from the different individual European jurisdictions, but an evolutionary pronunciation of legal principles, from a legal doctrinal perspective, as they contain *de lege ferenda* provisions.[23] Progressively, through their incorporation in contracts and application by judges and arbitrators, they can develop a self-contained European *lex mercatoria*.[24] It has to be underlined that PECL will assist courts in better addressing certain ambiguous or not well-regulated issues, and they will empower the judges to apply a solution /remedy that is either the common core of Europe or an evolutionary step from the common core into a better legal principle.[25] It is clear that PECL apply to commercial and not only

16 Ibid.
17 Ibid.
18 Ibid.
19 Ibid, p. xvi.
20 Ibid.
21 Ibid.
22 Ibid, pp. xvi and xvii. The classic example of difference is the principle of good faith which is primordial in most European jurisdictions, and which can be found only sporadically in English law, through specific cases and application to very concrete circumstances.
23 Roy Goode, *Transnational Commercial Law*, para 14.41.
24 Ibid, xviii.
25 Ibid.

transactions, and the court, should it so assess, may apply them on its own.[26] It is this latter element, the fact that PECL can be of assistance without being specifically referred to by the parties, in order to assist justice in proferring a judgment which addresses parties' interests and rights in the optimal way.

7. It has been submitted by Ole Lando that the principle of freedom of contract may be curved on the occasion of a contract where one of the parties is weaker, or evidently in consumer contracts.[27] Therefore, currently PECL are a soft law instrument[28] without the authority of national, a-national or supranational law,[29] but at the same time are aspired to be the stem-cell of the European Civil Code[30] and will help in the coordination of the existing and also stimulation and upcoming EU legislation in several areas of law. The next question to be addressed is how this fits in the area of maritime law. Therefore, the author will proceed to investigate how they can be first relevant and then applicable to maritime law in a fruitful and harmonised way.

## II. From Contract Law to Maritime Law

8. This relationship is worth exploring in order to understand the important crossovers between contract, commercial and maritime law. Commercial law constitutes the *sui generis* 'meeting point' of contract law and maritime law. Several definitions have been provided for commercial law.[31] According to Roy Goode, commercial law is the "the totality of the law's response to mercantile disputes. It encompasses all those principles, rules and statutory provisions, of whatever kind and from whatever source, which bear on the private law rights and obligations of parties to commercial transactions, whether between themselves or in their relationship with others."[32] Therefore, it is not just implied, but it has also been asserted that commercial law covers transactions for the international sale of goods.[33] These are the branches of commercial law that the author will focus on in this paper, namely the law of the international sale of goods and the law of international carriage of goods by sea.

26 Article 1(101).4 of PECL.

27 Ole Lando, 'European Contract Law', in Petar Carcevic (ed) *International Contracts and Conflicts of Laws: A collection of Essays* (Graham & Trotman, London, 1990) 1, 5.

28 Ole Lando, 'Salient Features of the Principles of European Contract Law: A comparison with the UCC', above 341.

29 Ole Lando and Beale (eds.), *Principles of European Contract Law*, Part I, p. 40.

30 Ole Lando, 'Salient Features of the Principles of European Contract Law', 340.

31 See 'The Nature of Commercial Law' in LS Sealy and RJA Hooley, *Commercial Law, Text, cases and materials* (4th edn, OUP 2009), pp. 3–8: HC Gutteridge, 'Contract and Commercial Law' (1935) 51 *LQR* 117 defined commercial law as "the object of commerce that is to deal in merchandise, [...] commercial law can be defined as the special rules which apply to contracts for the sale of goods and to such contracts are ancillary thereto, namely contracts for the carriage and insurance of goods and contracts the main purpose of which is to finance the carrying out of contracts of sale".

32 LS Sealy and RJA Hooley, *Commercial Law, Text, cases and materials* (4th edn, OUP 2009), p.4 citing this abstract from Roy Goode's speech in the 1997 Hamlyn Lectures.

33 Ibid, p.4.

9. As aforementioned, PECL are principles of contract law. Before we see whether PECL can offer solutions to maritime law, in the context set above, it is crucial to look at the idiosyncrasies of regulating maritime (trade) law. As we shall see, this on the one hand, has regard to the different forms of regulating this law and the disparate sources available. Unification and harmonisation in these areas of laws is usually attempted through different ways of regulation and by bodies with different composition and policy considerations.[34] As implied above, two streams of harmonisation have been observed internationally: through international conventions and model laws[35] and through standardisation.[36] Throughout this paper the author will be referring to either commercial or maritime law taken from the broad definition that Roy Goode and several other legal scholars have advocated.

## 2.1. *Forms of harmonisation of maritime and trade laws*

10. Harmonisation of commercial laws has been the great goal justifying the rule setting work in the area of international commerce. CMI, UNCITRAL, UNIDROIT are international organisations which have undertaken the codification of rules in this field, through drafting of international conventions. There are also rules originating from business self-regulation, such as from the ICC, GAFTA, and FOSFA. Sale contracts of commodities represent the majority of international commercial sales.[37] In these contracts, it is *locus classicus* to have English law as the governing law of the contract,[38] without the country of shipment or destination being necessarily the UK, and regardless of whether payment is to be made outside the UK, or in a currency other than the English pound.[39] The choice of English law as the governing law as well as the preference for English jurisdiction is also justified by the profound expertise of English courts in commercial law matters. When dealing with international commerce, English statutory as well as common law becomes incredibly relevant. Big commodity organisations use English law in their contracts.[40]

### 2.1.1. Sets of standard trade terms

11. Incorporation of standard trade terms is another feature of international commercial contracts on shipping terms. If a certain answer to a trade question cannot

34 See in detail, Charles Debattista, 'Legislative techniques in international trade: madness or method?' [2002] JBL 626.
35 LS Sealy and RJA Hooley, *Commercial Law, Text, cases and materials* (4th edn, OUP 2009), p. 28.
36 Ibid.
37 F. Lorenzon, Y. Baatz and Lynne Skajaa, *CIF and FOB contracts* (Sweet & Maxwell 2012), para 1.001.
38 M. Bridge, *The international sale of goods* (3rd edn, Oxford University Press 2013), para 1.39; F Lorenzon, 'When is a CIF seller's carriage contract unreasonable? – Section 32(2) of the Sale of Goods Act 1979' (2007) 13 (4) *JIML* 241, 242; M.Bridge, 'Uniformity and Diversity in international sale contracts' (2003)15 *Pace Int'l L. Rev.* 55, 57.
39 Ibid.
40 M. Bridge, *The international sale of goods* (3rd edn, Oxford University Press 2013), para 1.39.

be provided by a look at trade statutes and case law or carriage statutes, conventions and case law, then the study of other sales terms voluntarily incorporated may provide the answer.[41] Some of the most popular sets are the Incoterms and the UCP 600, which are drafted by the International Chamber of Commerce (ICC). The Incoterms were published for the first time by the ICC in 1936.[42] "Incoterms" provide a set of official rules for the interpretation of trade terms used in international trade.[43] They are drafted and revised by experts from several nationalities chosen for their outstanding contribution to international commercial law and to the International Chamber of Commerce over the years.[44] They are written in a very simple language for lay people lacking the specific knowledge of lawyers.[45] They are legal but non-binding instruments, widely used by practitioners and voluntarily incorporated into contracts.[46] Their importance has been acknowledged by the Court of Justice of the European Union.[47] Designed for use with the contract of sale, Incoterms have been adopted universally as a safeguard against misunderstandings and disputes between buyers and sellers.

**12.** Since they are business-oriented, Incoterms are more pragmatic. The ICC Commission on Commercial Law and Practice (CLP), which revises the Incoterms on the one hand and UNCITRAL on the other, work in completely adverse ways: CLP, on the one hand, starts from the individual experts coming from companies, then works actively with intergovernmental organisations and, only ultimately, collaborates with national organisations for the production of effective regulatory systems.[48] UNCITRAL,[49] on the other hand, and the mechanisms behind the creation of international conventions have a governmental, rather than an industry starting point.[50] The drives behind

41 See in detail, Charles Debattista, "Legislative techniques in international trade: madness or method?" [2002] *JBL* 626.

42 M. Bridge, *The international sale of goods* (3rd edn, Oxford University Press 2013), para 10.62.

43 For a considerable analysis of the distinctive characteristics of major ways of arranging payment for sale of goods overseas see M. Goldby, *Electronic documents in maritime trade: law and practice* (OUP 2013), paras 3.09–3.17.

44 'History of the Incoterms: From 1936 to today: the Incoterms® rules' online www.iccwbo.org/products-and-services/trade-facilitation/incoterms-2010/history-of-the-incoterms-rules/ accessed 25 March 2014.

45 M. Bridge, *The international sale of goods* (3rd edn, Oxford University Press 2013), para 1.19.

46 Laurence Ravillon, 'Chronicle of informal sources on Business Law' [2012] 5 *IBLJ* 519, 542.

47 *European Court of Justice (Case C-87/10) (Third Chamber) of 9 June 2011, Electrosteel Europe SA vs Edil Centro SpA;* 'Supply of goods in a distance selling contract: the Judicial competence and the role of the Incoterms' at <www.picozzimorigi.cn/main/reports.php?id=82> accessed 23 November 2013; Melis Ozdel, 'Multimodal Transport Documents in international sale of goods' (2012) 23(7) *I.C.C.L.R.* 238.

48 'What do we do?: Commission on Commercial Law and Practice' online www.iccwbo.org/about-icc/policy-commissions/commercial-law-and-practice/what-do-we-do-/ accessed 20 March 2014.

49 On the roles of UNCITRAL see in general G Herrmann, 'The role of UNCITRAL', in I Fletcher, L Mistelis and M Cremona (eds.), *Foundations and Perspectives of International Trade Law* (Sweet & Maxwell 2001).

50 Charles Debattista, 'Legislative techniques in international trade: Madness or method?', 637. This, however, does not mean that the UNCITRAL and ICC have a competitive relation. Quite the opposite, there is cooperation as shown by the recent endorsement of Incoterms 2010 by UNCITRAL. See Report of the Commission on the work of its 45th session (Doc A/67/17), 2012, paras. 141–144.

international conventions, the Rotterdam Rules included, are harmonisation,[51] whereas the rules created by private organisations/committees/bodies such as the ICC, are oriented to bring predictability in practice.[52]

**13.** UNCITRAL have the following aims:[53] first, harmonisation, in order to minimise disparity of laws and other obstacles among jurisdictions,[54] specialisation, in order to meet current needs of international transactions and disputes,[55] modernisation, in order to take on board changes in values, technology and commercial practices,[56] codification for the elimination of obstacles paving the way for methods of communication, commerce and finance,[57] and the overall enhancement of legal certainty and confidence of traders on the provisions. These lead to the following observations.

## III. Fusion of Legal Sources

**14.** The above categories of carriage and trade legal terms seem to be almost always relevant to a legal advisor.[58] This is because they add segments to the desired legal advice on an international commercial dispute, where goods are to be carried by sea. However, they may bear controversies or prove of controversial application. This is first because they are drawn up by rival market sectors[59] and in a "sector-specific"[60] manner. Carriage representatives support carriage interests whereas trade private bodies push for more commercial, rather than detailed shipping solutions. One should also be expecting synergies between all these sources, based on the fact that conventions have their own intricacies. Self-regulatory terms and conventions are drafted under different legislative techniques and as pointed out above, by organisations with different aims.[61]

**15.** All this international rule-setting agencies as well as the Lando Commission had certain objectives in common. They all aim to further uniformity of the application of the law,[62] to be sufficiently flexible in order to be timeless and embrace possible future developments[63], and as far as PECL are concerned, to sometimes serve as an ideal solution to a contract law problem, where the application of national laws would be insufficient.

51 Charles Debattista, 'Legislative techniques in international trade: Madness or method?', p. 636.
52 Ibid.
53 As listed by G Herrmann, 'The role of UNCITRAL' above.
54 Ibid, paras 2-010-2-012.
55 Ibid, paras 2-013-2-014.
56 Ibid, paras 2-015-2016.
57 Ibid, paras 2-017-2-020. This is the so-called "preventive unification".
58 See in detail, Charles Debattista, "Legislative techniques in international trade: madness or method?" [2002] *JBL* 626.
59 Charles Debattista, 'Legislative techniques in international trade: Madness or Method?', p. 632.
60 Ibid p. 634.
61 Ibid p. 635.
62 On PECL see O Lando and H Beale (eds.), *Principles of European Contract Law Parts I and II* ( Kluwer Law International 2000), p xxvi.
63 On PECL see, ibid. xxvii.

### 3.1. *Main underpinnings of international commercial law*

**16.** On the one hand the business community is interested in the flexibility, which is preserved by commercial freedom and party autonomy.[64] But this should not counter the national and international interest for certainty and predictability in the definition of rights and obligations as well as in the outcome in case of a dispute.[65] Goode submits that these two pillars of commercial law are often in conflict.[66] This can be prevented by fairly clear and comprehensive principles which affect the judicial decision-making.[67] Clearly, this is an area where PECL are welcome to assist.

**17.** Therefore it is in the interest of commercial law and of the business community to open the legal system to new practices and customs, without this minimising the ultimate interest in fairness and justice.[68] Flexibility can be very much achieved by the structure of English law and the use of standard contracts as a form of commercial harmonisation, but fairness can be ensured through the outline of principles permeated by a doctrinal approach that takes on-board the regulation that promotes justice to all parties.[69] The benefit of codification is that it simplifies and discerns the law, but it also offers the chance to assess it and optimise it.[70]

**18.** So far, international codification through conventions has been an important platform of harmonisation, but we have also moved towards other methods:[71] model laws, principles( see PECL), and best practice guides.[72]

**19.** Maritime law is permeated by the use of standard contracts and especially in the area of carriage of goods by sea, we have had international harmonisation attempts through conventions. Traditionally, these conventions, and particularly carriage of goods conventions were intended to introduce a fair balance of risk allocation between carriers and cargo interests. The Rotterdam Rules represent the most recent convention in the area of carriage of goods by sea, which encapsulates freedom of contract through provisions for customised agreements that may derogate from most of the mandatory provisions of the Rotterdam Rules, if certain conditions are met. These customised agreements are the so-called volume contracts. Derogations from the Rotterdam Rules

64 E McKendrick(ed.), *Goode on Commercial Law* (4th edn, Penguin 2010), p. 1348.
65 Ibid.
66 Ibid.
67 Ibid.
68 Ibid, pp. 1348, 1349.
69 Ibid.
70 Ibid. p.1352.
71 Herbert Kronke, 'The future of harmonisation and formulating agencies: The role of UNIDROIT' in Ian Fletcher, Loukas Mistelis, Marise Cremona (eds.), *Foundations and Perspectives of International Trade Law*, (Sweet & Maxwell 2001), para 5-018.
72 See also Loukas Mistelis 'Is Harmonisation a necessary evil? The future of harmonisation and new sources of international trade law' in I Fletcher, L Mistelis and M Cremona (eds.), *Foundations and Perspectives of International Trade Law* (Sweet & Maxwell 2001), para 1.029–1.030.

were initially conceived to apply to parties of equal bargaining power; however, this is not properly reflected in the text or the heading of the article. There are sections which are specifically devoted to the protection of third parties, but which are so broadly drafted that they will almost certainly be variably applied and interpreted by different national courts, when the Rotterdam Rules come into force.

**20.** In the opinion of the author this is an area where PECL can have a supplementary, if not salutary effect. In the following heading the author will discuss the application of PECL to a volume contract resort to PECL for the sake of interpretational help is justified by the fact that the volume contract provisions have raised eyebrows with regards to the potential that Article 80 of the RR leaves for the abuse of traders with little bargaining power.

## IV. Can PECL Promote the Smooth Application and Efficient Integration of the Rotterdam Rules in Europe?

**21.** This question is important but also relevant to the topic of the 8th European colloquium on maritime law. Better integration of European laws is anyway among the objectives of PECL. The Rotterdam Rules constitute the latest attempt of harmonisation in the area of maritime trade law, which has received criticism in certain aspects. Therefore, studying how a convention in carriage of goods can optimise its harmonisation effects and foster trade in Europe, through PECL is at the crux of this conference's debate. The place is also significant, as Rotterdam was at the centre of the world in September of 2009 for the signature of the Rules, and also this year with the most distinguished legal scholars of European maritime law gathered to discuss PECL, DCFR and the common law and the contribution they can make to maritime law. Therefore both the time and place are pertinent for the discussion the author wants to make.

**22.** First, the Rotterdam Rules, like PECL, constitute a legal piece of harmonisation,[73] but in the field of maritime law. The Rotterdam Rules were drafted to update and harmonise carriage of goods wholly or partly by sea and finally set aside the fragmented regimes which have been in existence so far.[74] The Rotterdam Rules recognise freedom of contract and want to secure the ability of shippers and carriers to tailor-make their agreements. Thus, they allow derogations from the mandatory provisions of the Rotterdam Rules, under certain circumstances.[75] Volume contracts are defined as volume contracts for the carriage of a specified quantity of goods in a series of shipments over a given period of time.[76] Given, that the definition of a volume contract is vague in certain respects, and because oppositions have been made during the preparatory works,

73 On the aims of the RR see the preamble to the Convention available at: www.uncitral.org/pdf/english/texts/transport/rotterdam_rules/Rotterdam-Rules-E.pdf accessed 9 September 2014.

74 Namely the Hague, Hague-Visby and Hamburg Rules.

75 See the proposal of the U.S. on the need and benefits to allow this contractual freedom in the preparatory works of the RR.

76 See Article 1(2) of the RR.

the draftsmen of the Convention have decided to set forth a list of formal conditions that the volume contract should satisfy so that the derogations prove to be consensual and valid.[77]

**23.** Article 80(2) reads:
A derogation pursuant to paragraph 1 of this article is binding only when:

*(a) The volume contract contains a prominent statement that it derogates from this Convention;*
*(b) The volume contract is (i) individually negotiated or (ii) prominently specifies the sections of the volume contract containing the derogations;*
*(c) The shipper is given an opportunity and notice of the opportunity to conclude a contract of carriage on terms and conditions that comply with this Convention without any derogation under this article; and*
*(d) The derogation is neither (i) incorporated by reference from another document nor (ii) included in a contract of adhesion that is not subject to negotiation*

*This prominence of the derogations along with the need of an express consent to such terms are specifically requested for the protection of a third party (usually assignee, subsequent holder of the transport document), since such parties will not have negotiated the contract.*[78]

**24.** The major criticism that the framework around derogations from the RR has received is that it affords carriers with a potentially extensive possibility to derogate from the RR.[79] This, in turn may empower them to impose this derogation standard in the market, "forcing" shippers to conclude contracts where the carrier undertakes little liability against usually a low freight rate, and thus expose especially parties without much bargaining power or experience to undesirable liability exclusions. It is especially small or medium sized shippers that need this protection and this naturally takes us to similar provisions of PECL that could be of help.

**25.** One such is Article 2:104: Terms Not Individually Negotiated. The article states the following:

> *(1) Contract terms which have not been individually negotiated may be invoked against a party who did not know of them only if the party invoking them took reasonable steps to bring them to the other party's attention before or when the contract was concluded.*

77 See Article 80(2) of the RR.
78 Article 80(5) of the RR.
79 See among others Asariotis, Regina Asariotis, 'Reflections on the Rotterdam Rules', in M.A. Clarke (ed.), *Maritime Law Evolving: Thirty Years at Southampton* (Hart Publishing 2013); Regina Asariotis 'UNCITRAL Draft Convention on Contracts for the Carriage of Goods Wholly or Partly by Sea: Mandatory Rules and Freedom of contract' Antapassis, Athanassiou and Rosaeg (eds.), *Competition and Regulation in Shipping and Shipping Related Industries* (Martinus Nijhoff, 2009), pp. 358 and 361–363.

*(2) Terms are not brought appropriately to a party's attention by a mere reference to them in a contract document, even if that party signs the document.*

**26.** Coming back to volume contracts, in the opinion of the author, the requirements for an opportunity and notice of the opportunity to contract in non-derogatory terms are impractical and perhaps confusing, especially in terms of evidence. A notice can be in writing, but the same cannot apply separately to the opportunity to contract on regular 'RR' terms; the opportunity per se cannot be evidenced through writing if there are no more specific indicators.[80]

Surprisingly, the rationale behind subsection 80(2) of the RR, instead of over-emphasising the need of protection of parties in an unprivileged bargaining position, focuses on the conclusion of contracts in a way which is compatible with commercial practice;[81] the fears of having small shippers exposed to volume contracts, almost on a standard basis, with the negotiations perhaps focusing on freight, was understood during the preparatory works.[82] It has to be clarified that a mere written indication that the contract has been individually negotiated does not necessarily mean that this has actually been the case, or more importantly that a more vulnerable party (for example a smaller shipper) has been reasonably directed to all or some of the derogations.

**27.** Parties could presumably sign a volume contract with a coversheet saying *"On date x, Y and Z have entered into individual negotiations and concluded a volume contract that derogates from the RR. Some terms are agreed outside the mandatory scope of the Rotterdam Rules. For details of the clauses see Annex attached"*. What is remarkable in the above scenario is that Article 80 may be *technically* satisfied, without the original drafting aims being properly solidified, hence, Article 80 of the RR has been hotly debated by practitioners and academics.

**28.** Evidently, such a contract *prima facie* satisfies the formality of an individually negotiated contract, whereas this may not be the actual case. Besides, there is only an indication of derogations, without exact knowledge of the different provisions. This obstacle can be avoided in two ways: either by way of interpretation, if it is inferred that the requirement for the opportunity is satisfied through the tender of a written notice of the opportunity; or by a specific provision in the volume contract with a simpler wording. For clarity, the parties can stipulate in their contract that the shipper was offered an opportunity to contract on standard terms and conditions subject to the RR, and he has rejected.

80 See preparatory works of the Rotterdam Rules, 15th session Report, A/CN.9/576, para 83, where there was an official suggestion for inserting indicators specifying the individuality of the negotiations, e.g., the bargaining power of the parties.

81 See, 15th session Report, A/CN.9/576, para 82, where *"a need to maintain a measure of commercial pragmatism"* was acknowledged. The draftsmen were cautious not to insert precautions that would be too onerous and thus commercially impracticable.

82 See preparatory works of the Rotterdam Rules, 15th session Report, A/CN.9/576, para 83.

However, even in that case, there does not seem to be a way to prove whether the intention of the carrier to enter into a non-volume carriage contract has actually occurred. If the terms of the volume contract are a lot more attractive (low freight rates for instance), there is potentially nothing to prevent the shipper from being induced by the carrier – or left without a viable alternative choice – because of the commercial pressure exercised or the standardisation of the freight market.[83] The reason why this is said is because Article 80(2) of the RR seems to insert steps showing that there is adequate consideration before the volume contract is concluded.

**29.** In the opinion of the author, individual negotiations needed to be a separate and independent precondition to assure that there is abundant clarification of the sections that will be derogated. The word "sections" used in Article 80(2)(b)(ii) of the RR mostly refers to the numbers of the derogations,[84] so, one could say that they are used figuratively. In the author's view, the logical and imperative order of steps which have to be proven in writing should have been: the opportunity to contract on conventional terms, individual negotiations about the content of the intended derogations and lastly, prominent statement of the content of the derogations on the contract itself. Eventually, even if a volume contract is entered into and satisfies these preconditions, it is difficult to know the particular preceding bargaining matrix, whether the party signed accepting or knowing all of the derogations and their substance, or whether the contract was offered on an actual take it or leave it basis, thus making it a contract of adhesion.[85]

**30.** It is the author's contention that the above formalities could be of practical help if they were read not only in light of the underlying principles of the RR, but essentially if they were read through the principle underlying Article 2.104 of PECL.[86] A European court could read the RR also in light of PECL, and go beyond the technicalities of Article 80 of the RR, giving justice to the parties and interpretational help to the RR, that are a bit vague on the matter. The fact that the principles represent the common core of European contract law would mean that an interpretation of Article 80 of the RR in light of PECL could be, and in fact should be followed by any European court. At the same time, this would increase trust of the trade community in the way disputes are resolved within the European jurisdiction and would indeed materialise PECL's objective to foster inter-European trade. Essentially, reading Article 80 of the RR under the light of articles of PECL such as the aforementioned would safeguard the laborious work of all the states,

83 This has been admitted by several commentators, but it was foreseen during the deliberations of the RR, as seen above.

84 See Y Baatz and others, *The Rotterdam Rules: A Practical Annotation* (Informa 2009), para 80.04.

85 The volume contract which derogated should not be in the form of a contract of adhesion according to article 80(2)(d) of the RR.

86 Articles 4. 109 and 4:110 of PECL are also in the same vein. Article 4:110 para 1, reads:
"A party may avoid a term which has not been individually negotiated, if contrary to the requirements of good faith and fair dealing, it causes a significant imbalance in the parties' rights and obligations arising under the contract to the detriment of that party, taking into account the nature of the performance to be rendered under the contract, all the other terms of the contract and the circumstances at the time the contract was concluded".

agencies and organisations towards the RR and the intensive need of the international trade community for one carriage regime, which is modern, all-embracive and leaves behind the jurisdictional chaos of the present, with multiple regimes applicable and the national courts still judging also through the lenses of the law proffered by their own jurisdiction.

## V. Suggestions and Final Recommendations

**31.** In this article, the author has embarked on a considerable analysis of the possible value of PECL, examining their hypothetical contribution to the application of justice under a vexing issue of maritime law. This concerned volume contracts not individually negotiated, as regulated under the Rotterdam Rules. Before that, the author illustrated the principles underlying PECL and described the main characteristics of maritime and commercial law, focusing on the fusion of legal sources by rule-setting agencies with different composition and objectives.

**32.** Opinions on PECL have usually been polarised: the principles have either been completely distrusted or appreciated from the prism of wishful thinking. The author has conceived a way of considering PECL and the RR as not just two more – fairly recent – legal pieces which may never be of practical use or application, but as a way of seeing if and how they could prove useful in the modern maritime law context.

**33.** At the moment there are concerns about the possible application of both PECL and the Rotterdam Rules. The idea of the author is to use PECL in an attempt to provide interpretational help to an international contract (volume contract with derogations) which may give rise to a dispute that will have to be resolved within Europe. Thus, the author explained how the article(s) of PECL on terms not individually negotiated may protect an unsophisticated commercial party which has entered into a volume contract under commercial pressure, with Article 80 of the RR being only seemingly complied with.

One should not look at the suggestions of the author as an attempt to add layers of checks and principles, but as an indicative illustration of how PECL, which are at the disposal of European courts and arbitrators for the achievement of legal certainty, may actually contribute to a fair and homogeneous resolution of maritime disputes within Europe.

Andrew Tettenborn

# GOOD FAITH, THE DCFR AND SHIPPING LAW

## I. Introduction

1. In the 1920s the Australian cartoonist H.M. Bateman gained fame and a large fortune in England with his cartoons of the disingenuous, whose innocent but unconventional pronouncements spawned universal shock and consternation. These days an English lawyer, if so inclined, can induce much the same effect in a civil lawyer by stating that the law in England gets on very well without the need for any general doctrine of good faith.

2. The purpose of this article is to investigate the potential effect on English shipping law of the introduction of just such a universal idea of good faith through the medium of possible European contract harmonisation. This is not too far-fetched. Among other proposals[1], the Principles of European Contract Law (PECL), openly EU-backed and billed as possible code material[2], and the vastly more ambitious Draft Common Frame of Reference (DCFR), a document not limited to contract and with a distinct whiff of a European Civil Code about it[3], are on the table. Both, as will be seen, have a great deal to say on the subject of good faith.

1 Notably the proposed 2011 Common European Sales Law adopted in February 2014 by the European Parliament. See, for a history: L. DiMatteo, "Common European Sales Law: a critique of its rationales, functions, and unanswered questions" [2012] *Journal of International Trade Law & Policy* 222.

2 See e.g. O. Lando, "Principles of European Contract Law: An Alternative to or a Precursor of European Legislation" (1992) 40 *Am. J. Comp. L.* 573, 577; J. Smits (ed), *The Need for a European Contract Code*, Chs 1,2. Of course, if the audience be Eurosceptic, the Principles can be presented as a mere scholarly demonstration of the hidden similarities between European jurists' thought patterns: see J. Basedow, "Codification of Private Law in the EU: The making of a Hybrid" (2001) 9 *Eur.Rev.Priv.L.* 35, and compare L. Miller, "The Common Frame of Reference and the feasibility of a common contract law in Europe" [2007] *JBL* 378, 381–2.

3 In particular it incorporates a good deal of the EU acquis, and greatly expands the contract section to encompass a good many specific types of contract, as well as general contract principles. See generally H. Eidenmüller et al, "The Common frame of Reference for European Private Law – Policy Choices and Codification Problems" (2008) 28 *OJLS* 659, esp 669 ff; N. Jansen and R. Zimmermann, "'A European Civil Code in All But Name': Discussing the Nature and Purposes of the Draft Common Frame of Reference" [2010] *C.L.J.* 98. S. Whittaker, "A framework of principle for European contract law?" (2009)

## II. Background: English Law, Civilians and Good Faith

**3.** Despite the above, this is not to say that "good faith" is unknown to English lawyers. On the contrary: the phrase is frequently used by them. Furthermore, over and over again rules which would be regarded by a civilian as stemming from a principle of good faith are replicated in some other form in England. But this still does not mean that English law[4] has anything like a doctrine of good faith as understood elsewhere. There are two vital differences in its approach.

**4.** First, "good faith" when referred to in the English law of obligations is used in a studiedly narrow way.[5] Normally it refers, not to some overall quality of a person's behaviour, but to a particular aspect of it: in most cases, his lack of knowledge of some given fact, or his lack of some specific intent. Typical instances concern knowledge of states of affairs that may affect rights under a specific type of contract: for example, the rule – sometimes expressed as one of "good faith" – that a claim under a performance bond is good, provided the claimant does not actually know there is no background liability[6], or the marine assured's "good faith" duty of disclosure, meaning merely that he must disclose adverse facts which are known to him[7] ). "Good faith" is also sometimes used as a portmanteau term for duties implicit in particular relationships, as with the special duty of trust and confidence in an employment contract[8], a trustee or fiduciary's duty to pay particular regard to his beneficiary's interests[9], or a receiver's

125 *L.Q.R.* 615, 623–624 regards with some disbelief the stout denial of the European Commission that a code is envisaged as the eventual outcome.

4 Note the limitation to English law. Elsewhere in the common law world the idea of some kind of general obligation of good faith is slightly more acceptable. US orthodoxy, for example, now recognises at least a limited doctrine, both at common law (e.g. *Wigand v Bachmann-Bechtel Brewing Co*, 222 NY 272 at 277 (1918), *Feld v Levy & Sons*, 37 NY 2d 466, 470 (1975)), and under the UCC, §1–203 and the Restatement 2d of Contracts, §205: on which, see generally R. Summers, "'Good faith' in General Contract Law and the sales provision of the Uniform Commercial Code", 54 *Va L.Rev.* 195 (1968) and J. Calamari & J. Perillo, "The Law of Contracts" (4th ed), 457 et seq. Australia seems to be going the same way in the common law of contract: see *Renard Constructions (ME) Pty Ltd v Minister for Public Works* (1992) 26 *NSWLR* 234, 268 (Priestley JA), Hughes Aircraft Systems International Ltd v Airservices Australia Ltd (1997) 76 *FCR* 151, 192–193 (Finn J) and the enthusiastic endorsement to be found in J. Carter, *Contract Law in Australia* (6th ed). Ch 2.

5 For a useful short comparative summary, see the *Max Planck Encyclopedia of European Private Law*, Vol. I, pp.792–793.

6 *Wuhan Guoyu Logistics Group Co Ltd & Anr v Emporiki Bank of Greece SA* [2013] EWCA Civ 1679; [2014] 1 Lloyd's Rep. 273,t [23] (Tomlinson L.J.). See too *Trafalgar House Construction (Regions) Ltd v General Surety and Guarantee Co Ltd* (1994) 38 ConLR 53, 58, 62 (Saville L.J. and Bingham M.R.) (reversed on other grounds, [1996] A.C. 199).

7 Marine Insurance Act 1906, ss.17 (marine insurance comports utmost good faith) and 18(1) (assured to disclose relevant facts *known to him*).

8 See e.g. *Lakshmi v Mid Cheshire Hospitals NHS Trust* [2008] *EWHC* 878 (QB); [2008] *I.R.L.R.* 956 at [27].

9 See e.g. *Bristol & West Building Society v Mothew* [1998] Ch 1, 18 (Millett LJ). In *Bradbury v BBC* [2012] EWHC 1369 (Ch); [2012] *Pens. L.R.* 283 at [90], Warren J referred to a trustee's duty of trust and confidence and good faith.

duty not to misuse a power of sale.[10] But there is emphatically no permissible appeal to good faith as a generalised free-standing principle supplementing or qualifying the exercise of particular rights.[11]

5. Secondly, whenever an English court encounters situations appearing to a civil lawyer as aspects of good faith, it frequently (and unsurprisingly) reaches the same result as the civilian would.[12] But in such a case it says specifically what rule it is applying and sees no need to generalise further, or try to enclose it under a single umbrella concept called "good faith" or anything else.[13] So (for instance) a contractor's implicit duty not to subvert the whole purpose of a contract is very much alive and well at common law[14], as is the rule protecting of those who rely to their detriment on assertions of fact[15] or on promises not to invoke rights such as prescription[16], or that contracts are construed according to business realities and the reasonable understanding of the parties to them.[17] But they are called for what they are: the implied term of co-operation, estoppel, and the rule of business interpretation. It would never occur to an English lawyer to put them all together under one rubric, or in one chapter of a book.[18]

6. When we turn elsewhere, by contrast, the difference with the civilian approach is patent. Of course civil law systems parallel English law in recognising good faith as an

10 See e.g. *Downsview Nominees Ltd v First City Corporation Ltd* [1993] *AC* 295, 312 (Lord Templeman).

11 For authorities making this point uncompromisingly, see e.g. *Interfoto Picture Library Ltd v Stiletto Visual Programmes Ltd* [1989] QB 433, 439 (Lord Bingham MR); *Timeload Ltd v British Telecommunications Plc* [1995] E.M.L.R. 459, 468 (Lord Bingham MR); *ING Bank NV v Ros Roca SA* [2011] *EWCA Civ* 353, [2012] 1 W.L.R. 472 at [92] (Rix LJ); *Horkulak v Cantor Fitzgerald International Ltd* [2004] *EWCA Civ* 1287; [2005] I.C.R. 402 at [30] (Potter LJ); *Chitty on Contracts* (31st edn), Vol 1, para. 1-039. The point is not lost on the drafters of the DCFR: *Principles, Definitions and Model Rules of European Private Law: Draft Common Frame of Reference (DCFR)* (hereafter DCFR Commentary), 36.

12 See e.g. A. Forte (ed), *Good Faith in Contract and Property Law*, Ch 3 (E. McKendrick, *Good faith: A Matter of Principle?*).

13 Despite occasional attempts: for a fully-argued advocacy of acceptance, see *Yam Seng Pte Ltd v International Trade Corp Ltd* [2013] EWHC 111 (QB), [2013] 1 C.L.C. 662 at [120]-[155] (Leggatt J). Not surprisingly, efforts to move the common law in the direction of accepting a doctrine of good faith normally take the form of arguing that disparate rules that might be regarded by a civilian as reflecting a good faith rule should be explicitly gathered together under that rubric, with the latter then being liable to be extended to cover other cases so far not dealt with. An example is J. Carter, *Contract Law in Australia* (6th ed), Ch 2, referred to above.

14 E.g. *Cory & Son Ltd v London Corporation* [1951] 2 KB 476, 484 (Lord Asquith); *CEL Group Ltd v Nedlloyd Lines UK Ltd* [2003] *EWCA Civ* 1716; [2004] 1 *Lloyd's Rep*. 381.

15 A rule neatly summarised in *Spencer Bower on Estoppel by Representation* (4th ed), Ch.1; and epitomised by cases such as *Pickard v Sears* (1837) 6 *A & E* 469.

16 See e.g. *The August Leonhardt* [1985] 2 *Lloyd's Rep*. 28, esp at 33–35 (Kerr LJ); also *The Antares (No 2)* [1986] 2 Lloyd's Rep. 633; M. Canny, *Limitation of Actions in England and Wales*, Paras. 1.13–1.14.

17 See in particular *Investors Compensation Scheme Ltd v West Bromwich Building Society* [1998] 1 *WLR* 896, 912–913 (Lord Lloyd).

18 These examples are taken, as any German lawyer will recognise, because they are regarded as three of the best-known examples of the application to contracts of the general duty of good faith under BGB, §242.

ingredient of specific rules (for example, those giving some innocent purchaser of goods good title to them[19] ). But far more importantly, civilians almost universally accept some overall requirement for parties to act in good faith, and a corresponding idea of generality of principle.[20] However wide or narrow its application[21], and despite the fact that in many systems good faith ideas cover very different and discrete areas, there is also always at least some theory of commonality between them (such as the idea in German law that in the context of private obligations good faith has the function of supplementing the parties' rights, preventing their abuse and allowing their adjustment to meet future developments[22]). Admittedly the application varies. In France, for example, until relatively recently the doctrine was of comparatively little importance in practice[23], whereas in Germany it has always marked a central point of departure.[24] Again, in some systems its application is limited to specific areas such as existing contracts: this is particularly the position under French law.[25] But elsewhere the principle applies more widely or even universally. Hence in German law it affects all rights of any description, contractual or otherwise and whatever their source[26]; and this is often reflected

19 See e.g. the general provision in BGB §932 (person taking possession of a thing from a non-owner nonetheless gets good title "unless at the time … he would obtain title he is not in good faith" (" … *es sei denn, dass er zu der Zeit, zu der er… das Eigentum erwerben würde, nicht in gutem Glauben ist*")).

20 "The principle of good faith anchored in §242 BGB puts an intrinsic limitation on the content of all rights" ("*Das in §242 BGB verankerte Prinzip von Treu und Glauben bildet eine allen Rechten immanente Inhaltsbegrenzung*"). See BGH, 16. 2. 2005 – IV ZR 18/04, 2005 TranspR 170, 172 quoting from Palandt/Heinrichs, BGB, 64 ed, §242 Rn. 38. See too in the Swiss context BGE 83 II 345, 348 (17.6.1957) (requirement of good faith under Article 2 of the Swiss Civil Code graphically described as a "basic assumption of the most general possible type" ("*Grundsatz allgemeinster Art*").

21 And the application of good faith varies enormously between different systems: for brief coverage see *Max Planck Encyclopedia of European Private Law*, Vol. I, pp.791–792.

22 That is, its functions of *Ergänzung, Schränkung, Anpassung*, In turn loosely derived from the Papinian's comment on the *ius honorarium* (or *ius praetorium*) as an institution *adiuvandi vel supplendi vel corrigendi iuris civilis* (see F. Wieacker, *Zur rechtstheoretischen Präzisierung des §§242 BGB*, Tübingen 1956).

23 See P. Malaurie & L. Aynès, *Les Obligations*, 4th ed, §764. But times are changing: ibid. or a reference to the application of good faith varies enormously between different systems, see *Max Planck Encyclopedia of European Private Law*, Vol. I, pp.791–792.

24 See BGH, 16. 2. 2005 – IV ZR 18/04, 2005 *TranspR* 170, 172, referred to in Note above.

25 Where the only direct codal application of a duty of good faith is Code Civil, Article 1134(3) ("[Contracts] must be kept in good faith" ("*[Les conventions] doivent être exécutées de bonne foi*")). See particularly the decision in Civ 3e 14.9.2005, 04–10.856. In those common law jurisdictions that have accepted the idea of good faith, the position tends to be the same. See, in the US, UCC 1–304 ("Every contract or duty within the Uniform Commercial Code imposes an obligation of good faith in its performance and enforcement"), and the *Restatement 2d of Contracts*, Article 205. In Australia too, however much the doctrine may be accepted in the law of contract, there is little sign of its spreading outside it.

26 Although BGB, §242, is in terms limited to the performance of obligations ("The debtor is bound to perform according to the requirements of good faith … " ("*Der Schuldner ist verpflichtet, die Leistung so zu bewirken, wie Treu und Glauben … es erfordern*")), it has been consistently interpreted as applying to the exercise of all rights as well.

elsewhere, especially in systems following or aping German law[27] ). Yet again, in the contractual context, while it is generally accepted that the duty of good faith cannot be excluded as such, how far it effectively constrains freedom of contract can vary extensively. In some jurisdictions what amounts to good faith may in effect itself depend on the terms of the contract, in which case freedom is hardly affected at all[28]: on the other hand, at the other end of the spectrum, notably again under German law, attempts to exclude particular duties may be regarded as ipso facto inadmissible bad faith.[29]

## III. The PECL, the DCFR and Good Faith

7. On the question of good faith, there is no doubt where the DCFR stands. (This article will concentrate on the DCFR as the fuller and more recent document, though reference will be made where necessary to the PECL, whose provisions in the contract context are in any case fairly similar, though not identical). The basis is solidly civilian, rather than common law, in conception. Good faith is regarded as an absolutely fundamental principle[30], that runs through the whole text. It is introduced through a general provision (III-1:103), under which a person "has a duty to act in accordance with good faith and fair dealing in performing an obligation, in exercising a right to performance, in pursuing or defending a remedy for non-performance, or in exercising a right to terminate an obligation or contractual relationship". On freedom of contract, it is said specifically that this duty "may not be excluded or limited by contract or other juridical act".[31] Furthermore, this is repeatedly supplemented by parallel provisions elsewhere: there are direct references to obligations of good faith and fair dealing in the treatment

27 Notably Swiss law. See Civil Code, Article 2 ("In exercising his rights and performing his duties everyone is bound to observe the principles of good faith") ("*Jedermann hat in der Ausübung seiner Rechte und in der Erfüllung seiner Pflichten nach Treu und Glauben zu handeln*")). Dutch law is even clearer in emphasising that good faith trumps everything else: see BWB, Book 6, Article 2 ("*Een tussen hen krachtens wet, gewoonte of rechtshandeling geldende regel is niet van toepassing, voor zover dit in de gegeven omstandigheden naar maatstaven van redelijkheid en billijkheid onaanvaardbaar zou zijn*").

28 See UCC, 1-302 ("The obligations of good faith, diligence, reasonableness, and care prescribed by [the Uniform Commercial Code] may not be disclaimed by agreement. The parties, by agreement, may determine the standards by which the performance of those obligations is to be measured if those standards are not manifestly unreasonable"). A similar rule has been held to apply under the *Restatement 2d of Contracts*, Article 205: see e.g. *VTR, Inc. v. Goodyear Tire & Rubber Co*, 303 F.Supp. 773 (1969, DC NY).

29 As will appear below, in particular in connection with matters such as carriers' attempts to exonerate themselves from the obligation to provide a seaworthy vessel.

30 See e.g. DCFR Commentary, 67–68, referring to a fundamental principle of "[n]ot allowing people to rely on their own unlawful, dishonest or unreasonable conduct."

31 Parallel is PECL1:201: "(1) Each party must act in accordance with good faith and fair dealing. (2) The parties may not exclude or limit this duty." See for criticism H. Beale, "General Clauses and Specific Rules in the Principles of European Contract Law: The Good Faith Clause", in *General Clauses and Standards in European Contract Law* 205, 218 (S. Grundmann & D. Mazeaud eds., 2006) (remarking that "Article 1:102 needs to be revised to make clear that good faith and fair dealing is not an overarching control mechanism.").

of liabilities arising from pre-contractual negotiations[32]; of interpretation and implied terms[33]; of the duty to co-operate with a co-contractor[34]; of conditional contracts[35]; of error[36], fraud[37], and change of circumstances[38]; and of the treatment of clauses exonerating parties from contractual[39] and other[40] liabilities.

8. Indeed, there is little room for doubt that the DCFR conception of good faith is not only civilian, but is intended to track the wide-ranging German (and German-related) approach referred to above. What the two have in common includes the idea that good faith affects all rights without exception[41]; the practice of explicitly incorporating good faith duties not only in general clauses but also in numerous particular provisions[42], such as (importantly) exemption clauses[43]; a large degree of parallelism in the matters dealt with[44]; and a clear willingness to allow good faith considerations to trump

32 DCFR, II-3:301 (also PECL, 2:301).

33 DCFR, II-8:102(1)(g) (also PECL, 5:102).

34 DCFR, III-1:104. This is in all but name a duty of good faith, even if the word "good faith" is not used: see DCFR 715 and e.g. L. Macgregor, *Report on the Draft Common Frame of Reference: a report prepared for the Scottish Government*, University of Edinburgh, Part 4.

35 DCFR, III-1:108(4) (also PECL, 16:102).

36 DCFR, II-7:201 (also PECL, 4:103).

37 DCFR, II-7:205 (also PECL, 4:107).

38 DCFR, III-1:110 (also PECL, 6:111).

39 See DCFR, II-7:215, II-9:405 (also PECL, 4:110, 4:118, 8:109).

40 See e.g. DCFR, III-3:105 and VI-5:401. The former is remarkable, in that in III-3:105(2) it allows a court to disapply a remedial restriction even where valid under the other parts of the DCFR.

41 The width of DCFR, III-1:103, under which a person "has a duty to act in accordance with good faith and fair dealing in performing an obligation, in exercising a right to performance, in pursuing or defending a remedy for non-performance, or in exercising a right to terminate an obligation or contractual relationship", is a clear deliberate parallel to the references in Notes – above.

42 Thus, as with the DCFR, good faith under German law explicitly extends to the rules of contract interpretation (BGB, §157); to the duty not to subvert conditional contracts (BGB, §162); to the test of what is an unfair and unenforceable standard term (BGB 307); to what happens in the case of change of circumstances (BGB, §313); and to the right to withhold performance (BGB, §320). In addition, other provisions de facto apply good-faith-derived rules despite not expressly mentioning the words "good faith": for instance, BGB, §311.2, on pre-contractual duties. In at least one case, the unavailability of a claim to performance unsupported by any adequate interest on the claimant's part, the rule is regarded as explicitly as good-faith-based in Germany (see BGB, §275.2) but not under the DCFR (III-3:302): but even here the DCFR thinking is on the lines of good faith (see O. Lando, "Salient Features of the Principles of European Contract Law: A Comparison with the UCC" 13 *Pace Int'l L. Rev.* 339, 350 (2001) on the equivalent provision in PECL, 9:101).

43 Compare DCFR, II–9:405 ("A term in a contract between businesses is unfair… if it is a term forming part of standard terms supplied by one party and of such a nature that its use grossly deviates from good commercial practice, contrary to good faith and fair dealing") with BGB, §307 ("Provisions in a party's standard terms of business are ineffective if they unduly disadvantage the party other than the one employing them contrary to the requirements of good faith and fair dealing" ("*Bestimmungen in Allgemeinen Geschäftsbedingungen sind unwirksam, wenn sie den Vertragspartner des Verwenders entgegen den Geboten von Treu und Glauben unangemessen benachteiligen*")).

44 See the previous note. In some other cases a duty only impliedly good-faith-based in the DCFR (such as the duty to co-operate in DCFR, III-1:104) matches a duty expressly so based elsewhere, as in Germany (e.g. RGZ 8.5.1926, 113 RGZ 403, 405 and *Münchener Kommentar zum BGB* (6th ed), §242, Rn 167–169).

commercial freedom of contract.[45] The point is a significant one, since it means that when considering the possible effect of good faith *à la* DCFR on English law, it is relevant to cite not only the commentary on the DCFR but also the (very extensive) German and related authorities on the same matter.

## IV. The Effect on English Shipping Law

**9.** This subject of this paper is how the introduction of a general obligation of good faith as part of the DCFR might affect shipping law. The concentration will be on English law, for three reasons. First, as appears above the doctrinal contrast is greatest here. Secondly, in contrast to the nuanced world of give-and-take embedded in the idea of good faith, shipping lawyers traditionally think in terms of black and white (a charter can either be cancelled or not; a time-bar provision either does, or does not, apply; and so on). And thirdly, there is a practical point: for several reasons[46] shipping disputes have gravitated to the English courts through explicit choice of law clauses, and an entirely disproportionate number of them are therefore decided – or at least arbitrated – under its rules.

### *4.1. Starting-point: in many ways, change may be surprisingly limited*

**10.** Despite the yawning intellectual gulf between civil and common lawyers on the subject, it is suggested that the overall effect of introducing good faith as envisaged by the DCFR would not necessarily be as radical as one might expect.

**11.** One reason for this has already been hinted at. Many of the classic applications of good faith doctrine, even as it appears in the extensive DFCR version, are entirely familiar to English lawyers. So, for example, with a contractor's good faith duty to co-operate[47] and not to subvert the purpose of the contract[48], readily admitted in English law under the different but similarly-oriented rubric of an implied term[49]; or with the rule that a

45 E.g. BGB, §307 (see above). For instances see BGH 28.02.1983, II ZR 31/82, *VersR* 1983, 549 (charterparty limitation of seaworthiness obligation annulled: cf too OLG Köln 3.7.1998, 3 U 105/93); BGH 20.03.1978, II ZR 19/76 (contractual time-bar in inland water carriage disregarded); also the famous *Reichsgericht* case of the *Hansa*, 117 RGZ 354, 356 (29.6.1927) (no right to cancel charter for harmlessly late delivery, despite contract term to that effect).

46 London has at least two unfair advantages here. One is its comfortable temporal geography, nestled in Europe, neatly between American and eastern time-zones. Another is the fact that vastly more businesspeople speak English, as either a first or a second language, than any other tongue on the globe. No European language, however logical the law expressed in it, comes anywhere near, and neither does Mandarin Chinese.

47 See DCFR, III–1:104.

48 Above, Note.

49 See in particular *CEL Group Ltd v Nedlloyd Lines UK Ltd* [2004] 1 Lloyd's Rep. 381 (sea carrier's duty to entrust all onshore haulage business requirements to claimant infringed when, owing to merger, it argued that it no longer had any requirements to entrust). Standard implied terms necessary to make a contract work come in this category: e.g. the wharfinger's duty to provide a safe mooring in *The*

defendant cannot take a time-bar point after having clearly lulled a claimant into thinking it will not be relied on[50], or invoke less than prompt payment of instalments having repeatedly accepted earlier late payments without complaint[51], reproduced in England through the doctrine of estoppel.[52] And so also with the rule that a recipient of a time-critical notice cannot buy time by deliberately delaying receipt[53]; and with the principle that one cannot connive at the breach of a carriage contract and then claim damages for it.[54] Again, take a case where a carrier consistently deals with his shipper the basis that a particular legal relationship applies between them, even if it would not otherwise do so. Few lawyers would disagree that in such a case the mutually-accepted relationship governs. To a civilian the carrier would be acting in bad faith were he to deny this relationship[55]; to a common lawyer it is due to contractual interpretation or estoppel by convention (or both)[56]: but the result is the same. On a similar basis, take the fact, clear to anybody who has ever seen a container ship, that deck cargo – indeed, high-above-deck cargo – is the norm. Obviously a cargo-owner's claim that such carriage is wrongful, as it is with other kinds of vessel, must fail. Why? To a civilian such a plea amounts to bad faith[57]; to a common lawyer the right to carry on deck is an obvious implicit term in the contract.[58] Moreover, this can also apply to more sophisticated doctrines too. A neat instance is the situation where a goods owner acquiesces in carriage being subcontracted on the usual terms. There is clear German authority that, notwithstanding the lack of any contract between owner and actual carrier, good faith

*Moorcock* (1889) 14 PD 64, or the duty on a fob buyer to nominate a ship (*The Kriti Rex* [1996] 2 Lloyd's Rep. 171). See DCFR Commentary, 606, 713.

50 See e.g. OLG Frankfurt, 15.9.1999 – 21 U 259/98 (time-bar under Warsaw Convention): also OLG Köln, VersR 1970, 1005 and O. Vortisch & W. Bemm, *Binnenschiffahrtsrecht: Kommentar*, para 118, p 627 (inland water transport); DCFR Commentary, 706–707. For the similar English position see Note above.

51 OLG Nürnberg 22.6.2010 – 13 U 947/10, 10 MDR 2010, 1442.

52 See the English cases cited at Note above; also, e.g., *The Ion* [1980] 2 *Lloyd's Rep.* 245 (Hague Rules time-bar under charter). Similarly, under both systems a promise not to rely on a time-bar can be withdrawn (BGH 19.4.2001, I ZR 340/98, *TranspR* 2001, 375 and dicta in *The Ion* [1980] 2 *Lloyd's Rep.* 245, 250–251 clearly accepting the same principle).

53 One of the few examples from shipping law in the DCFR Commentary: see p.136 (shipowner deliberately delaying picking up charterer's telephone message extending charter). Compare the similar discussion of an analogous point (receipt of a notice of withdrawal), and the similar conclusion, in *The Brimnes* [1975] QB 929, 945–946 (Edmund Davies LJ).

54 BGH, 27. 2. 2003, I ZR 145/00, *TranspR* 2003, 298, 299 (carrier in Germany conniving in parking of vehicle by sub-contractor in ill-secured compound owned by carrier, contrary to strict terms of sub-contract). Compare the English authorities saying the same thing in *Hickman v Haynes* (1875) LR 10 CP 598, 604; and *The Kanchenjunga* [1989] 1 Lloyd's Rep. 354, 358 (Lloyd LJ) (affirmed [1990] 1 *Lloyd's Rep.* 391).

55 See the German land carriage decision in BGH 06.12.2007 – I ZR 174/04 (IT equipment dropped and damaged during loading: good faith duty meant responsibility possibly on trucker owing to long-standing practice, despite risk normally being on shipper under HGB 412(1)).

56 Cf *The Vistafjord* [1988] 2 Lloyd's Rep. 343 (assumption that different contractual regime applied: parties bound as if it did); *The Henrik Sif* [1982] 1 Lloyd's Rep. 456 (estoppel preventing reliance on demise clause).

57 As in Germany: OLG Hamburg 04.08.2000, 6 U 184/98.

58 See N. Gaskell, R. Asariotis & Y. Baatz, *Bills of Lading: Law and Contracts*, Para.10.28.

precludes the owner from disregarding the subcontracted terms limiting the carrier's liability.[59] By way of parallel, the English courts have filled the logical lacuna in the same way using the doctrine of sub-bailment on terms.[60]

12. Another reason is that, while (as will be seen below) good faith *can* spectacularly trench on freedom of contract[61], or invalidate the unjustified exercise of an otherwise clear contractual right[62], even under the DCFR interventions of this sort in shipping law may well be comparatively rare.[63] Even in the German jurisprudence, trivial or undeserving attacks on terms as contrary to good faith are regularly rejected[64] in favour of the view that they should be upheld whenever there is a plausible commercial justification for them.[65] Again, the German jurisprudence is tolerant of them where they deal with matters specifically exempted from regulation under international transport regimes[66]: for instance, in the case of simple negligence exclusions[67], reasonable time-bars[68], exemptions applying outside the "tackle-to-tackle" regime of

59 See the colourful land carriage decision in KG Berlin, 19.3.1998 – 2 U 4685/97 (owner of Renaissance sculpture bound as a matter of good faith by terms of subcontracted carriage for exhibition in Frederick the Great's erstwhile palace at Sans-Souci at Potsdam); also e.g. BGH, 21. 12. 1993, VI ZR 103/93, *TranspR* 1994, 162, 166.

60 See notably *The Pioneer Container* [1994] 2 *AC* 324.

61 See Notes and. See also DCFR Commentary, 708–709, referred to below, where English law is singled out for opprobrium for allowing freedom of contract here.

62 See DCFR Commentary, 67 et seq.

63 Something the drafters of the DCFR clearly have in mind: DCFR Commentary, 136 ("In many commercial contracts the rights and obligations of the parties will be so carefully regulated that in the normal course of events considerations of good faith and fair dealing will remain entirely in the background").

64 In the transport context see e.g. BGH 4.5.1995, I ZR 90/93, 1995 *TranspR* 381 (unsuccessful attack on haulier's six-month time-bar); OLG Köln, 30.05.2008, 3 U 7/07, *TranspR* 2009, 37, 41 (river cargo by arrangement carried appreciably short: when intermediate carriage contractor failed, no objection to actual carrier charging, and exercising lien against owner for, full original freight). And cf the quixotic plea of a carrier defendant that accusing it of gross negligence in the context of limitation of liability was *treuwidrig* and *rechtsmissbräuchlich* – i.e. contrary to good faith – merely because the plaintiff had later continued to employ it for further work: OLG Hamm, 28.9.1995 (18 U 195/94), *TranspR* 1996, 156, 159.

65 For instance, in the case of anti-set-off clauses; see OLG Nürnberg 27.10.1993 12 U 1951/93, *TranspR* 1994, 154 (anti-set-off clause in trucking contract); and see DCFR Commentary, 671.

66 See too OLG Nürnberg 27.10.1993 12 U 1951/93, *TranspR* 1994, 154, above (anti-set-off clause allowed in CMR contract re late delivery, in the light of fact that not prevented by CMR Art 23.4).

67 E.g., OLG Bremen 1.1.1973, *VersR* 1985, 759, 761 (negligence exemption in towage contract). And compare the 1968 Swiss decision in BGE 94 II 197 (while carriers' exonerations may offend good faith if effect intolerable (*unerträglich*), no possible objection to simple negligence exemption in inland water-carriage of raw plastic).

68 BGH 17.11.1980, *VersR* 1981, 229 (six-month time-bar re inland waterway carriage). (Oddly enough, this would be different under the DCFR, which has a hard-to-defend blanket ban on any agreed time-bar of less than a year: III–7:601(2)).

the Hague-Visby Rules[69], or "weight unknown" stipulations in a bill of lading.[70] Similarly the good faith limitation on the exercise of contractual rights, while undoubtedly existent, is not lightly invoked. The mere fact of relying on a clear legal right ungenerously or even unfairly is not, of itself, enough[71]; thus there is seen to be nothing wrong as such in refusing to perform substantial contracts of sale for non-payment of a relatively small part of the price[72], in insisting that payment time-limits in a settlement agreement are strictly observed[73], in taking advantage of an opportunity to terminate a contract relating to property in order to make the maximum sum of money[74], or (in the case of an insurer) denying cover for an accident when premiums are overdue, even if they are then very hurriedly paid.[75] In similar vein, the temptation has been resisted to use good faith to impose any further requirements on beneficiaries of bank guarantees than a prohibition on operating them in the face of clear evidence of what an English court would regard as fraud.[76]

## 4.2. *Moving on: some significant effects of a requirement of good faith*

**13.** Nevertheless, despite the unobtrusive nature of much of the general doctrine of good faith law, there are still a noticeable number of areas where its introduction on the model of German law or the DCFR might well have a worryingly unsettling effect. A few representative topics are discussed below.

### 4.2.1. The law of contract: formation and formalities

**14.** English commercial law, including shipping law, regards it as axiomatic that at any one time either there is or is not a formal contractual relationship between parties. If there is such a relationship, then the usual panoply of contractual obligations obtains.

69 See the German decisions in BGH, 26. 6. 1997 – I ZR 248/94, 1997 *TranspR* 379 and OLG Hamburg, 02.11.2000, 6 U 277/99. (This is reversed by German legislation from 2013 – see HGB, § 512(1) in its new form – but this is not relevant to the point in the text). Nevertheless, even here we might not be entirely safe from good-faith intervention: see the French decision in Aix, 18.7.2013, DMF 2013, 905 (even where tackle-to-tackle clause, good faith demands carrier take some steps to protect cargo owner's interests after discharge, and prevents him invoking one-year Hague-Visby limitation from discharge).

70 BGH 27.10.1960, II ZR 127/59.

71 BGH 3.3.2011 – I ZR 50/10, *TranspR* 2011, 220, 223 ("It is also not clear why the defendant should be in breach of the duty of good faith, if all he is doing is relying on the liability regime established by law and contractually agreed between the parties" ("*... [es] ist auch nicht ersichtlich, warum die Bekl. gegen Treu und Glauben verstoßen soll, wenn sie sich auf das gesetzliche und vertraglich vereinbarte Haftungsregime verlässt*")). See e.g. BGH, 6.10.2005 – I ZR 14/03 (not bad faith peremptorily and harshly to invoke Warsaw Convention time-bar against recourse claimant).

72 BGH 8.7.1983, 88 BGHZ 91, 95.

73 BGH 19.12.1979 – VIII ZR 46/79, *NJW* 1980, 1043.

74 BGH, 18.4.1980, WM 1980, 1073.

75 OLG Nürnberg *VersR* 1966, 1125, 1126.

76 BGH 10.8.2000, BGHZ 145, 286, 291 (to prevent enforcement, misuse must be "clear and obvious, i.e. either there for all to see or evidenced with crystal clarity" ("*klar erkennbar, dh offensichtlich oder liquide beweisbar*").

If not, for instance because the parties are still negotiating[77], or because some necessary contractual formality remains unobserved[78], only the most skeletal duties can apply – effectively tortious duties not to mislead, and possibly duties not to break confidence. Under the DCFR, and in most civilian systems, the contrast is stark. Negotiating parties explicitly owe a duty (which cannot be excluded) to negotiate "in accordance with good faith and fair dealing", to refrain from negotiating without intent to contract, and not to break off discussions contrary to good faith and fair dealing, on pain of liability to substantial damages.[79] Although the commentary to the DCFR supposedly limits to egregious cases these exceptions to the right not to negotiate[80], the potential for liability should still give pause to a businessperson seeking to protect himself – for example, in the case of simultaneous negotiations by an owner with a number of potential charterers, or where the appearance of an apparent obstacle to agreement introduces a threat of liability for a tardy warning of it. Furthermore, under the jurisprudence emanating from jurisdictions where this head of good faith is already taken seriously, there would also be a threat to the long-standing practice of assuming no liability until a stipulated formal contract is signed.[81] To be added to this is the potential of a fairly open-ended jurisdiction to allow reliance losses to be claimed by those relying on even the most cautiously-drafted letter of comfort issued by, for example, a charterer's holding company[82], or for that matter a mere letter of intent.[83] Furthermore, there are indications that under the DCFR there would also be potential incursions into the rule that an offeror can put what conditions he likes on what

77 See generally the non-carriage case of *Regalian Properties Plc v LDDC* [1995] 1 *WLR* 212.

78 Such as writing in the case of an agreement amounting to a contract of guarantee: *Actionstrength Ltd v International Glass Engineering SpA* [2003] UKHL 17; [2003] 2 *AC* 541.

79 DCFR, II–3:301.

80 DCFR Commentary, 71.

81 See e.g. BGE 105 II 75 (Switzerland, *Bundesgericht*, 6.2.1979) (bank liable for agreeing in principle, explicitly subject to formal signature, then changing its mind). As the same court later put it in another unreported 2002 case, "It is inconsistent with the rules of good faith to give one's unreserved assent in principle to the conclusion of a formal contract and then at the last minute to refuse to put one's agreement in the necessary form without vouchsafing any reason" ("*Il est contraire aux règles de la bonne foi de donner sans réserve son accord de principe à la conclusion d'un contrat formel et de refuser in extremis, sans raison, de le traduire dans la forme requise*"): TF SJ 2002 I 164, c.3a, quoted in N. Rouiller, *Droit suisse des obligations et les principes du droit européen des contrats*, 267.

82 See the analogous decision in BGE 120 II 331 (Switzerland, *Bundesgericht*, 15.11.1994) (letter of comfort by Swissair concerning land deal by subsidiary); N. Rouiller, *Droit suisse des obligations et les principes du droit européen des contrats*, 153–4. Compare the uncompromising English decision in *Kleinwort Benson Ltd v Malaysia Mining Corp Bhd* [1989] 1 WLR 379, effectively insulating the issuers of such letters from legal liability.

83 See R. Schlosser, *Les lettres d'intentions: portée et sanction des accords précontractuelles*, in *Mélanges en honneur de Baptiste Rusconi*, Lausanne 2000, 345, at 362. Compare once again the very sceptical English approach in cases such as *Milner (J.H.) Ltd v Percy Bilton Ltd* [1966] 2 *All ER* 894: and see generally M. Furmston, T. Norisada and J. Poole, *Contract Formation and Letters of Intent*, Ch 6.

amounts to valid acceptance[84], and into the rule that formal requirements mean what they say.[85]

### 4.2.2. The right of withdrawal

**15.** In England the right to withdraw from a contract where counter-performance is not received is instinctively regarded, not as a legal remedy for non-performance, as in the civilian tradition[86], but as a matter of conditionality of the obligation undertaken. In other words, how far, properly interpreted, is a party's obligation to observe a contract conditional on receipt of proper performance by the other side? If the interpretation is clear, so is the answer. The point matters in shipping law. As anyone who has dealt with ship sales or charter disputes knows, certainty as to when a contract can be cancelled is vital, and a great deal of money turns on it.[87] Businessmen appreciate the rule of English law that this boils down to interpretation and autonomy: if the matter is clearly provided for, the law's task is not to look to motives, reasons or justice but simply to give effect to what the parties have agreed.[88] This world-view is, however, regarded as anathema by the

84 DCFR Commentary, 706 (in certain cases, mandatory rule of good faith means that acceptance valid even if not using stipulated method, if no prejudice to offeror). The ECJ for its part seems to accept a similar approach: see *Berghoefer GmbH v ASA SA, Case 221/84* [1985] *ECR* 2699; [1986] 1 *CMLR* 13 at [15] (contrary to good faith for defendant to deny presence of written agreement on its part where it simply failed to answer letter sent to it). In English law, while there may be room for an inference that an offeror cannot invoke an entirely non-prejudicial failure to follow the prescribed means of acceptance, this entirely a matter for the terms of the offer: if these are clear that only one method of acceptance will do, they must be given effect. See *Manchester Diocesan Council for Education v Commercial & General Investments Ltd* [1970] 1 *WLR* 241, 246 (Buckley J).

85 A point of some little importance as regards guarantees. With the robust decision in *Actionstrength Ltd v International Glass Engineering SpA* [2003] UKHL 17; [2003] 2 AC 54 (unenforceability of guarantee for lack of writing under Statute of Frauds 1677 cannot be sidestepped, even by estoppel), compare DCFR, II–1:106 (defendant may be liable for not informing claimant that claim against him unenforceable on formal grounds). The general duty of good faith in DCFR, III-1:103 may also be relevant here: again compare German jurisprudence, which while generally allowing even unreasonable reliance on formal requirements (e.g. BGH, 16.07.2004 – V ZR 222/03) nevertheless sees nothing wrong with dispensing with them where good faith so demands: e.g. BGHZ 48, 396 (27.10.1967) (defendant allowed claimant to believe contract for sale valid despite lack of necessary notarisation).

86 To see this, take German law. There it is regarded as obvious that the right to withdrawal (*Rücktritt*) presumptively only arises after a claimant faced with non-performance has formally demanded it and failed to get it (BGB, §323(1)), the right to escape in other circumstances being exceptional (BGB, §323(2)). As regards the DCFR, termination under Article III-3:501 et seq appears explicitly under "Chapter 3: Remedies for non-performance".

87 Notably, where after a long-term charter is entered into shipping rates rise: the owner will typically be on the look-out for reasons to withdraw the vessel and re-charter, often to the same charterer, at the higher rate.

88 The English attitude is nicely encapsulated in the opening lines of the judgment in *The Li Hai* [2005] *EWHC* 735 (Comm); [2005] 1 *CLC* 704 at [1]: "This case represents commerce, red in tooth and claw. The issue is whether the Defendant owners were entitled to withdraw the [vessel] from the Claimant time charterers ... for non-payment of US$500, after the market had risen in the space of 10 months to about 2½ times the charter rate. ... [T]here can be no doubt that if it was owing and the appropriate 'anti-technicality' notice was given... the Owners were entitled to withdraw the vessel. The Court has no

DCFR. This not only takes the civilian view that cancellation is simply a facility given by the law as an adjunct to the right to performance[89], but also specifically under Article III.–1:103 subjects all rights to terminate or refuse performance to a (non-negotiable) duty to "act in accordance with good faith and fair dealing." Specifically attacking the English way of thinking[90], the authors do not mince their words: "the English approach based on construction of the agreement," they say, "is a weak one as it cannot prevail against clear contrary provisions in the agreement," from which it follows (of course) that their new article "represents an advance" on the English position.[91] And as if this element of control were not enough, the DCFR rules then go further to apply a converse control: it may be contrary to good faith to invoke an express right not to have a contract terminated for a breach that would generally allow it, even if the stipulation is otherwise unexceptionable.[92]

**16.** Moreover, it seems that this viewpoint, if adopted, would potentially have considerable practical effect. In the German case-law[93], one of the few shipping cases in which good faith featured concerned just this. A charterer was held liable for refusing to load a cargo of rye in Stettin when the ship declared readiness some half-an-hour later than the final cancelling time: although the charter gave him precisely this right, it was held contrary to good faith to invoke it in the circumstances.[94] Indeed, cancellation for harmless infractions of time-limits, however standard in English shipping and sales law[95], provides one of the commonest instances of good-faith limits on the right to withdraw, whether in sales[96] or other contracts.[97]

power to relieve from forfeiture on the grounds that this is a harsh case." These lines, surprising to a continental European lawyer, neither contain nor are intended to convey the slightest trace of irony.

89 See Note above.

90 In the shape of the well-known (at least to English lawyers) fob sale case of *Bunge Corporation v Tradax SA* [1981] 1 *WLR* 711, allowing sellers to cancel when buyers gave 10 as against 15 days' notice of readiness to ship, even though sellers suffered no prejudice.

91 DCFR Commentary, 708–9. A similar mistrust of freedom of contract in this connection lies behind the PECL: see comment to PECL 1:201 ("even if the non-performance of an obligation is fundamental because strict compliance with the obligations is of the essence of the contract under Article 8:103, a party would not be permitted to terminate because of a trivial breach of the obligation") and O. Lando, "Salient Features of the Principles of European Contract Law: A Comparison with the UCC" 13 *Pace Int'l L. Rev.* 339, 362–363 (2001).

92 DCFR, III–3:105(2). Unfortunately, no relevant examples are given. But compare the Swiss decision in BGE 97 II 58 (*Bundesgericht*, 30.3.1971) (removal of right to cancel contract to let and improve motel for late performance contrary to good faith since it left lessees "in the arbitrary power of the lessor" ("*au pouvoir discretionnaire de la bailleresse*").

93 On which see generally *Münchener Kommentar zum BGB* (6th ed), §242 Rn 413 et seq. ("*geringfügigkeit*").

94 RGZ 117, 354 (RG 1927) (sometimes known as the *Hansa* case). See too the later converse case in BGHZ 11, 80 (BGH 1953), (cancellation under GENCON charter for failure to provide cargo: no bad faith because breach sufficiently serious).

95 Straightforward instances are *The Brimnes* [1975] QB 929 and *The Chikuma* [1981] 1 *WLR* 314.

96 E.g. RGHZ 76, 150 (RG 1911) (cancellation of sale of bleached yarn for non-payment of small sum in dispute); RGZ 169, 140, 143 (RG 1941) (instalment on truck) (cf BGH 8.7.83 – V ZR 53/82). See too DCFR Commentary, 708–709.

97 Traditionally this applies in leases, as in BGH 2.3.72, NJW 1972, 1324. But more recently, and potentially more seriously for commercial law, see OLG Stuttgart, 2.5.2005 – 5 U 10/05, MDR 06, 378 (settlement

**17.** Furthermore, in at least one respect the effect of good faith may go subtly further even than this. The English view that a contractor's right to withdraw is simply a matter of interpreting the limits on his obligation to perform has an important corollary. If a party has the right to refuse performance, that is an end of the matter. He need provide neither notice nor reason for not performing; and if he does give a reason he is not bound by it.[98] Hence in the shipping context, if an owner or charterer says he is withdrawing from a charter and in fact has good reason to do so, he is protected from liability even if the reason he actually gave was insufficient[99]; and in the related context of commodity sales, if shipping documents are in fact in some way defective they may be rejected by a buyer, even if the latter purported to do so on some entirely different, and insufficient, ground.[100] This point is not mentioned as such in the DCFR, but almost certainly the result would be different. In particular, the commentary to the relevant article of the DCFR[101] regards it as an obvious corollary of the obligation of good faith that a contractor relying on the right to withdraw cannot simply do nothing, but must give both notice that he is refusing to perform[102] and in many cases reasons for the refusal.[103] And if the lack of any reason means that is contrary to good faith to rely on what would otherwise be a right to escape a contract, it seems to follow a fortiori that defending withdrawal on

agreement dependent on prompt payment: contrary to good faith for claimant to claim right to disregard agreement when late payment fault of bank rather than payer).

98 See e.g. *Manbré Saccharine Co Ltd v Corn Products Co Ltd* [1919] 1 KB 198; *Glencore Grain Rotterdam BV v Lebanese Organisation for International Commerce* [1997] 4 *All ER* 514 (sellers cancel on inadmissible pretext of late arrival of buyers' ship: can rely on technical inaccuracy of buyer's letter of credit). This right is independent of the equities of the situation: see *Glencore Grain Rotterdam BV v Lebanese Organisation for International Commerce*, above, at pp. 529–531 (*Evans LJ*). See generally *Chitty on Contracts* (31st ed), Para.24–014. In fact it is difficult to see any injustice. If the creditor has done something that justifies the other party in refusing his performance, then, even if the other party has no notice of this fact, it is difficult to justify awarding the creditor damages. He is essentially asking to be compensated for the loss of something he had no right to obtain in the first place.

99 See e.g. *The Mihalis Angelos* [1971] 1 *QB* 164 (charter cancelled ostensibly for force majeure: even though in fact no force majeure, charterers entitled to rely on breach by charterer of readiness condition); see also the owners' cancellation case of *Universal Cargo Carriers Corporation v Citati* [1957] 2 QB 401, 443–444 (Devlin J).

100 *Manbré Saccharine Co Ltd v Corn Products Co Ltd* [1919] 1 KB 198 (shipping documents rejected on legally-insufficient ground that cargo lost at time of tender: when sued, buyer could instead rely on technical inadequacy of documents, even though point not raised earlier); *Glencore Grain Rotterdam BV v Lebanese Organisation for International Commerce* [1997] 4 *All ER* 514 (sellers cancel on inadmissible pretext of late arrival of buyers' ship: can rely on technical inaccuracy of buyer's letter of credit).

101 DCFR, III-3:501.

102 A requirement specifically stated in the case where further time is given for late performance under DCFR, III-3:503: DCFR Commentary, 883 (and at DCFR Commentary, 902, it is added that good faith requires another notice also at the end of the extended period, if the promisor is still intending to perform (!)). By parity of reasoning it might well also apply elsewhere.

103 "The duty to exercise rights in accordance with good faith and fair dealing... may, in appropriate cases, require the notice [0f termination] to indicate the reason for the termination" (DCFR Commentary, 898).

the basis of a different reason from that given must equally be regarded as an abuse of the right to withdraw.[104]

### 4.2.3. The effect of a change of circumstances

**18.** If there is anything clear in English commercial law, it is that the ability of a person to escape from a contract on the basis of change of circumstances is exceedingly limited[105]; that enormous attention is paid to the wording of any agreement where the point is argued[106]; and (of course) that any right that might otherwise exist to escape can be, and often is, ousted by the terms of the bargain between the parties.[107] The instinct of the civil law is different.[108] Long before the PECL and the DCFR, German law regarded it as axiomatic that whenever circumstances had radically changed, the duty to enforce rights and perform obligations in good faith carried with it a duty in the advantaged party to renegotiate in good faith and a corresponding curial power to relieve a contracting party and if necessary re-write the contract.[109] As might be expected, the DCFR deals with the matter expressly. Book III, Article 1:110, provides that where an obligation "becomes so onerous because of an exceptional change of circumstances that it would be manifestly unjust to hold the debtor to the obligation" there is a power to adjust or terminate it. Theoretically this is a rather muted provision, carrying no actual duty to negotiate in good faith, but merely allowing a court to decline to enforce an obligation if there has been a radical change and the creditor refuses a reasonable offer to re-negotiate.[110] Nevertheless, even in this form it could be important in a number of cases where English commercial and shipping law currently chooses certainty over

104 Hence German courts have held in other contexts that an illegitimate reason my vitiate the exercise of a right to withdraw from a contract: e.g. BAG NJW 1995, 275 (employment contract). Generally, *Münchener Kommentar zum BGB* (6th ed), §242 Rn 214.

105 E.g. in the shipping context the Suez Canal cases, typefied by decisions such as *The Eugenia* [1964] 2 QB 226: generally G. Treitel, *The Law of Contract* (13th ed), Para.19–006.

106 For an instance, see *Kuwait Supply Co v Oyster Marine Management Inc* [1994] 1 Lloyd's Rep. 637 (whole issue turned on interpretation of boilerplate in charterparty war clause).

107 E.g. *Kuwait Supply Co v Oyster Marine Management Inc* [1994] 1 Lloyd's Rep. 637; *The Sea Angel* [2007] 2 Lloyd's Rep. 517: ship management case; G. Treitel, *The Law of Contract* (13th ed), Para.19–069 et seq.

108 K. Zweigert & H. Kötz, *Introduction to Comparative Law* (3rd ed), Ch 37; J. Gordley & A. von Mehren, *An Introduction to the Comparative Study of Private Law*, 494 et seq.

109 A power originally based on the general good faith clause, and now codified in BGB, §313(1); for useful analysis see *Münchener Kommentar zum BGB* (6th ed), §313 Rn 1–2 and P. Ridder & M-P. Weller, "Unforeseen Circumstances, Hardship, Impossibility and Force Majeure under German Contract Law" (2014) 22 ERPL 371. Indeed, even French law, with its less developed ideas of good faith, had in certain cases condoned the exercise of a similar power by lower courts: see e.g. Cass. Com, 3.11.1992, D. 1995, Somm. 85 ("*arrêt Huard*") (good-faith-based duty to renegotiate petroleum distribution contract in the light of the oil crisis); and more recently Cass Civ 1ère, 16.3.2004, D. Jurisp. 1754, note Mazeaud.

110 See DCFR Commentary, 738–739: compare the earlier PECL, which under Article 6.111 had included an actual duty to renegotiate. How significant this difference is is, however, open to some question: see R. Uribe, "Change of Circumstances in International Instruments of Contract Law. The Approach of the CISG, PICC, PECL and DCFR", 15 *Vindobona Journal of International Commercial Law & Arbitration* 233, 256–257 (2011).

justice. For instance, in *The Sea Angel*[111], a short-term charter for the very temporary purpose of lightening a salvaged tanker was expressed to last until the vessel was redelivered to her owners (which everyone expected to be after about 14 days). Nevertheless, an English court had no difficulty in holding that the contract remained fully in force, obliging the charterers to pay hire, even though a combination of impenetrable Pakistani bureaucracy and trumped-up claims delayed redelivery for some four months. It is hard to see such a result being replicated under the DCFR. Again, the DCFR when discussing change of circumstances makes a very pointed reference to a closure of the Suez Canal as a classic instance.[112] It is difficult to see this as anything other than a thinly-disguised attack on the common law mindset. There, it will be remembered, one of the most remarkable features was a steadfast refusal to take account of this as a frustrating event in either shipping or sale cases, even where this skewed costs and benefits and made the economics ruinous to one or other party.[113]

**19.** Furthermore, there is further, though less obvious, question here: namely, how far the terms of the parties' agreement should trump any other rules as to the risk of a change of circumstance. At first sight under the DCFR, the answer is that it should: the "renegotiation" rule is ostensibly a mere default rule, and if the terms of the contract put the risk of a particular event on one party, that is conclusive.[114] But there is a possible difficulty. It has to be remembered that under the DCFR the exercise of any right whatever is subject to the overriding control of good faith[115], and it must be arguable that relying an agreement to put the entire risk of a game-changing event on one party[116] might be regarded as unfair and thus incompatible with it. This seems particularly plausible since the revised version of the PECL[117], with at least some academic approval[118], specifically provides that unreasonable allocations of risk, which of course have the effect of sidelining the good faith power of modification, are ineffective[119]; and indeed certain jurisdictions, such as Germany, have accepted that the modification power is mandatory law which cannot be altered by mere agreement.[120]

111 [2007] 2 Lloyd's Rep. 517.

112 DCFR Commentary, 739 ("The excessive onerosity may be the direct result of increased cost in performance – for example, the increased cost of transport if the Suez Canal is closed and ships have to be sent round the Cape of Good Hope").

113 The two most notable examples are *The Eugenia* [1964] 2 QB 226 (a charter case) and the sale decision in *Tsakiroglou & Co Ltd v Noblee Thorl GmbH* [1962] AC 93.

114 DCFR Commentary, III–1:110(3)(c) (necessary that "the debtor did not assume, and cannot reasonably be regarded as having assumed, the risk of that change of circumstances").

115 DCFR, III-3:103.

116 As was held to be the case in *The Sea Angel*, above.

117 This revised version was prepared in 2008 by the French Association Henri Capitant, under the direction of Guillaume Wicker and Jean-Baptiste Racine. For the influence of this on the DCFR, see DCFR Commentary, 11 et seq.

118 E.g., R. Uribe, "Change of Circumstances in International Instruments of Contract Law. The Approach of the CISG, PICC, PECL and DCFR", 15 *Vindobona Journal of International Commercial Law & Arbitration* 233, 266 et seq (2011).

119 See PECL (revised), 7:102.

120 See *Münchener Kommentar zum BGB* (6th ed), §313 Rn 112 et seq.

### 4.2.4. Exclusion of liability and similar clauses

**20.** English law not only starts from a strong presumption of commercial freedom of contract, both substantively[121] and in its enforcement against businesses of terms in the small print of a contractual document.[122] It has also taken enormous care to preserve it in international commercial transactions, notably by expressly disapplying any legislative protections and limitations that would otherwise obtain.[123] The same cannot be said of the DCFR, which under the good faith rubric calculatedly seeks to undermine freedom of contract[124] and provide for significant general controls on almost all[125] terms in business-to-business arrangements. To begin with, there is a general provision under which standard terms[126] are unenforceable if "unfair"[127], a word used to describe any term which by reference to transparency[128] and otherwise to all the circumstances of the case[129] is (under Article II-9:405) one "forming part of standard terms supplied by one party and of such a nature that its use grossly deviates from good commercial practice, contrary to good faith and fair dealing". Secondly, and quite independently, Article III–3:105 says, with pointed emphasis[130], that a commercial party may also be prevented

121 "[I]f there is one thing which more than another public policy requires it is that men of full age and competent understanding shall have the utmost liberty of contracting, and that their contracts when entered into freely and voluntarily shall be held sacred and shall be enforced by Courts of justice." (Jessel MR in *Printing & Numerical Registering Co v Sampson* (1875) LR 19 Eq 462, 465).

122 A point made many years ago, with particular reference to shipping law in the shape of bills of lading, in *Crooks v Allan* (1879) 5 QBD 38.

123 The Unfair Contract Terms Act 1977, which applies certain reasonableness controls to business-to-business contracts, specifically exempts from control contracts for international sales and contracts governed by English law solely by virtue of party choice: see ss.26, 27.

124 Admittedly so. Having accepted that the matter is politically charged, the authors of the DCFR Commentary at p.670 comfort themselves with the assurance that such controls are an EU competence under the EU acquis, and then say, rather disingenuously, that their proposed controls are "not justified by a general assumption of unequal negotiation power between the parties but by the assumption that the use of standard terms drafted in advance by one party enabled the party supplying these terms to restrict the other party's contractual freedom."

125 True, there is no explicit control over the "definition of the main subject matter of the contract" or the "adequacy of the price to be paid" (DCFR, II-9:406): but this restriction is unlikely to be important in practice.

126 That is, standard terms drafted by a *proferens* on which he then seeks to rely. It must be admitted that the coverage is not absolute, since in some shipping cases this will not be the case. See the German decision in BGH 28.02.1983, II ZR 31/82 (the German controls in BGB, §§305 et seq. being similarly limited, where there is an attack on term in GENCON charter exonerating carrier for unseaworthiness, it must be open to carrier to argue that charter form in fact proposed *by cargo owner*). But this qualification is not very significant in practice.

127 DCFR, II-9:408.

128 DCFR, II–9:402(1) (person using standard terms "has a duty to ensure that they are drafted and communicated in plain, intelligible language"). This is transposed from Article 5 of the Unfair Terms Directive 1993/13/EEC applicable to consumers. It is not immediately obvious that a transposition of this requirement from consumer to business law is appropriate.

129 DCFR, II–9:407.

130 The DCFR Commentary states explicitly at p.818 that "it is useful to make clear the potentially powerful effect of the good faith requirement in this area."

from relying on any term whatever restricting a remedy for non-performance[131], even one not caught by the previous section and hence otherwise perfectly valid, "if it would be contrary to good faith and fair dealing to do so."

**21.** The potentially subversive effect of both these provisions on the present English approach to shipping and similar contracts is, to say the least, condiserable. We can take first the general rule allowing a court to disapply terms held to be unfair. The reference to the requirement of transparency might well be used to invalidate (for example) a jurisdiction or arbitration clause on the back of a closely-printed bill of lading[132], which in English law would fairly clearly be effective.[133] Hence it would jeopardise the present assurance of those contracting under English law that a formal contract of carriage is "exactly what it says on the tin": if a clause is unambiguously contained in it, the only issue is interpretation, with no further room left for argument over effectiveness. Similarly with the general rules on unfairness. Although little guidance appears in the commentary to the DCFR, the nearly parallel practice of German courts in invalidating standard terms on good faith grounds is telling[134]; the interventionist background is clearly, and disconcertingly, in evidence, in that even where no mandatory liability regime exists, courts have regularly disallowed terms excluding liability for breach of what are regarded as fundamental obligations. Victims have included terms in non-ocean carriage[135] exonerating the carrier from liability in the case of a failure to provide a seaworthy vessel[136], or of gross negligence by himself or his servants[137], or delay[138], not to mention clear contractually-agreed time-bars.[139] More importantly, this has also happened with charterparties, in stark contrast to the common law tradition of freedom of contract. So in 1968 a Hamburg court had no

131 Despite the apparently limited term "non-performance", the drafters of the DCFR clearly regard this provision as covering all forms of defective performance too: hence the DCFR Commentary at pp.818–821 refers to clauses dealing with such matters as late performance, improper performance of a carriage contract and the supply of defective goods.

132 Compare the German decision in BGH 30.5.1983, NJW 1983, 2772, 2773, disapplying on good faith grounds (under what is now BGB, §§305 et seq) an unambiguous, and entirely understandable, Indian jurisdiction clause in the small print of a contract by an Indian sea carrier to carry rugs from Calcutta to Hamburg. Suit was thus allowed in Germany.

133 Because of the principle in *Crooks v Allan* (1879) 5 QBD 38, referred to above.

134 Under BGB, §§305 et seq (controls over standard terms (*Allgemeinen Geschäftsbedingungen*)). The practice is not exactly parallel, since under those provisions the effect need simply be to unfairly disadvantage ("*unangemessen benachteiligen*") the counterparty, whereas under the DCFR that test is reserved for consumers, with businesses having to go further and prove a "gross deviation" from good commercial practice. However, whether this is a very substantial distinction, particularly since in practice under German law consumers were more generously treated than businesses anyway when asking whether there was an unfair disadvantage, only time will tell.

135 I.e., terms to which the Hague-Visby Rules do not apply.

136 See e.g. BGH 08.12.1975, II ZR 64/74 (inland transport: uncargoworthy ship causes wetting of rice cargo by rain); also OLG Hamburg 8.1.1976, *VersR* 1977, 221 and OLG Köln 03.07.1998, 3 U 105/93 (inland transport: unseaworthy collier).

137 See the non-marine decision in BGH, 3. 2. 2005 – I ZR 276/02 (recklessness by carrier).

138 OLG Hamburg, 13.01.2011, 6 U 150/09.

139 See e.g. BGH 20.03.1978, II ZR 19/76.

hesitation in refusing to allow a carrier to invoke an exculpatory clause in a voyage charter to protect itself against liability for what was characterised as gross negligence.[140] Again, in a 1983 case[141] foul weather in the Bay of Biscay started hatch-covers and caused sea-water damage to a cargo of iron fabrications being carried under a Gencon voyage charter. Cargo successfully recovered on the basis of unseaworthiness, despite the standard Gencon owner's responsibility clause disclaiming liability except where personal want of due diligence was proved: good faith, it was said, precluded exclusion of fundamental obligations of this sort. With authorities of this sort in the background, it remains to be seen what would happen (for example) to the very extensive exemptions from liability contained in some more modern forms of offshore charter, such as SUPPLYTIME 2005[142], not to mention the drastic curtailments of rights to damages inherent in knock-for-knock clauses in that and similar agreements, whose very aim is to prevent claims even where there is gross fault on the defendant's part.[143] One thing is clear: under the DCFR regime it would be very difficult for participants to rely on the effectiveness of such arrangements and make the necessary savings in liability insurance costs.

**22.** Turning to Article III–3:105 of the DCFR, that is the good faith reliance clause, the indications are that this too may be highly relevant to shipping lawyers. This is true for at least two reasons. First, despite a disarming statement in the general unfair terms clause (i.e. Article II-9:405) that it represents the sole ground on which a business-to-business contract term can be disapplied as unfair[144], the commentary to Article III–3:105 makes it quite clear to those negotiating and later seeking to rely on contractual provisions that it too can invalidate a term a priori, even if that term would pass muster impeccably under Article II-9:405, or for that matter is specifically immune to attack under it (for example, because it is individually negotiated and hence not a standard term). The reasoning is apparently that a term may be so one-sided that the very act of invoking it is automatically contrary to a party's general obligation to act in good faith. The example given is informative: a contract for the sale of goods where the seller, in common with all other sellers, insists on excluding liability for consequential losses (despite the availability of insurance cover) and the buyer unhappily acquiesces.[145] But extensive exclusion of liability for consequential losses is a standard feature of many

140 OLG Hamburg, 1968 *VersR* 552.

141 BGH 28.02.1983, II ZR 31/82, VersR 1983, 549.

142 See Clause 14(b)(ii), exempting owners from almost any liability to charterers.

143 For an account of such clauses, and a robust defence of their enforcement without question, see B. Soyer & A. Tettenborn (Eds), *Offshore Contracts and Liabilities*, Chap. 8 ("Wilful Misconduct and Gross Negligence Exclusions in "Knock-for-Knock" Provisions in Offshore Contracts", by E. Blackburn & J. Lightfoot).

144 "A term in a contract between businesses is unfair for the purposes of this Section *only if* it is a term, etc..."

145 DCFR Commentary, 821.

kinds of shipping contract, from shipbuilding[146] to towage[147] to specialised charters.[148] And even where these are not standard form, there may be many advantages in a party insisting on a bespoke provision that leaves the counterparty to bear the risk of consequential loss of profits consequential on breach – even breach due to gross negligence – but allows it to quote competitively by saving a fortune in liability insurance costs.[149] If such provisions are now to be thrown in doubt, the effects could be to say the least considerable.

**23.** Secondly, Article III–3:105 incidentally raises another issue well-known to English commercial lawyers: namely, the relation between exculpatory clauses and fundamental breach of contract. To sum up the background history, there has always been a strong presumption in English law that exculpatory clauses should be construed as inapplicable where breach was blatantly deliberate, or where there had been no serious attempt to comply with the contract at all.[150] Prior to 1966, the view had sometimes been expressed that this was actually a matter of law, and that no clause, however explicitly drafted, could ever exonerate a contractor from liability for the consequences of such a breach. But in a well-known decision that year[151], the House of Lords roundly rejected this view, holding that the whole issue indeed concerned interpretation. While it might be unlikely that properly construed a clause covered a fundamental breach[152], on principle freedom of contract in a commercial context should allow an agreement to exonerate a party for the effects of any breach whatever. Since then, while English law always disallows exclusion of liability for personal fraud[153], and continues to view sceptically claims to

146 E.g. Cl.IX.4 of the widespread SAJ form of shipbuilding contract (builder shall not "in any circumstances be responsible or liable for any consequential or special losses, damages or expenses, including, but not limited to, loss of time, loss of profit or earning or demurrage directly or indirectly occasioned to the BUYER by reason of [defects] or due to repairs or other works done to the VESSEL to remedy such defects"). A similar clause was without compunction applied *au pied de la lettre* by an English court in *China Shipbuilding Corp v Nippon Yusen Kabukishi Kaisha* [2000] 1 *Lloyd's Rep.* 367.

147 TOWCON 2008, Cl.25. Compare the robust comment of Morison J in *Smit International (Deutschland) GmbH v Josef Mobius Bau-GmbH* [2001] *CLC* 1545 at [19] "The knock-for-knock arrangement is a crude but workable allocation of risk and responsibility: even where the tug or tow is wholly responsible for the accident liability depends entirely upon the happenstance of which of the two collided with the third party."

148 E.g. SUPPLYTIME 2005, Cl.14(b); WINDTIME, Cl.16(a).

149 See above, Note.

150 *The Cap Palos* [1921] P. 458 (abandonment of tow by tugs). See generally the non-marine case of *Karsales (Harrow) Ltd v Wallis* [1956] 1 *WLR* 936.

151 *Suisse Atlantique Société d'Armement SA v NV Rotterdamsche Kolen Centrale* [1967] 1 *AC* 361. The seal was set on this development in a later case, *Photo Production Ltd v Securicor Transport Ltd* [1980] *AC* 827, where an exception clause was indeed applied to exonerate a security company in a case of deliberate arson by one of its employees.

152 *Suisse Atlantique Societe d'Armement SA v NV Rotterdamsche Kolen Centrale* [1967] 1 *AC* 361, 434–435 (Lord Wilberforce).

153 *HIH Casualty & General Insurance Ltd v Chase Manhattan Bank* [2003] UKHL 6; [2003] 2 *Lloyd's Rep.* 61 at [16] and [78] et seq (Lords Bingham and Hoffmann). Note that this does not include the fraud of employees and others for those for whose acts one is responsible, where exclusion remains entirely permissible: see e.g. *Frans Maas (UK) Ltd v Samsung Electronics (UK) Ltd* [2004] 2 *Lloyd's Rep.* 251.

exoneration by those guilty of deliberate or wanton breach[154], there has been no difficulty in applying exculpatory clauses even to cases of intentional breach[155], as (for example) in a recent case where a tug abandoned its tow in mid-ocean but the towage contract on a proper reading covered even a breach of this sort.[156] On the other hand, this solution, which at least has the benefit of simplicity, seems to have been roundly rejected by the DCFR. Article III–3:105, it will be remembered, refers to cases where what is contrary to good faith is not the inclusion of a term but its invocation. The examples suggested in the commentary nearly all involve precisely this: deliberate breach of one sort or another. Moreover, the idea of deliberate breach is construed widely. Thus in the carriage context the drafters of the DCFR are adamant that, even where the contract contains an exoneration or limitation, liability must be unlimited in the case of a carrier who knowingly provides inadequate protection thinking, often with reason, that the goods will probably come to no hurt.[157] Moreover, this is willy-nilly and independent of what the parties actually want: there is no way of avoiding this conclusion by drafting, since the duty to observe good faith on which it all depends cannot be excluded by agreement.[158] The result is a large hole in freedom of contract and, in effect, that the pre-1966 English position on fundamental breach is to be forcibly restored by a European side-wind. The point can matter considerably in shipping law. It is not uncommon that (for instance) where a shipowner is in breach of provisions in a charter someone in his employ will know of it: if so, any agreed limitation of liability for cargo damage immediately becomes suspect. The same goes for a carrier who knows that there may be a defect in his vessel's ability to protect the cargo properly: again, all limitations and exemptions are called in question. And indeed, reading between the lines, the suggestion seems to be made in the DCFR that a voyage charterer who deliberately keeps a ship on demurrage rather than loading or unloading it, unless he has an excuse such as port congestion, immediately loses the right to rely on the demurrage clause and becomes liable to damages at large for detention.[159] Now, this may actually be desirable: it may indeed be right that the ability to invoke the protection of a contractual clause should depend, willy-nilly, on a close

154 See e.g. the shipbuilding case of *China Shipbuilding Corp v Nippon Yusen Kabukishi Kaisha* [2000] *CLC* 566 at 577–580 (Thomas J).

155 See *Photo Production Ltd v Securicor Transport Ltd* [1980] *AC* 827, above.

156 See *A Turtle Offshore SA v Superior Trading Inc* [2008] *EWHC* 3034 (Admlty); [2009] 1 *Lloyd's Rep.* 177.

157 *Ibid* (trucking company providing inadequately refrigerated vehicle). See too other significant non-maritime examples, namely the insistence that that a building contractor must lose the right to limit liability for late completion to a stipulated daily amount where the delay is due to his concentrating on other competing work (DCFR commentary to Article III–3:105, p.819), and that a security company knowingly providing a lower level of protection than the contractual one loses the right to invoke a limitation of liability even if there is no intent to harm (DCFR commentary to Article III–3:105, p.820).

158 As, indeed, is explicitly recognised. See DCFR commentary on Article III–3:105, p.821 ("It should not be possible to set aside by agreement the restrictions on the availability of terms under the Article; this exclusion would be contrary to the duty of good faith and fair dealing.").

159 See DCFR Commentary, 820, on DCFR, III–3:105, Illustration 4, where the emphasis on the presence of some unavoidable hazard like port congestion suggests that if it is absent the charterer is liable in full. As any English lawyer will have noticed, this effectively means that not only the reasoning in *Suisse Atlantique Société d'Armement SA v NV Rotterdamsche Kolen Centrale* [1967] 1 *A.C.* 361, but the result itself, is to be overturned: and this again despite any contrary agreement by the parties.

investigation of the conduct of the person seeking to do so (though this is something on which P and I clubs, who work on the basis of as much certainty as possible in matters of liability, may well have an opinion). But the potentially drastic effect on English shipping law as currently understood should not be underestimated.

### 4.2.5. Other matters

**24.** Apart from the rather substantial points of principle mentioned above, a look at the DCFR and the idea of good faith embodied in it will reveal a number of other miscellaneous, but nevertheless important, potential effects on the present English approach to shipping law. These are all worth mentioning, as they could possibly have considerable effects.

**25.** (a)**Time-bars.** The application of time-bars in English commercial practice is essentially a mechanical exercise: a time-bar either applies in its terms or it does not. If it does obtain then the point can be taken, however unfairly, by the defendant unless there has been a clear and unequivocal statement by him that it will be waived, amounting to an estoppel.[160] The DCFR, by contrast, recognises that even if a time-bar does apply, its invocation may be prevented under the general duty of good faith.[161] Although much of this "good faith" qualification simply mirrors the English estoppel rule[162], this may not always be true. A couple of examples from German law, which observes a similar principle[163], show what might happen. In one 2011 case from Munich, concerning a carrier's misdelivery of a consignment of mobile phones, the time-bar on claims had been waived in lawyers' correspondence, but in error this had been done on behalf not of the actual defendant but of a different though associated company (a corporate re-organisation had intervened). Good faith, it was held, nevertheless prevented the real defendant then taking advantage of the time-bar, which in the meantime had expired.[164] And in a 2005 decision, the owner of a stolen yacht mistakenly brought suit on a marine policy, not against the underwriters, but against the brokers who had set it up. By the time the mistake came to light, the six-month time-bar for claims against the underwriters had expired. The Supreme Court of Germany upheld a decision in the policyholder's favour, finding nothing amiss in a Celle court's determination that the underwriters, who had in no way been taken by surprise, were barred in the circumstances by the rules of elementary good faith from invoking the time-bar.[165]

160 *Seechurn v Ace Insurance NV* [2002] 2 *Lloyd's Rep.* 390, esp at [26], [55]-[58] (Ward LJ); *Fortisbank SA v Trenwick International Ltd* [2005] *EWHC* 399 (Comm) at [30]-[42]; generally, M. Canny, *Limitation Periods in England and Wales*, Paras.1.13–1.14. For shipping cases where an estoppel was established, see e.g. *The Ion* [1980] 2 *Lloyd's Rep.* 245 and *The Stolt Loyalty* [1995] 1 *Lloyd's Rep.* 598.

161 See DFCR commentary on Article III-7:307, p.1223.

162 Above, text around note 16.

163 E.g. BGH, 06.06.1966 – II ZR 66/64, *VersR* 1966, 723 (section V).

164 See OLG München, 26.1.2011, 7 U 3426/10, *TranspR* 2011, 147.

165 See BGH, 16.02.2005 – IV ZR 18/04, 2005 *TranspR* 170, 172. See too similar reasoning in BGH 12.6.2002, VIII ZR 187/01.

26. **(b) Limitation of liability.** Limitation of liability is vital in shipping law, applying as it does to cargo claims (whether brought under bills of lading, waybills, charterparties or other documents), collision claims, salvage claims and so on. The matter is now governed fairly comprehensively by the 1976 Convention on Limitation of Liability for Maritime Claims, ratified by most European countries. Under that convention, the right to limit can be lost, but only "if it is proved that the loss resulted from [the defendant's] personal act or omission, committed with the intent to cause such loss, or recklessly and with knowledge that such loss would probably result.".[166] Although no mention is made of this in the DCFR, its introduction of a general duty of good faith in Article III-1:103 may indirectly affect it in one important way. Under the 1976 Convention, the burden of proof is fairly, squarely and deliberately put on the claimant: if he wants to break limitation, he must positively prove knowing wrongdoing. But practice in Germany suggests that good faith may considerably muddy these waters. Historically, in a series of cases[167] on road transport (in which both the standard internal regime and the CMR similarly provide for a monetary limit breakable on proof of enhanced fault)[168], German courts developed the doctrine that where the significant facts were probably within the exclusive knowledge of the carrier, good faith prevented the latter, when faced with an allegation of wilful fault by a claimant seeking full recovery, from simply saying "prove it." On the contrary: he had to ascertain what had happened and provide an explanation consistent with the lack of enhanced fault, and if he could not, then such fault was held established.[169] This highly significant outgrowth of good faith doctrine has since migrated to sea carriage, as witness (for example) a 2009 case where wind turbine parts shipped from Australia to Germany for repair were damaged at sea because insufficiently secured. The carrier, being unable to give sufficient details to indicate that there had been no systemic organisational failings leading to the loss, was held liable in full.[170]

166 Article 4. A similar rule applies under Article 22 of the Montreal Convention 1999 governing carriage of goods by air. The original Warsaw Convention 1929, still applicable to some carriage, in Article 25 referred to "wilful misconduct" as the factor necessary to break limitation.

167 LG Wuppertal, 13.07.1995, 9 S 275/94, 1996 *TranspR* 212; BGH, 18.12.2008 1 ZR 128/06; BGH, 10.12.2009 1 ZR 154/07; BGH, 13.06.2012 · I ZR 87/11(also the Austrian decision in OGH, 14.07.1993, 7 Ob 540/93). Air carriage was treated in the same way: see the Warsaw Convention case of OLG Köln, 27.06.1995, 22 U 265/94, *TranspR* 1996, 26.

168 See ADSp, Articles 23, 27; CMR, Article 29.

169 As the courts repeatedly put it, "The burden lying on the claimant to establish the facts and prove his case is nevertheless qualified on the basis that, given the contracting parties' disparate access to information, the carrier is bound on the basis of good faith to elucidate the immediate circumstances surrounding the casualty, as far as this is possible and can reasonably be expected." ("*Die dem Anspruchsteller obliegende Darlegungs- und Beweislast kann jedoch dadurch gemildert werden, dass der Frachtführer angesichts des unterschiedlichen Informationsstands der Vertragsparteien nach Treu und Glauben gehalten ist, soweit möglich und zumutbar, zu den näheren Umständen des Schadensfalls eingehend vorzutragen*"). See e.g. BGH, 13.06. 2012 · I ZR 87/11.

170 BGH 29. 7. 2009 – I ZR 212/06, 2009 *TranspR* 331. See too, for cases accepting the same doctrine, BGH, 03.11.2005 – I ZR 325/02, 2006 *TranspR* 35, 37; BGH 11.04.2013 – 1 ZR 61/12, 2013 *TranspR* 437, 439; and OLG Stuttgart, 20.08.2010 – 3 U 60/10, 2010 *TranspR* 387, 393, 394.

27. (c) **Lien.** Under English practice, the lien is very a powerful weapon in the hands of a carrier. Provided that the terms on which it is given are clear, there are no inherent limits on its exercise. It can be exercised over any goods, for any debt, whether or not owed by the goods owner, and (in the case of a general lien, which a number of carriers and warehousemen employ) in respect of any transaction whatever with the shipper, and not simply the carriage of those particular goods.[171] By contrast, whereas in the English context the only serious issue is one of interpretation, where an extensive doctrine of good faith applies then there may well be important limits placed on the lienholder's freedom of action. First, the lien must it seems be exercised with a good deal of regard for the interests of the owner of the goods: there is, for example, German authority that it may be contrary to good faith to exercise a right of retention merely as a means of pressure for payment in circumstances where sale would yield little or nothing.[172] And secondly, a lien may it seems be exercised by a carrier only over that part of the cargo reasonably necessary to cover the amount for which the lien is held: it is not open to him simply to sell the cargo as a whole, reimburse himself and account for the rest.[173] If he does this, he may find himself liable in tort to the owner for any loss that the latter can prove due to his failure to receive the excess goods.[174]

28. (d) **The right to perform and the rule in *White & Carter v McGregor.*** As any English lawyer will know, one peculiarity of English law is the rule in *White & Carter (Councils) Ltd v McGregor*[175]; that is, the principle that a contractor who can perform his contract without the consent of the other party[176] can ignore any purported termination by the latter[177], render performance albeit unwanted and claim payment in full. The fact that he thereby acts unreasonably is irrelevant[178]: the only exception is in extreme cases

171 For an example, see *Jarl Trä AB v Convoys Ltd* [2003] EWHC 1488 (Comm); [2003] 2 Lloyd's Rep. 459.

172 OLG Karlsruhe, 8.8.72 – 8 U 69/71, BB 1972, 1163 (goods valuable to debtor but almost valueless on the market).

173 See O. Vortisch & W. Bemm, *Binnenschiffahrtsrecht: Kommentar*, p 352 (regarding this as a matter of good faith in the context of inland carriage); also OLG Köln, 30.05.2008, 3 U 7/07, *TranspR* 2009, 37, below.

174 As happened in OLG Köln, 30.05.2008, 3 U 7/07, *TranspR* 2009, 37 (carrier of maize cargo had lien for about 22,000€: liable in damages to owner when sold maize worth three times that amount and simply accounted for excess).

175 [1962] 2 AC 413. Technically this was a Scots decision, but there is no doubt that it represents English law.

176 If he cannot so perform, even owing to breach by the defendant, then no right to payment can arise at all: see e.g. the sale case of *Colley v Overseas Exporters* [1921] 3 KB 302. The common law, in other words, does not recognise the civilian doctrine that a debtor who wrongly prevents a condition of his liability being satisfied is liable as if it had been fulfilled.

177 The absolute nature of this right (which will be surprising to civil lawyers, where the right to terminate is regarded as inherent in the idea of good faith: see e.g. BGB, §314(1)) was established beyond argument by the UK Supreme Court in *Geys v Société Générale* [2012] *UKSC* 63; [2013] 1 AC 523.

178 "It might be, but it never has been, the law that a person is only entitled to enforce his contractual rights in a reasonable way, and that a court will not support an attempt to enforce them in an unreasonable way" – *White & Carter (Councils) Ltd v McGregor* [1962] 2 *A.C.* 413, 430 (Lord Reid). This sentence indeed encapsulates the difference between the civil and common law approaches to contracts.

where he has no conceivable interest in continuing with the contract.[179] The point is particularly significant where a time or bareboat charterer purports to cancel early; assuming the charterer is solvent, the owner need do nothing at all to accept the return of the vessel or mitigate his loss, but can simply invoice monthly for hire and sue if unpaid.[180] Similarly, it is arguable that in a standard shipbuilding contract where instalments of the price are payable at stated stages of construction, the builder may continue to build and cause instalments of the price to fall due even though it is no longer clear that the buyer will accept.[181] And there is also authority that a carrier once in possession of goods may carry them to destination even though reasonably requested not to do so, with a view to setting up a general right of retention and thus gaining security for existing indebtedness.[182]

**29.** This position is, predictably, rejected in the DCFR. Under Article III-3:301(2)(b) the right to render unwanted performance and then claim fulfilment of the duty to pay is specifically excluded where performance would be "unreasonable in the circumstances"[183]; and in the specific case of leases of chattels (a category presumably including bareboat charters) a claim for rent is unavailable against a lessee who wishes to return the goods if it would be reasonable for the lessor to accept them.[184] Although the words good faith are not directly mentioned in this respect, this seems to be the underlying idea[185]: and indeed in a number of existing legal systems the limits on the right to claim the price are put on this basis.[186]

179 "It may well be that, if it can be shown that a person has no legitimate interest, financial or otherwise, in performing the contract rather than claiming damages, he ought not to be allowed to saddle the other party with an additional burden with no benefit to himself" – *White & Carter (Councils) Ltd v McGregor* [1962] 2 *A.C.* 413, 431 (Lord Reid). See generally *The Aquafaith* [2012] *EWHC* 1077 (Comm); [2012] 1 *C.L.C.* 899 at [6]-[25] (Cooke J).

180 *The Aquafaith* [2012] *EWHC* 1077 (Comm); [2012] 1 *CLC* 899 (attempt at redelivery a few months before the end of a 5-year time-charter: owner entitled to ignore and sue for remaining instalments as they fell due). See too *The Dynamic* [2003] EWHC 1936 (Comm); [2003] 2 *Lloyd's Rep.* 693 (time trip charter). It seems that on principle the same principle applies to a bareboat charter, unless the owner takes back possession of the vessel (see *The Aquafaith* [2012] *EWHC* 1077 (Comm); [2012] 1 *CLC* 899 at [40] (Cooke J, discussing *The Puerto Buitrago* [1976] 1 Lloyd's Rep. 250), and compare *Reichman v Beveridge* [2006] *EWCA Civ* 1659; [2007] 1 *P. & C.R.* 20 (same re lease of land)).

181 *Stocznia Gdanska SA v Latvian Shipping Co* [1996] 2 *Lloyds Rep* 132, 139 (Staughton LJ).

182 See *George Barker (Transport) Ltd v Eynon* [1974] 1 *W.L.R.* 462, 468 (Edmund Davies L.J.) (concerning road transport, but equally applicable to carriage by sea).

183 And indeed the facts of *White & Carter (Councils) Ltd v McGregor* [1962] 2 AC 413 are given in the DCFR commentary at p.846 as just such a case: see too *ibid* at pp.847–848.

184 DCFR, Article IVB-6:101(1) (also PECL, Article 9:101(2)(b)).

185 O. Lando, "Salient Features of the Principles of European Contract Law: A Comparison with the UCC", 13 *Pace Int'l L. Rev.* 339, 350 (2001), discussing the equivalent PECL provisions, regards this as a matter of good faith; see too G. Dannemann & S. Vogenauer, *The Common European Sales Law in Context*, p.679, and H. Weidt, *Antizipierter Vertragsbruch: eine Untersuchung zum deutschen und englischen Recht*, p.160.

186 E.g. Belgium, where it is regarded as bad faith or abusive to insist on unwanted performance (Cass 16.01.1986, Arr Cass 317, *RW* 1987–8); and it would seem Germany (H. Weidt, *Antizipierter*

## V. Conclusion

**30.** The conclusion to be drawn from this is largely apparent from what has gone before. One may accept the argument that English law in practice accepts a good many of the rules civilians regard as stemming from good faith, and hence that overall the effect of introducing it might not be as cataclysmic as appears at first sight. Nevertheless, in the rough-and-tumble of shipping law there is enough potential uncertainty and restriction on the freedom of parties to arrange their affairs the way they wish to give rise to disquiet. In this context at least, the instinctive mistrust of English commercial lawyers of good faith as an overarching conception[187] may well have a good deal more going for it than meets the civilian eye.

*Vertragsbruch: eine Untersuchung zum deutschen und englischen Recht*, p.160.; 425 munchk6 on 242: mention of "generell bei einer zwecklos gewordenen Leistung").

187 For instances, see e.g., R. Goode, *Commercial Law in the Next Millennium*, 19–20; M. Bridge, "Doubting Good Faith" [2005] *New Zealand Business Law Quarterly* 426; A. Forte, *Good Faith in Property and Contract Law*, Ch.4 (J. Thomson, *Good Faith in Contracting: A Sceptical View*).

Elena Orrù*

# UNEXPECTED CIRCUMSTANCES IN SHIPPING CONTRACTS

## I. Premises

1. Change of conditions after the conclusion of a contract particularly interests shipping contracts, because of the long-term duration of many of them. The article's aim is to contribute to determine if and to what extent the emerging European Contract or Private Law (PECL, DCFR, *etc*), according to the nature of each set of rules, could govern Maritime Law issues concerning supervening events unbalancing the parties' obligations or making their performance impossible. For this purpose, the speciality and autonomy of Maritime Law and the possible effects of PECL and DCFR on international and national law and case-law should be considered. The topic therefore refers to the exceptions to the principle *pacta sunt servanda* depending on unexpected events that are not within the parties' control and that were not and could not be reasonably foreseen by the parties when negotiating and concluding the contract, but affect the allocation of risks deriving from the contract, making the performance of an obligation impossible or altering the balance between the parties' obligations, or one party's use of the goods or services the contract was concluded for, or however the contract's specific purposes.[1]

2. On the contrary, this article does not deal with issues concerning the formation of the parties' consent and the circumstances according to which it could be considered invalidly developed or a misrepresentation of existing circumstances could entitle to the termination of the contract. The relevance and effects of unexpected circumstances, after the contract was concluded, are not uniformly ruled, depending on the law governing the specific contract. Civil Law and Common Law provide for very considerably different regulation of the effects on the contract's performance of supervening events after its conclusion. Moreover, both among Civil Law Countries,

* Tenured Assistant Professor (Ricercatrice confermata) of Maritime, Air and Transport Law, Department of Legal Studies, Alma Mater Studiorum – University of Bologna, Italy. PhD in European Transport Law, 2007, Department of Legal Studies, Alma Mater Studiorum – University of Bologna.

1 E. Hondius, H. C. Grigoleit, 'Introduction: An approach to the issues and doctrines relating to unexpected circumstances', in E. Hondius, H. C. Grigoleit (Eds), *Unexpected Circumstances in European Contract Law* (Cambridge University Press, 2011) 3, 3 f.

from the one hand, and among Common Law ones, from the other, the differences in regulating this issue are still quite remarkable.

3. Supervening events, altering the economical and legal balance between the parties' interests and consideration or causing the impossibility of performance of all or part of a party's obligations, could be regarded as circumstances enabling the party to cancel the specific contract or admitting a re-negotiation of the contract's terms or the Court's adjustment of them. It is therefore necessary to identify the relevant concept of supervening events that could affect the contractual relationship, according to each legal system, and to ascertain which remedies are provided for this case. For example, not all the legal systems expressly admit the termination of the contract or the modification of its terms as a consequence of an event that does not imply that the performance has become impossible, but only that it is suddenly excessively burdensome, because this circumstance is deemed to belong to the original contractual balance the parties freely agreed on.[2]

In addition, whereas the right to terminate the contract seems to be quite well-established among the different legal systems, often no obligation to re-negotiate the contract's terms is provided for.

Moreover, Maritime Law has been developed and is still often considered as a special or even autonomous law with respect to Contract/Private Law, and has developed its own rules governing shipping contracts. Another issue is therefore if the general principles and rules developed within Contract/Private Law could reflect on shipping contracts.

## II. Unexpected Circumstances in Shipping Contracts

4. With regard to the sector in issue, due to its particular features, specific international conventions were concluded, and EU law and often national law (especially for Civil Law Countries) include quite detailed and specific provisions particularly concerning (at least some aspects of) the contracts and the activities that are typical and specific of this sector, determining also the main events that enable each party to be exempted from liability. These international conventions are the result of the negotiations among the different States and categories involved in the operations: therefore they should be better able to correspond to the interests involved in the subject-matters they were drafted to govern, than provisions referring to general situations and prevail over the latter under the principle *lex specialis derogat generali.*

5. More over the parties usually regulate possible supervening events in the contracts they conclude, mainly with the use of forms developed, often at international level, by entrepreneurial organizations or associations. The effects of the clauses and terms included by the parties in their contract however depend on the limits each legal system

2 F. P. Traisci, *Sopravvenienze contrattuali e rinegoziazione nei sistemi di Civil e di Common Law* (Edizioni Scientifiche Italiane, 2003) 9.

sets for contractual freedom.[3] In each national system the events, concerned by this article, are also governed by Contract or Private Law in general: these rules, which do not specifically concern shipping contracts, but contracts in general, are often applied within legal systems when a matter is not exhaustively governed by Shipping Law provisions or by the parties in their contract.

## III. Unexpected Circumstances Within Forms

6. Specific contract clauses concerning supervening events and frustration or impossibility of performance are often incorporated in contracts, usually consisting of forms developed within the shipping sector.

They could consist in hardship clauses, provided in favour of one party or both, in force majeure clauses, in clauses allocating the risks related to the contract performance, in off-hire clauses included in time charterparties, or in clauses ruling out any possible frustrating or relieving effects of supervening events on the contract for the benefit of one party.[4] Some clauses could refer both to hardship and to impossibility of performance.[5] Hardship clauses, in particular, do not contemplate termination as the direct consequence of the frustrating event, but provide for the parties to re-negotiate the contract's terms and terminate the contract only if they do not reach an agreement or do not confer to a Court or to arbitrators the power to adapt the contract as a consequence of the unexpected supervening event.[6] Usually, events enabling the hardship clause to apply must be 'external, unexpected and frustrating'.[7]

7. Some contracts identify the supervening frustrating events that are put at one party's risk, but also specify that these events extend to 'any other cause preventing the full working of the vessel'.[8] This wording is interpreted as referring to causes of the

3 Many of the forms that are herein examined are also based on the model of the ICC Force Majeure Clause 2003, ICC Publication No 650, February 2003, Paris.

4 *Budgett & Co v Binnington & Co* [1891] 1 *QB* 35; *Larrinaga & Co Ltd v Société Franco-americaine des Phosphates de Medulla* [1923] 14 *Lloyd's Rep* 457; Y. Baatz, 'Charterparties', in *Southampton on Shipping Law* (Informa, 2008) 45, 79; A. Tettenborn, 'Frustration in Voyage Charters – Silted-up Backwater or Vital Navigation Resource?', in R Thomas (Ed), *The evolving law and practice of voyage charterparties* (Informa, 2009) 325 ff. On hardship clauses, also G Giacobbe, 'La presupposizione', in N. Lipari, P. Rescigno (Ed), *Diritto Civile* (vol 3, Giuffrè, 2009) 485, 496.

5 M. Almeida Prado, *Le* hardship *dans le droit du commerce international* (Bruylant, FEC, 2003) 165.

6 M. Almeida Prado (5) 129 ff; Ph. Delebecque, 'Flexibility, foreseeability, reasonableness in shipping contracts: the civil law approach' [2013] *DM* 281, 283 ff.

7 Ph. Delebecque (6) 283; Ch Arb Paris, 3 February 2010, No 1172; Ch Arb Paris, 3 December 2010, No 1170.

8 Clause 25 BIMCO Barecon 2001 relates to requisition for hire, compulsory acquisition or requisition for title of the vessel 'by any governmental or other competent authority', putting on the charterers the risks of such event: they shall continue to pay the hire according to the Charter itself until the time it would have been terminated under its own provisions, but any requisition hire or compensation shall be paid to the charterers during the remaining charter period or the requisition for hire period, whichever is the shorter. In Barecon 89, the charterers were liable for the hire during the requisition for hire period only from the time the requisition hire was payable to them [M Davis, *Bareboat Charters* (II

same type of those explicitly listed before, when the word 'whatsoever' is not added after 'any other cause'.[9] Examining some examples of shipping contracts, shipbuilding contracts can be mentioned: referring to the present subject-matter, as for the first type of clauses, the various forms concern the possible variations to the original projects, included those deriving from subsequent orders of Public Authorities, such as the Classification Societies, or depending on materials or technicalities.[10] The forms concern also delays in delivering the built ship, caused by events the contractor is not responsible of. These events are described in detail in the forms and include political, natural and technical causes the contractor must give evidence of. With regard to the latter, they must not depend on the contractor's organization, but must derive from causes beyond his control. The contractor must timely notify the principal about the event, specifying also the probable delay deriving from it, when possible. In these cases, the contractor has the right to a further amount of time for fulfilling his commitment, but if the delay exceeds the period provided for by the contract, the principal has the right to cancel the contract.

**8.** Concerning, for example, ship or crew management contracts, many forms rule out any liability of either party for any loss, damage or delay due to the listed events that are considered fitting the concept of force majeure, provided that any of them has prevented or hindered the party invoking it from performing any or all of his obligations under the contract. The party whose obligations are affected by one of the events described in the form must make all reasonable efforts to avoid, minimize or prevent those effects or conditions.[11] The same forms expressly limit the manager's liability to the owners only to the losses, damages, delays or expenses arising from his negligence, gross negligence or wilful default or those of his employees, agents or of the sub-contractors employed by the manager in connection with the vessel.[12]

Edn, LLP, 2005) 139 f, who suggests to amend this clause, in order to mitigate the charterers' regime, which otherwise shall remain liable for paying the charter hire even if it exceeds the requisition one and for the ship's maintenance and insurance, providing that they shall be liable for the charter hire only up to the requisition hire's level and giving them the option to terminate the contract if the requisition exceeds a certain period].

9 *The Laconian Confidence* [1997] 1 *Lloyd's Rep* 139; M Davis (8) 158.

10 Some of the main forms are the AWES Form, drafted by the Association of West European Shipbuilders, the SAJ Form, by the Shipbuilders' Association of Japan, the NSA Form of the Norwegian Shipowners' Association and the Norwegian Shipbuilders' Association and the Shipbuilding Contract by the Italian Fincantieri. On this topic, F Lorenzon, 'The European contract law project and maritime law', in *The Emerging European Maritime Law. Proceedings from the Third European Colloquium on Maritime Law Research, Ravenna, 17 – 18 September 2004* [2005] MarIus 330 137, 147 ff, G Boi, *I contratti marittimi. La disciplina dei formulari* (Giuffrè, 2008) 15 ff; S Curtis, 'Force Majeure Provisions in a Shipbuilding Contest', in E McKendrick (Ed), *Force Majeure and Frustration of Contract* (Informa Law, 2013) 139.

11 Cl 14(a) of Crewman A (Cost plus Fee) 2009; Cl 13(a) of Crewman B (Lump Sum) 2009; Cl 17(a) of Shipman 2009.

12 Cl 14(b) of Crewman A (Cost plus Fee) 2009; Cl 13(b) of Crewman B (Lump Sum) 2009; Cl 17(b) of Shipman 2009.

Charterparties and contracts of affreightment usually contain several clauses concerning frustration, too.[13]

As for charterparties, they usually include terms relating to frustrating delay ruling out the right to demurrage.[14] As it has been above-mentioned, time charterparties usually contain off-hire clauses, providing for the hire to cease to be payable when certain events (such as the breakdown of the vessel's engines, the detention by average accidents, the ship's arrest) prevent the ship's working without any fault of the owner.[15] When the events, an off-hire clause provides for, depend on the charterer's fault, he must compensate the shipowner of the damages he suffered as a consequence. Other clauses, on the contrary, are meant to have the freight payable even when the goods are lost, by making it payable in advance or adding the clause 'ship/goods lost or not lost': therefore in the first case the freight is deemed to have been earned on the goods' shipment instead of on their delivery to destination.[16]

9. Other clauses enable the parties to cancel the contract when any of the events, there listed or identified, occur.[17] Some clauses expressly refer to compulsory orders, recommendations, advices, etc of public Authorities, which are able to affect the contract's performance.[18] Great importance have also the war risk clauses, which allow the party whose performance is affected by this risk to interrupt it or enable either party

13 For example, they refer also to war (and similar) risks, incorporating clauses on war risks similar to clause 26 of Barecon 2001 [BP Time 3 terms; the Chamber of the Shipping War Risks Clause 1952; the Conwartime 93 terms; Gencon clause 17; clause 35 of Shelltime 4 (1984); Shellvoy 5, para 34; K Michel, 'War, terror, piracy and frustration in a time charter context', in R Thomas (Ed) (4) 199, 207]. Some clauses concern also acts of public enemies and can operate in favour of either party. Others relate, for example, to the unavailability of the vessel, from the one hand (Gencon 94, para 9; Shellvoy 5, para 11; *Jackson v Union Marine Insurance Co Ltd* [1874] LR 10 CP 125), or of the cargo to load, carry or unload, on the other (Gencon 94, para 16; *The Nema* [1982] 2 AC 724; *Budgett & Co v Binnington & Co* [1891] 1 QB 35; *Isles Steam Shipping Co Ltd v Theodoridi & Co* [1926] 24 Lloyd's Rep 362), otherwise the owners or the charterers would be liable (A Tettenborn (4) 325, 327).

14 Eg: Gencon 1994, clause 7.

15 Eg: *The Laconian Confidence* [1997] 1 Lloyd's Rep 139; *Nippon Yusen Kaisha Ltd v Scindia Steam Navigation Co Ltd (The Jalagouri)* [2000] 1 Lloyd's Rep 515; *The Mastro Georgis* [1983] 2 Lloyd's Rep 66; *The Apollo* [1987] 1 Lloyd's Rep 200; Y Baatz (4) 76 f. See Baltime form, clause 11; NYPE 1946, clause 15; NYPE 1993, clause 17; Shelltime 4 form, clause 21.

16 M N Howard, 'Frustration and Shipping Law – Old Problems, New Contexts', in E McKendrick (Ed) (8) 123, 124.

17 BIMCO Barecon 2001 concerns also the case of the ship's loss. Clause 28(c) entitles the parties to terminate the contract when the vessel becomes a total loss or is declared as a constructive or compromised or arranged total loss. According to clause 11(e) of the same form, in case the vessel is lost or missing, the hire's payment cease from the date and time it 'was lost or last heard of' and any hire paid in advance must 'be adjusted accordingly'. M Davis (8) 158.

18 For example, as for compulsory acquisition (requisition for title is disciplined in the same manner), since it deprives the owners of the vessel's ownership, the clauses of bareboat charters provide for the charter's termination, irrespective of the date when those events occur during the Charter Period and the hire shall be 'considered as earned and to be paid up to the date and time of' the event (Ibid).
Moreover, clause 26 of BIMCO Barecon 2001 prohibits to load contraband cargo or pass through any blockade whatsoever type it is or purpose it has, or to proceed to an area where it shall be subject to a belligerent's right of search and/or confiscation or is likely to be subject to this right.

to terminate the contract.[19] War risks definition is usually broad, including 'any actual, threatened or reported: war, act of war, civil war or hostilities; revolution; rebellion; civil commotion; (...) acts of piracy (...); acts of terrorists; acts of hostility or malicious damage; blockades (...)' by any kind of physical or legal person, including the Government of any State.[20] In order to have relevance, these risks 'may be dangerous or are likely to be or become dangerous' to the ship, its cargo, crew or other persons on board.[21]

**10.** As for the contracts of affreightment, usually forms include clauses referred to impediments beyond the parties' control that rule out any liability of the party, whose performance is affected by them, for interrupting his performance: as a consequence the cargo's quantities not carried because of force majeure are deducted from its remaining amount of cargo and its shipment cannot be demanded and neither it can be carried afterwards.[22] Some forms deal more specifically with the issue, explicitly providing that the performance shall not be resumed if it is evident that the hindrance's effect will not cease until the end of the contractual period and that the party not responsible for the breach of the contract has the right to cancel it, when the hindrance lasts or is evident that will last for more than six months.[23]

The bareboat charterers have the liberty (and – obviously – not the option) to comply with all orders, directions, recommendations or advices concerning, for example, 'departure, arrival, routes, sailing in convoy, ports of call, stoppages, destinations, discharge of cargo, delivery' by the Government whose flag the ship is sailing, by any war risks underwriters with the authority to give such orders, etc. according to the war risks insurance, and with the terms of any resolution of the UN Security Council, of the European Community, of any Supranational body that has this authority and with national laws aimed at enforcing the same the owners are subject to. M Davis (8) 146.

19 As for the first type of clause, according to clause 26 of BIMCO Barecon 2001, the vessel shall not continue to or go through any port, place, area or zone, where it reasonably appears that it, its cargo, crew or other persons on board may be or are likely to be exposed to war risks, according to the owners' reasonable judgement [M Davis (8) 143]. But, according to some English case-law, the place should be considered dangerous 'by reference to the standards and circumstances which existed at the date of the charterparty' [*The Product Star* [1991] 2 *Lloyd's Rep* 468, especially 478; K Michel (11) 208]. If the vessel is in this kind of place when a war risk occurs and that area becomes dangerous or is likely to become so, the owners have the right to require that it leaves the place. Only owners could consent, in writing, for the ship to continue to or go through such a port, place area or zone.
Eg also Clause 17 of GENCOA, clause 20 of VOLCOA. is a war cancellation clause.
The forms include also war cancellation clauses, providing for the right of either party to cancel the contract in case of the outbreak of war between any two or more of the Countries there listed. This is the case of the clause 26, par (f), of BIMCO Barecon 2001 and of INTERCOA's clause K.
On this topic, also B Davenport, 'War Clauses in Time Charterparties', in E McKendrick (Ed), *Force Majeure and Frustration of Contract* (Informa Law, 2013) 153.

20 Voywar 2013. Identical definition is in the Conwartime 2013 and very similar definition in clause 26 BIMCO Barecon 2001. On the concepts of wars, terrorism and similar events, eg: K Michel (11) 199 ff.

21 On the meaning of these expressions, recently *Pacific Basin Ihx Ltd v Bulkhandling Handymax AS (The Triton Lark)* [2012] *EWHC* 70 (Comm), that led to a modification of Conwartime and Voywar terms.

22 Clause 15 of GENCOA, clause 19 of VOLCOA.

23 Cl 19 of VOLCOA.

Unexpected circumstances, enabling the parties to terminate the contract without any liability, have been considered occurred, even when not explicitly mentioned by the contract, for example, in case of adventures concerning trades with alien enemies.[24]

## IV. National Law. English Law

11. As it has been above mentioned, the consequences of unexpected circumstances on shipping contracts are, first of all, dealt with by the relevant international conventions the single State is bound to. In the following paragraphs the domestic law of some Countries is briefly examined, starting with English law.

### *4.1. The doctrine of frustration*

12. Common Law provides for the general rule of the strict duty of performing an obligation, despite of supervening events.[25] With regard to English law an exception to this rule is the doctrine of frustration, which is considered to apply also to charterparties and to other shipping contracts, such as towage.[26] This doctrine is based on at least five theories, the most renowned of which is the 'test of a radical change in the obligation', according to the parties' intentions, objectively construed and 'in the light of the circumstances existing when [the contract] was made'. The change must occur to the extent that the obligation falls outside the contract's scope, in its true construction.[27] Therefore, the event must affect the whole contract altering its commercial basis, so that it becomes a different contract, being irrelevant events that have simply made one party's performance more burdensome.[28]

24 M Davis (8) 147.

25 The first case where this principle was stated is considered to be *Paradine v Jane* [1647] Aleyn 26, mentioned by W Swadling, 'The Judicial Construction of Force Majeure Clauses', in E McKendrick (Ed) (8) 3. L J Bingham, in *J Lauritzen AS v Wijsmuller BV (The Super Servant Two)* [1990] 1 *Lloyd's Rep* 1 [mentioned by E McKendrick, 'Force Majeure and Frustration – The Relationship and a Comparative Assessment', in E McKendrick (Ed) (8) 33, 37] referred to 'the rigour of the common law's insistence on literal performance of absolute promises'.

26 *National Carriers Ltd v Panalpina (Northern) Ltd* [1981] AC 675; R Shaw, M Tsimplis, 'The Liabilities of the Vessel', in *Southampton on Shipping Law* (Informa, 2008) 155, 179. The doctrine could apply both to time charters and voyage charters, even if for the latter it could be more difficult [A Tettenborn (4) 319].

27 *Davis Contractors Ltd v Fareham UDC* [1956] AC 696; *Sir Lindsay Parkinson & Co Ltd v Works & Public Buildings Comrs* [1950] 1 All ER 208; *National Carriers Ltd v Panalpina (Northern) Ltd* [1981] *AC* 675; *J Lauritzen AS v Wijsmuller BV (The Super Servant Two)* [1990] 1 *Lloyd's Rep* 1; M Davis (8) 241 f; Y Baatz (4) 63 ff; A Tettenborn (4) 323; E Hondius, H C Grigoleit (1) 3, 7.

28 *Bank Line Ltd v Arthur Capel & Co* [1919] *AC* 435; M Davis (8) 142; Y Baatz (4) 64; K Michel (11) 209; A Tettenborn (4) 319 ff, 323; S Baughen, *Shipping Law* (Routledge, 2012) 255. US law, on the contrary, admits commercial impracticability within the scope of the doctrine of frustration: C Brunner, *Force Majeure and Hardship under General Contract Principles: Exemption for Non-performance in International Arbitration* (Wolters Kluwer, 2009) 93.

**13.** The circumstance altering the contract must be unforeseen and unforeseeable by the parties when they stipulated the agreement and must not depend on the default of the party seeking for enforcing the doctrine of frustration or on one party's action.[29] It is questioned if the doctrine of frustration is ruled out in case of events falling within the scope of the party's organization of personnel and means or work.[30]

More over this doctrine does not concern excepted perils or other situations where a party's liability is excluded according to the provisions of international conventions or other relevant law. This could be the case of restraint of princes, which could indeed entail to consider the contract frustrated, but in any case is also the basis for excluding the owners' liability without any necessary reference to the doctrine of frustration.[31]

**14.** The actual existence of all the requirements for the doctrine of frustration to be enforced to each single case is also a matter of facts, which must be assessed by the Court, on the basis of what the parties knew or ought to know and should reasonably expect at the time of the event.[32] According to English case-law, frustration must be narrowly interpreted because it determines the contract's termination.[33] Under English law, the subject-matter is governed also by the Law Reform (Frustrated Contracts) Act 1943, which supplemented and partly superseded the doctrine of frustration.[34] It expressly applies to time charters[35] and charters by demise, but not to voyage charters or contracts for the carriage of goods by sea.[36]

29 *Maritime National Fish Ltd v Ocean Trawlers Ltd* [1935] *AC* 524; *Monarch SS Co Ltd v A/B Karlshamns Oljefabriker* [1949] AC 196, HL; *Imperial Smelting Corporation Ltd v Joseph Constantine Steamship Line Ltd* [1940] 2 KB 430; *Tsakiroglou & Co Ltd v Noblee Thorl GmbH* [1962] *AC* 93;*The Eugenia* [1964] 2 QB 226; *The Evia (No 2)* [1983] 1 *AC* 736, HL; *The Captain George K* [1970] 2 *Lloyd's Rep* 21, QB; *Hyundai Merchant Marine Co Ltd v Furness Withy (Australia) Pty* [2006] 2 *Lloyd's Rep* 175 (CA); A Tettenborn (4) 328.

30 *Davis Contractors Ltd v Fareham UDC* [1956] AC 696; *J Lauritzen AS v Wijsmuller BV (The Super Servant Two)* [1990] 1 Lloyd's Rep 1; A Tettenborn (4) 328. With regard to the case the vessel is loss or missing, the doctrine of frustration shall apply (when the situation is not provided for in the contract such as in the Barecon 2001) if the event occurred without any party's fault, thus not in case it derives from unseaworthiness or negligence of one party [*Joseph Constantine Steamship Line Ltd v Imperial Smelting Corporation Ltd* [1942] AC 154; *Monarch Steamship Co, Ltd v Karlshamns Oljefabriker (A/B)* [1949] *AC* 196). Other examples of frustration are, especially for voyage and time charters, delay or strikes not depending on one party or supervening illegality in English law or in the law of the place of performance (*Ertel Bieber & Co v Rio Tinto Co Ltd* [1918] *AC* 260; *Foster v Driscoll* [1929] 1 *KB* 470; *Ralli Bros v Compania Naviera Sota y Aznar* [1920] 2 *KB* 287), but it is believed that supervening illegality in the law of the Country where one party resides or is national is not ground for frustration [M Davis (8) 248].

31 *Nobel's Explosives Co v Jenkins & Co* [1896] 2 *QB* 326; *The Lefthero* [1991] 2 *Lloyd's Rep* 599; A Tettenborn (4) 326.

32 *Tamplin Steamship Co. v Anglo-American Petroleum Products Co Ltd* [1916] 2 *AC* 397 and *Bank Line Ltd v Arthur Capel & Co* [1919] AC 435; *Universal Cargo Carriers v Pedro Citati* [1957] 1 *Lloyd's Rep* 174, in particular 192; *Edwinton Commercial Corporation, Global Tradeways Ltd v Tsavliris Russ (Worldwide Salvage & Towage) Ltd* [2007] *Lloyd's Rep* 517, which concerned also cl 9 (iii) of the SCOPIC clause.

33 *J Lauritzen AS v Wijsmuller BV (The Super Servant Two)* [1990] 1 *Lloyd's Rep* 1.

34 M Davis (8) 243.

35 Disagreeing: A Tettenborn (4) 329.

36 S 2(5). M Davis (8) 17 and 242; S Baughen (28) 258; M N Howard (14) 123.

The Act refers to contracts that became 'impossible of performance or [have] been otherwise frustrated'.[37]

English law enables the parties to rule out the doctrine of frustration through a sufficiently detailed clause, in other words 'in such a way as shows that it is provided for, only for the purpose of dealing with one of its effects and not all'.[38] Through a hardship clause, the parties can provide for the renegotiation of the contract's content, in order to re-balance their obligations, because, even when the performance is still possible, the doctrine of frustration and the Law Reform (Frustrated Contracts) Act 1943 imply the automatic termination of the contract, irrelevant of the parties' awareness and willingness of it.[39]

15. The 1943 Act and the doctrine of frustration shall consequently apply only when consistent with the contract's provisions, but for this purpose force majeure clauses are usually strictly and narrowly interpreted.[40] S 1(2) of the Law Reform (Frustrated Contracts) Act 1943 provides for the recovery of 'all sums paid or payable in pursuance of the contract before the time when the parties were so discharged', because of the frustrating event. Moreover, the same section enables the Court, taking in consideration all the circumstances, to allow the party, who received the above-mentioned sums, to retain or recover any or part of them up to the amount of the expenses incurred before the time of discharge in, or for the purpose of, the performance of the contract.

37 S 1(1).

38 *Bank Line Ltd v Arthur Capel & Co* [1919] AC 435, in particular 456; *Bremer Handelsgesellschaft mbH v Vanden Avenne-Izegem PVBA* [1977] 1 *Lloyd's Rep* 133; M Davis (8) 247 ff; A Tettenborn (4) 324 *et seq.*; S Baughen (28) 256; E McKendrick (25) 34.
Therefore, a force majeure clause does not rule out in itself the enforcement of the doctrine of frustration, depending on its content. For example, in a case of a charter providing for the charterers' option to terminate the contract if the vessel was not timely delivered or if it was commandeered by the government during the charter period, the House of Lords decided, by majority, that these sorts of clauses did not rule out the doctrine of frustration (*Bank Line Ltd v Arthur Capel & Co* [1919] AC 435).
According to some Authors, BIMCO Barecon 2001's clause 25(a) should be sufficiently clear to exclude the doctrine of frustration to apply, but it is still discussed, whereas clause 26 is deemed not to preclude its operation [M Davis (8) 142, 249 ff; S Baughen (28) 255, mentioning some examples of war and acts of war which caused frustration, such as the First World War, the war between Israel and Egypt, the 1980 war between Iran and Iraq; K Michel (11) 199 ff, mentioning also the First Gulf War, the wars between China and Japan in 1894 and in 1937, between Turkey and Greece in 1912 and the 1936 Spanish Civil War].
Clauses 28 and 11(e) of BIMCO Barecon 2001 provides for the termination of the contract in case of a constructive, compromised or arranged total loss.
When such clause is not incorporated in the contract, especially for voyage charter, the doctrine of frustration could however hardly apply, but it is not excluded (*Texas Co v Hogarth Shipping Corp'n* [1921] 256 US 619; *Ellamar Mining Co v Alaska SS Co* [1925] 5 F.2d 890).

39 *Hirji Mulji v Cheong Yue SS Co Ltd* [1926] *AC* 497; *Blane Steamships v Minister of Transport* [1951] 2 *Lloyd's Rep* 155; *Atlantic Maritime Co v Gibbon* [1954] 1 *QB* 88; *J Lauritzen AS v Wijsmuller BV (The Super Servant Two)* [1990] 1 *Lloyd's Rep* 1; M Davis (8) 243. Frustration's consequences are the parties' discharge of any further obligation and their duty to return what has been performed until the frustrating event where here has been a total failure of consideration, with no right to damages [A Tettenborn (4) 315; S Baughen (28) 255].

40 S 1(3); *Metropolitan Water Board v Dick Kerr & Co* [1918] AC 119; *The Playa Larga* [1983] 2 *Lloyd's Rep* 171, both mentioned by E McKendrick (25) 35 f.

**16.** The 1943 Act provides for another mean to recover the expenses met in or for the performance of a charter falling within its scope: s 1(3) enables the Court to decide that a party, having obtained a valuable benefit (other than a payment of money) 'by reason of anything done by any other party thereto in, or for the purpose of, the performance of the contract', before its discharge, shall pay to the other party a suitable 'sum, not exceeding the value of the said benefit'.[41] On the contrary, according to the previous case-law, especially with regard to voyage charterparties, no payment in part could be made.[42]

**17.** The above-mentioned provisions of the Law Reform (Frustrated Contracts) Act 1943 are considered still not easy to interpret, since there is not much case-law concerning charterparties.[43] However, according to some case-law, s 1(3) implies a three-step approach: identifying the valuable benefit (which could consist in the end product or the services themselves[44]) valuating it and deciding about the award of a just sum.[45]

This approach is somewhat similar to the Italian provisions concerning unjust enrichment, according to Article 2041 and 2042 of the Civil Code, but it should be noted that some English case-law has rejected the statement that the Court's aim should always be the 'prevention of the unjust enrichment of the defendant at the plaintiff's expense', because each judge can decide what is just.[46]

Finally, another important provision of the 1943 Act is its s 2(4), according to which the Court has the power to severe part of a contract from the others and consider that part as not having being frustrated.[47]

## *4.2. The doctrine of impossibility of performance*

**18.** A brief reference should be done to the doctrine of impossibility of performance, which some Authors distinguish from that of frustration: the latter should refer to frustration of purpose, whereas the former to supervening impossibility of performance, which can occur only if unexpected contingencies determining the performance's impossibility have not been dealt with by the contract or by usages.[48] Other Authors do

[41] The benefit is assessed taking into consideration the party's position after the frustrating event [*BP Exploration Co (Libya) Ltd v Hunt (No 2)* [1979] 1 *WLR* 783; S Baughen (28) 258].

[42] *St. Enoch Shipping Co Ltd v Phosphate Mining Co* [1916] 2 *KB* 624; A Tettenborn (4) 329 f.

[43] M Davis (8) 245 f.

[44] In a bareboat charter, it could consist in the services performed by the owner to make the ship available for the charter and their value could be assessed according to the hire's contractual rates [M Davis (8) 246].

[45] *BP Exploration Co (Libya) Ltd v Hunt (No 2)* [1979] 1 *WLR* 783.

[46] Court of Appeal on *BP Exploration Co (Libya) Ltd v Hunt (No 2)* [1983] 2 AC 352, mentioned by M Davis (8) 246.

[47] S Baughen (28) 258, who takes as an example the case of a twelve-month charter frustrated in the sixth month, whose performance during the first five months could be considered not frustrated.

[48] G Treitel, *Frustration and Force Majeure* (Sweet & Maxwell, 1994) 231; M D Bayles, *Principles of Law: A Normative Analysis* (Kluwer Academic Publishers, 1987), 193 and 357.

not separate the two doctrines: in this sense they refer also to the case-law where impossibility of performance is considered one of the basis – and the first developed by Courts – for deeming a contract frustrated. The doctrine of impossibility is therefore sometimes considered the precursor of the frustration's one.[49]

## V. Unexpected Circumstances in Civil Law

### *5.1. Shipping law*

**19.** Civil Law legal systems often have special provisions concerning shipping contracts and expressly identifying the consequences of certain supervening events affecting their performance and the parties' powers thereof. For example, in Belgium, France, Germany, Spain and Sweden specific provisions govern Maritime Law and shipping contracts, too (along with – of course – specific international conventions): they could just be a part of the Civil or Commercial Code or consist in a separate law.[50]

Italy is an interesting case where two distinct sets of rules exist, with the consequent question related to their relation. Shipping contracts are governed by the international and EU law on the contract of carriage of passengers and goods and by the Navigation Code.[51] Many provisions of this Code are based on Common Law and international forms. More over some provisions enable the parties to terminate the contract because of unforeseeable supervening impediments, not depending on the fault of the party seeking for the enforcement of this right.[52] Other provisions enable the party to refuse the performance because of supervening circumstances involving risks for the vessel or the

[49] *Taylor v Cadwell* [1863] 3 B & D 826, 833; T Southerington, 'Impossibility of Performance and Other Excuses in International Trade', in M Maggi (Ed) *Review of the Convention on Contracts for the International Sale of Goods (CISG) 2002–2003* (Kluwer Law International, 2004) 249, 308; C Castronovo, S Mazzamuto, *Manuale di diritto privato europeo* (2nd Vol, *Proprietà, obbligazioni, contratti*, Giuffrè, 2007) 526 ff; Y Kwon, 'Judicial Modification of Contract in Relation to the Change of Circumstances', in G Duttge, S W Lee (Eds), *The Law in the Information and Risk Society* (Universitätsverlag Göttingen, 2011) 69.

[50] In Belgium, the subject matter is mainly governed by the Commercial Code (*Code de Commerce*), II Book, also known as *Loi Maritime*, but it is going to be reformed with the proposed enactment of a Maritime Code (www.droitmaritime.be/; E Van Hooydonk (Dir), *Livre Vert. Nouvelle Loi Maritime Belge* (Association belge de droit maritime Institut européen de droit maritime et des transports (Université d'Anvers) Anvers, October 2007). With regard to France, the subject-matter is mainly governed by the Transports Code (*Code des Transports*), enacted on the 3rd November 2010, V Part, IV Book. In Germany, a new Maritime Law entered into force on the 25th April 2013. As for Spain, recently was enacted the Law No 14 of 24 July 2014, on the Maritime Navigation (*Ley 14/2014, de 24 de julio, de Navegación Marítima*), in BOE, 25 July 2014. Similarly, in Sweden, Maritime Law is governed by the Maritime Code and by special Acts.

[51] Eg: The Hague-Visby Rules on the bill of lading, the 1978 Hamburg Rules, Regulation (EU) No 1177/2010 of the European Parliament and of the Council of 24 November 2010 concerning the rights of passengers when travelling by sea and inland waterway and amending Regulation (EC) No 2006/2004, OJ L 334/2010 1.

[52] Eg: Article 348 ff; 382, 400 ff, 427 ff.

persons on board.[53] Other articles govern the consequences of temporary impediments to performance.[54] More over other provisions rule out any frustrating nature of an event.[55] The articles often govern the consequences of the events there described.

**20.** For the aspects not expressly dealt with by the Navigation Law, the relation between it and Private/Contract Law in the Italian legal system is discussed. Italian law, in fact, splits the main provisions on the contracts of transport and those related to the transport sector in the Civil Code and the Navigation Code. Whereas the Italian Civil Code rules the transport contract of persons and goods in general, the Italian Navigation Code governs the maritime and air contracts of carriage and charters, along with other sectoral issues.[56] The main issue is therefore if Navigation Law's speciality – to the extent that it is covered by a specific and distinct code – makes it an autonomous sector of law, with the exclusion of the application of Civil Code's provisions for complementing Navigation Law before the interpretation according to the analogy criterion.[57] Some Authors believe that, under Article 1 of the Navigation Code, the rules concerning the contracts of voyage and time charters and the contract of carriage should prevail over the Civil Code's articles.[58] The Italian case-law and legal literature disagreeing with this theory believes, on the contrary, that the aspects not explicitly governed by the Navigation Code should be governed by the compatible provisions of the Civil Code. This is the case, for example,

53 Article 388(1) enables the owner to refuse to operate a voyage involving risks for the vessel or the persons on board, which where unforeseeable when the contract was concluded.

54 Article 391 relates to temporary impediments in time charters: this provision is similar to off-hire clauses within international forms. A Lefebvre D'Ovidio, G Pescatore, L Tullio, *Manuale di diritto della navigazione* (XII edn, Giuffrè, 2011) 408. With regard to carriage of goods, Article 428 relates to a temporary impediment in the departure or during the voyage, not depending on the carrier, ruling out any termination of the contract.

55 Article 429.

56 Article 1 of the Italian Navigation Code expressly provides that the Civil Code applies to the maritime and air transport sectors only for those cases not regulated by the Navigation Code itself, the special law on maritime and air navigation, the customs and through their application by analogy. Similarly, article 1680 of the Italian Civil Code states that maritime and air transports are regulated by the Italian Navigation Law and the special law (including international Conventions in force in Italy) governing the maritime and air sector and the shipping and air industry and that the Civil Code's articles on the contract of transport would apply only on topics not specifically covered by the above-mentioned sources of law. Therefore, the Civil Code provisions concern mainly the contract of transport by road.

57 On the issue concerning the Navigation Law's autonomy or its merely specialty within the Italian legal system, S M Carbone, 'L'internazionalità e la specialità delle fonti del diritto della navigazione nel terzo millennio', in A Antonini (Ed) *Trattato breve di diritto marittimo* (I vol, *Principi – Soggetti – Beni – Attività*, Giuffrè, 2007) 15.

58 L Tullio, 'I contratti di utilizzazione della nave e dell'aeromobile', in *Studi per Romanelli* (Giuffrè, 19979) 1195, 1208. Disagreeing: Cass, 21 December 1953, No 3804 [1954] *Riv Dir Nav* II 183, with comment of G Riccardelli, 'Locazione di nave e noleggio'; S Ferrarini, *I contratti di utilizzazione della nave e dell'aeromobile* (Foro Italiano, 1947) 23; E Spasiano, 'I contratti di utilizzazione della nave: note per la revisione della disciplina attuale' [1977] GI IV 49, 301; C Tosoratti, 'La locazione di nave', in A Antonini (Ed) (57) 1; D Ragazzoni, 'La locazione di nave', in F Morandi (Ed), *I contratti del trasporto* (I vol, Zanichelli, 2013) 397.

of ship chartering, whose provisions are complemented with the Civil Code's articles on the contract of lease.[59]

21. Articles 1 of the Navigation Code and 1680 of the Civil Code are applied as source for identifying the law governing some aspects not covered by the former code, such as the multimodal transport contract, through the application of the Civil Code's articles on the contract of transport of goods.[60] This interpretation is based also on Article 1680's reference to the Navigation Code and the special law on maritime and air transport, with the consequence of ruling out provisions applied through the analogy criterion.[61]

22. Another example could be shipbuilding contracts, because the Italian legal system provides for only some limited aspects, making in general reference to the Civil Code provisions concerning, in particular, the contract for the provision of work and materials or of services (*appalto*).[62] This reference is indeed very interesting, because for this contract Italian law provides for the right of both the parties to demand a modification of the contract's price. Article 1664(1) of the Civil Code entitles, respectively, the contractor or the principal to demand such a modification when the costs for the materials or the personnel augmented or decreased and the difference exceeds the ten per cent of the initial price. But the revision can affect only the amount exceeding the ten per cent. The second paragraph of the same article sets the contractor's right to demand an equitable fee in case of unforeseen (and unforeseeable) difficulties for the contract's performance, deriving from by geological, hydro-geological and similar causes, making his accomplishment considerably more onerous.

59 S Bonduà, 'Applicabilità delle disposizioni sull'affitto alla locazione di nave' [1942] DM 66, 170; A Graziani, 'Locazione di nave e noleggio' [1950] *RTDPC* 155, 156; E Spasiano (62) 296. Disagreeing: S Ferrarini (62) 23; A Fiorentino, *I contratti navali: locazione di nave e di aeromobile, noleggio, trasporto di persone e di cose, rimorchio* (II Edn, Jovene, 1956) 4; G Romanelli, *La locazione di nave e di aeromobile* (Giuffrè, 1965) 95 ff. See also: A Lefebvre D'Ovidio, G Pescatore, L Tullio (55) 385 f.

60 Articles 1678 and 1683–1702 of the Italian Civil Code. Recently, Cass 6 August 2013, No 18657 [2013] DM 861–867, with comment of F Tajani. See also Cass, 6 May 1956, No 656, with comment of S Ferrarini, 'Trasporto misto terrestre-marittimo' [1956] *DM* 197; Cass, 17 November 1978, No 5363 [1979] Porti, mare e territorio 5 92, with comment of E Turco Bulgherini, 'Trasporto combinato delle merci'; Cass, 14 January 1986, No 887 [1987] *DM* 290, [1998] Dir Trasp I 120, with comment of N Adragna, 'Qualificazione del trasporto ed individuazione del termine di prescrizione applicabile'; Cass, 8 July 1993, No 7504; Cass 26 May 1994, No 5156 [1995] DM 1012; Cass, 14 February 2005, No 2898 [2007] *DM* 1115; Cass 2 September 1998, No 8713 [2000] DM 1349, with comment of L Ravera, 'Trasporto multimodale: un preoccupante vuoto normativo'; CA Genoa, 8 March 2002 [2002] Contr 907, with comment of M Ruggeri, 'La disciplina applicabile al contratto di trasporto multimodale'; Trib Gorizia, 28 May 2003 [2005] *Dir Trasp* 755; Trib Genoa, 11 April 2005 [2006] DM 1300, [2007] *Dir Trasp* 627; Trib Avellino, 1 June 2005 [2006] *Dir Trasp* 931. Disagreeing: G Romanelli, *Il trasporto aereo di persone. Nozione e disciplina* (CEDAM, 1959), 16; G Righetti, *Trattato di diritto marittimo* (II vol, Giuffrè, 1990), 84, n 36; G Caturani, A Sensale, *Il trasporto*, Jovene, 1960, 101.

61 Another example is the above-mentioned ship charter contract, whose law, according to some case-law and legal literature, can be complemented by the Civil Code's provision on the contract of lease.

62 Articles 1655–1677 of the Italian Civil Code.

**23.** It is questioned if Article 1664 of the Civil Code could apply also to the contract of carriage, which falls within the general category of contracts for the provision of services: some Italian case-law and legal literature has tried to figure out a possible extension of some provisions concerning the latter contract to the former, especially when the contract of carriage concerns more transport services.[63] The consequence would be that the sets of rules on contracts for the provisions of services should complement the provisions on the contract of carriage. One of the objections to this interpretation is the relation between the two sets of provisions, because that concerning the contract of carriage should supersede the other, according to the principle *lex specialis derogat generali* and the absence of certain provisions, unlike the service agreements' discipline, should be deemed not as a gap but as intentional.[64] The Italian case is therefore an example of how Maritime Law developed as an autonomous system, where great importance have forms drafted by the trade and maritime sector, and of the issue concerning its relation with general Contract Law, in particular on the possibility for the latter to complement the former.

## 5.2. *General contract/private law*

### 5.2.1. Italian law: the juridical and economical balance of the parties' obligations

**24.** According to Article 1372 of the Italian Civil Code, the contract is as binding between the parties as law and can be terminated only when both the parties agree or a party has a right to withdraw from it[65] or in the cases the law provides for. Supervening unexpected and unforeseeable events can affect the economic and juridical balance between the parties' obligations in contracts with obligations of both the parties (*causa*) or their content (*oggetto*).[66] The remedies the Italian Civil Code sets for the cases of imbalance of the parties' obligations due to these events are various.

**25.** First of all, the Italian law provides for the termination of the contract either because the performance of at least one party has become impossible after its conclusion

63 G Romanelli (60) 564 ff; L Murtas, 'Il contract of affreightment: problemi di qualificazione' [1988] Dir Trasp 173; G Vermiglio, 'L'appalto di servizi di trasporto', in G Silingardi, A Antonini, F Morandi (Eds), *Dai tipi legali ai modelli sociali nella contrattualistica della navigazione* (Giuffrè 1996) 393 ff; M Brignardello, 'Vecchia e nuova ipotesi di disapplicazione delle tariffe a forcella' [2000] DM 1456; N Callipari, *Il contratto di autotrasporto di merci per conto terzi* (Giuffrè, 2009), 97 ff; Corte Cost, 5 November 1996, No 386 [1997] Dir. Trasp 463, with comment of C Tincani, 'Applicabilità delle tariffe a forcella all'appalto di servizi di trasporto'; Cass, 30 November 2010 No 24265; Cass, 13 September 1997, No 9128; Cass, 25 May 1986, No 3581 [1986] I FI 2137. On the matter, also S Busti, *Contratto di trasporto terrestre* [A Cicu, F Messineo, L Mengoni (past Dirs), P Schlesinger (Dir), *Trattato Diritto Civile e Commerciale*, XXVI vol, Giuffrè, 2007], 45 ff; E G Rosafio, *Il trasporto aereo di cose: riflessioni sul nuovo regime legale* (Giuffrè, 2007), 261 ff.

64 L Tullio, 'Una fattispecie improponibile: l'appalto di servizi di trasporto' [1993] *Dir Trasp* 89, 92 ff; M Riguzzi, *Il contratto di trasporto* [M Bessone (Dir), *Trattato di diritto privato, I contratti speciali*, vol 14, Giappichelli, 2006] 22 ff;.

65 The general provision is Article 1373 of the Italian Civil Code.

66 Articles 1325, No 3, and 1346–1349 of the Italian Civil Code.

(*risoluzione per impossibilità sopravvenuta*) or because it has become excessively onerous after the contract was stipulated (*risoluzione per eccessiva onerosità*). Both the cases refer to contracts where both the parties are bound to perform obligations, which are deemed to have been originally balanced in the contract's content according to the parties' intent.

The first case concerns an event altering the contract's content: the performance of a party becomes impossible contrary to Article 1346 of the Civil Code. According to Article 1463, when the performance became completely and definitively impossible, without any fault of the disadvantaged party, this party loses its right to the other party's performance and must return what he have already received. When the performance becomes impossible only in part, the other party has the right to have his performance proportionally diminished (with regard to its economic value) or can withdraw from the contract if he has no more considerable interest on its partial performance.[67]

**26.** The other case relates to contracts for continuous or periodic performance or for deferred performance: according to Article 1467, when the performance of a party suddenly becomes excessively burdensome because of extraordinary events, that party may ask for the contract's termination. Hence, the unexpected circumstances must not fall within the usual risks the parties (also implicitly) accept when concluding the contract.[68] This case therefore concerns the alteration of consideration. The other party can avoid the contract's termination, offering to equitably modify its content.

**27.** When only the disadvantaged party is bound to performance according to the contract, he has the right to ask for an equitable reduction of his obligation's content or an equitable variation of its performance.[69]

Other remedies provided by the Italian legal system refer to the general principles of good faith and fair dealing, which deeply permeate juridical relationships according to Italian law.[70]

On the principle of good faith is founded the doctrine of *presupposizione*, developed by the case-law and the legal literature with regard to supervening unforeseeable events depriving the contract of its actual purposes according to the inner reasons that induced a party to conclude it and that were known to the other party, taking into consideration the circumstances existing at that time, without affecting the other elements of the contract, which is still formally valid.[71]

67 Article 1464 Civil Code.

68 Consequently, according to Article 1469 Civil Code aleatory contracts cannot be terminated under Article 1467.

69 Article 1468 Civil Code.

70 The general principles are expressed in Articles 1175 and 1375 of the Code, but also Articles 1337, 1338, 1358, 1366 provide for them with regard to specific issues, such as the interpretation of contract clauses, the behaviour of the parties while a condition precedent or subsequent is pending, but also during the negotiations before the (possible) conclusion of a contract.

71 This could, for example, the case of a person who is going to work in another city and for this reason rents a house, if the landlord knows about it. Other famous cases concerned the rent of balconies in a particular street to see the coronation march, which subsequently changed route or did not happen on the day the balcony was rent for. In English Law the latter cases fall within the doctrine of frustration,

**28.** When those circumstances radically change as to deprive the contract of any interest for the disadvantaged party, the parties are free to renegotiate the contract's content, but if they do not reach any agreement, the party, to the detriment of whom the unexpected event occurred, can ask for its termination, provided that the other party knew or ought to know the reasons that induced him to conclude that contract. According to some Authors, the principle of good faith would more over entail a duty to renegotiate the contract's content because of supervening events altering the balance between the parties' obligations.[72]

**29.** It is also discussed if the principle of good faith could imply a duty of cooperation in the other party's performance. This duty is admitted by the prevalent case-law and legal literature for certain cases, as a consequence of the content of the specific contract and of the parties' obligations,[73] or as the result of the prohibition of abusing of his own rights (*abuso del diritto*). The latter has been established as a general rule and concerns the prohibition of exercising his own rights in a manner exceeding reasonableness and aimed to the other party's detriment. This duty is considered as having a general scope and is based on express provisions of the Civil Code concerning the property and similar rights.

However, some authors and case-law interpret the duty of co-operation as consisting not only in avoiding all those behaviours or omissions that can impede the debtor's performance, but also in cooperating with him.

**30.** Finally, it must be noted that the disadvantaged party could not avail himself of the unjustified enrichment (*arricchimento senza giusta causa*) under Articles 2041 and 2042 of the Civil Code, for governing cases of supervening imbalance of contractual obligations, because it concerns a subsidiary remedy for cases where the party has no other claim found on another title, such as a contract.[74]

when all its requirements are met. In the case *Chandler v Webster* [1904] 1 KB 493, the Court rejected the plaintiff's claim, because the obligation was considered to have arisen before the frustrating event and was not affected by it. According to M Davis (8) 243 f, these cases contributed to the drafting of the Law Reform (Frustrated Contract) Act 1943. Now the issue is governed also by s 1(2) of the Act. In Italian law some authors disagree on the reference to the inner reasons, the contract's conclusion was based on, for *presupposizione*, such as, recently, F Macario, 'La risoluzione per eccessiva onerosità', in N Lipari, P Rescigno (Eds), *Diritto Civile* (vol 3, Giuffrè, 2009) 1175, 1177 ff.

72 R Sacco, *Il contratto* [in R Sacco, G De Nova (Dir), *Trattato di diritto civile*, I vol, *Le fonti delle obbligazioni*, UTET, 2004], 686; F Macario, *Adeguamento e rinegoziazione nei contratti a lungo termine* (Jovene, 1996), 293 ff, 316 ff. Other Authors, such as P Barcellona, *Profili della teoria dell'errore nel negozio giuridico* (Giuffrè, 1962), 216 and 225 ff; C Castronovo, S Mazzamuto (49) 531 ff, disagree.

73 Cass, 4 August 2000, No 10261; Cass, 24 May 2007, No 12079; Cass, 15 February 2013, No 3830; Cass, 15 May 2014, No 10702; G D'Amico, 'Mancata cooperazione del creditore e violazione contrattuale' [2004] RDC 1.

74 Articles 1:101 and 2:101 DCFR use the word 'unjustified' instead of 'unjust'; V Gorla, F Silva 'La causa come elemento essenziale del contratto: assente o solo "nascosta"?', in C Marchetti (Ed), *Il DCFR: lessici, concetti e categorie nella prospettiva del giurista italiano* (Giappichelli, 2012) 127, 135 f.

### 5.2.2. French law

**31.** French law is based on the strict principle of the contract's binding force, under Article 1134 of the Civil Code, which admits derogations only in case of the parties' agreement or in the cases the law provides for.[75] One of them is the supervening impossibility of the obligation due to unexpected and unavoidable circumstances with the requirements of *force majeure* and *cas fortuit.*[76] On the contrary, with regard to commercial contracts, according to the prevailing but not uniform case law and literature, French law does not provide for any right of termination or re-negotiation when, after the conclusion of the contract, an obligation or its performance has become unexpectedly excessively burdensome with regard to the original contractual balance, with the exception of specific cases identified by the law or case law.[77]

According to the above-mentioned article, contracts must be performed in good faith, which is interpreted by case-law as the loyal performance of a contract, too: in French law, a duty of cooperation in the other party's performance of his own obligations is still discussed.[78]

### 5.2.3. *Wegfall der Geschäftsgrundlage* and the doctrine of assumption (Germany, Denmark and Sweden)

**32.** In Germany the principle of good faith (*Treu und Glauben* ) originally applied only for the cases expressly providing for it, but according to some Authors, through the doctrines developed in German case-law and legal literature, it has acquired ample importance in Contract Law.[79] German law was recently interested by a reform of the obligations law, the *Schuldrechtsreform*, expressly introducing the concept, already developed by the case-law and the legal literature, of *Geschäftsgrundlage*.[80] According to this doctrine, the contract's binding nature is suspended when the parties' fundamental expectations are not fulfilled.[81] This doctrine provides for separate rules concerning supervening impossibility of the obligation, from the one hand, and the excessive burden

75 M Almeida Prado (5) 14.

76 Article 1148 of the French Civil Code.

77 The so-called *théorie de l'imprévision* could apply only to contracts concluded with Public Authorities. M Almeida Prado (5) 14, 16 ff, 30 ff; F P Traisci (2) 11; C Castronovo, S Mazzamuto (49) 527; Y Kwon (49) 68.

78 The doctrine of *solidarisme contractuel*/contractual solidarism, opposed to that of the *autonomie de la volonté*/contractual freedom based on the will of the parties. Ph Delebecque (6) 283 ff. Also Prof. Delebecque's lecture *Foreseeability, flexibility and reasonableness in shipping contracts: a civil law approach*, on the 7th April 2014, as Visiting Professor at the Alma Mater Studiorum – University of Bologna, Italy.

79 L Antoniolli, 'General Duties', in L Antoniolli, A Veneziano (Eds), *Principles of European Contract Law and Italian Law* (Kluwer Law International, 2005) 49; C Castronovo, S Mazzamuto (49) 499.

80 C Castronovo, S Mazzamuto (49) 527; E Hondius, H C Grigoleit (1) 7 and 'Overview: concepts dealing with unexpected circumstances', in E Hondius, H C Grigoleit (Eds), *Unexpected Circumstances in European Contract Law* (Cambridge University Press, 2011) 55.

81 E Hondius, H C Grigoleit (1) 7 f and (81) 55.

of performance, from the other. Like the doctrine of frustration, this remedy applies only if the matter is not already and fully provided for in the contract or in other law provisions.

German law contemplates the Court's power to re-balance the contractual obligations (under a specific request of the party) or enable a party to terminate the contract.[82]

**33.** In Danish and Swedish legal systems, the doctrine of assumption has strong resemblances with German law. The assumption must be material and perceived by the other party.[83] The party can ask for the contract's termination, but in Sweden and other Countries, such as the Netherlands, the Court could also adapt the contract to the new circumstances.

## VI. Unexpected Circumstances in PECL, DCFR and UPICC

**34.** The emerging EU Private and Contract Law deals also with the change of circumstances after the conclusion of a contract. Both the Principles of European Contract Law (PECL)[84] and the Draft Common Frame of Reference (DCFR)[85] confirm the principle that parties are bound by the obligations undertaken with the contract, even if they became more onerous, 'whether because the cost of performance has increased or because the value of what has to be received in return has diminished'.[86] According to both of them the relevant change of circumstances cannot exist when the contract was concluded, as on the contrary in German law, but must unexpectedly arise after that moment, in other words it could not have been reasonably foreseen when the contract was negotiated and concluded, taking into consideration the contract's nature and market's conditions.[87] Another issue both of them deal with is subsequent unexpected impossibility of performance not depending on the debtor.

**35.** With regard to the first case, Article 6:111 PECL relates to Change of Circumstances and applies when the contract's performance has become excessively onerous because of a change of circumstances and two conditions are met, in other words the supervening event could not be reasonably taken into account at the time the contract was concluded and such a risk is not one that must be borne by the disadvantaged party according to the contract. Therefore, it is not sufficient that performance merely became more onerous. In this sense, Article III-1:110 DCFR, which is based in part on PECL[88] but applies also to

82 Ibid; Y Kwon (49) 68.

83 This prerequisite is similar to the Italian doctrine of *presupposizione* and the Portuguese *presuposição* [E Hondius, H C Grigoleit (1) 8].

84 O Lando, H Beale (Eds), *Principles of European Contract Law, Parts I and II combined and revised* (Kluwer Law International, 2000).

85 C von Bar, E Clive, H Schulte-Nölke, H Beale, J Herre, J Huet, M Storme, S Swann, P Varul, A Veneziano, F Zoll (Eds), *Principles, Definitions and Model Rules of European Private Law. Draft Common Frame of Reference (DCFR)* (Outline Edition, Sellier, 2009).

86 Article III.-1:110(1) DCFR.

87 C Castronovo, S Mazzamuto (49) 540.

88 C von Bar, E Clive, H Schulte-Nölke, H Beale, J Herre, J Huet, M Storme, S Swann, P Varul, A Veneziano, F Zoll (Eds) (86) 30.

obligations arising from unilateral juridical acts, confirms that an obligation must be performed notwithstanding any increase of its burdensomeness, because of the increased costs for its performance or because of the decrease of the value of the other party's performance. The same article provides for an exception to this principle for the case of a change of circumstances after the time the obligation was incurred: if performance becomes so onerous that it would be manifestly unjust to hold the debtor to it, provided that the debtor himself did not and could not reasonably take into account 'the possibility or scale of that change of circumstances' and did not assume or cannot be reasonably considered as having assumed the risks of such supervening events.

**36.** The drafters of the two Soft Law instruments chose to conjugate two methods that emerge from some EU member States' legal systems: the renegotiation of the contract's content and the right to terminate it if no agreement is reached. According to Article 6:111 PECL, the parties are bound to enter into negotiations with a view to adapting the contract or end it, if the above-mentioned conditions occur. The same article provides that, in case the parties do not reach an agreement within a reasonable period, the Court may end the contract at a date and on terms determined by the Court itself or adapt it and may also award damages for the loss suffered through a party refusing to negotiate or breaking off negotiations contrary to good faith and fair dealing, hence resorting to the principles, typical of Civil Law, of good faith and fair dealing.

The ways chosen by Article III-1:110 DCFR, with regard to supervening events altering the burden over one party or the balance of value between the performances, are, first of all, negotiations: the debtor must try, 'reasonably and in good faith, to achieve by negotiation a reasonable and equitable adjustment of the terms regulating the obligation'. When he does not succeed, he can sue the other party before the Court having authority over the case, which may 'vary the obligation in order to make it reasonable and equitable in the new circumstances', or 'terminate the obligation at a date and on terms to be determined by the Court' itself. PECL and DCFR refer both to the principles of reasonableness and good faith with regard to the assessment of the debtor's behaviour. Reasonableness and equity are the criteria, the modification of the more onerous obligation must be based on.

**37.** Under Article 1:201 PECL, 'each party must act in accordance with good faith and fair dealing'. Therefore, in the drafters' view, good faith and fair dealing not only are expressly mentioned in some provisions of PECL, but are general principles, according to which PECL articles must be interpreted, 'in order to enforce community standards of decency, fairness and reasonableness in commercial transactions'.[89] According to some Authors, this article implies also a principle of mutual consideration, in other words each party 'must show due regard for the interest of the other party, particularly in the case of subsequent contingencies which were not contemplated in their contract'.[90] More over,

89 O Lando, H Beale (Eds) (85); L Antoniolli (79) 49.
90 L Antoniolli (79) 50.

under Article 6:102, good faith and fair dealing are considered the basis for complementing the contract with implied terms.

**38.** DCFR has expressly introduced the principles of good faith and fair dealing both as general principles and in provisions related to specific matters, too.[91] According to Article I-1:103, these principles refer 'to a standard of conduct characterized by honesty, openness and consideration for the interests of the other party to the transaction or relationship in question'. They inform DCFR's interpretation and promotion, the negotiation between the parties, the contract's stipulation and interpretation.[92]

**39.** When setting the requirements for their provisions on change of circumstances to apply, the above-mentioned articles make reference also to the criterion of reasonableness for assessing the parties' behaviour. According to Article 1:302 PECL reasonableness is based on the behaviour of 'persons acting in good faith and in the same situation as the parties would consider to be reasonable', having regard to 'the nature and purpose of the contract, the circumstances of the case, and the usages and practices of the trades or professions involved'. Under Article I-1:104 of DCFR, reasonableness must be objectively ascertained, taking into consideration 'the nature and purpose of what has been done', 'the circumstances of the case' and 'any relevant usages and practices'.

**40.** Both PECL and DCFR expressly set a duty of cooperation with the debtor in his performance. According to Article 1:202 PECL 'each party owes to the other a duty of co-operation in order to give full effect to the contract'. As for DCFR, their third Book, s 1, not only provides for both the debtor and creditor 'to act in accordance to good faith and fair dealing' in performing an obligation, in exercising a right to performance, in pursuing or defending a remedy for non-performance, or in exercising a right to terminate an obligation or contractual relationship', but also for an explicit duty of cooperation 'when and to the extent that this can reasonably be expected for the performance of the debtor's obligation'.[93]

**41.** The origins of this duty are indeed the doctrines developed in some Civil Law Countries: the intent of PECL and DCFR seems to express them as a general principle of law, as an effect of the importance they confer to the above-mentioned principles.

**42.** With regard to temporary or definitive subsequent impossibility of performance, both Article 8:108 PECL and Article III-3:104 of DCFR enable a debtor having breached his obligation to excuse himself when that breach is due to an impediment beyond his control and, with regard to contracts, he could not reasonably be expected to have taken

91 C von Bar, E Clive, H Schulte-Nölke, H Beale, J Herre, J Huet, M Storme, S Swann, P Varul, A Veneziano, F Zoll (Eds) (86).
92 Articles I-1:102, II-3-301, II-1:106, II-9:101: II-8:101, B II, s 4.
93 Articles III-1:103 and 1:104.

into account it at the time when the obligation was incurred and to have avoid or overcome it or its consequences. When the excusing impediment is only temporary, the excuse's effect is limited to its duration and the creditor is enabled to treat the delay as a fundamental non-performance, if so provides the contract or the law governing it. The permanent excusing impediment entails the extinction of the obligation, together with that of any reciprocal obligation.[94] According to Article III-3:101 of DCFR, when non-performance is excused, the other party cannot demand specific performance and damages.

**43.** Finally, it could be interesting to examine Unidroit Principles of International Commercial Contracts, which face the issue of supervening hardship of a contract, too. Their Article 6.2.1 binds the parties to observe the contract, even in case it became more onerous for one of them, but in this case their relationship is subject to the following articles, concerning hardship, which can occur only in case of a fundamental alteration of the contractual equilibrium either because the cost of a party's performance has increased or because the value of the performance a party receives has diminished and the requirements set by Article 6.2.2 are met. The event must happen after the conclusion of the contract, when it was not reasonably foreseeable. Moreover, the occurrence must be beyond the disadvantaged party's control, which must not have assumed its risks.

**44.** Article 6.2.3 of Unidroit Principles provides for the consequences of hardship, enabling the disadvantaged party to demand renegotiations without undue delay and specifying its grounds. This request, however, does not entitle the disadvantaged party to withhold performance. If renegotiations fail, after a reasonable time, either party can sue the other before the Court with authority to hear the case, which could 'terminate the contract at a date and on terms to be fixed', or adapt its content 'with a view to restoring its equilibrium', according to what appears the more reasonable solution.

**45.** Unidroit Principles provide for a duty to act according to good faith and fair dealing in international trade, too.[95] These principles operate to such an extent that Article 5.1.3 sets a duty of cooperation with the other party in performing the latter's obligation, too, when this cooperation may be reasonably expected. Unidroit Principles not only make reference to exemption clauses, but also to force majeure for excusing one party's non-performance of its own obligations.[96] The requirements are similar to those provided for by PECL and DCFR.

**46.** In order to try to infer what could be the actual outcome of PECL, DCFR and similar Soft Law instruments, it is fundamental to identify their nature. PECL, like Unidroit principles, were born, first of all, as a collection and elaboration of the alleged common traits of the existing national Contract Law by a group of renowned experts,

94 Articles 9:301(1) and 9:501(1) PECL, III-3:104(4) and III-3:101(2) DCFR.
95 Article 1.7.
96 Article 7.1.6 and 7.1.7.

with no intent of repealing national law.[97] They are indeed not limited to a mere anthology of national provisions, since their articles sometimes go further, providing for new rules, also on the basis of the theories that have been developed within national law.[98] They can be chosen by the parties as the law governing the contract and in so far as they do not contrast with mandatory provisions of international or national law, they shall apply.

DCFR's main purpose was 'to serve as a draft for drawing up a 'political' Common Frame of Reference (CFR)'.[99]

## VII. Conclusions

**47.** The above outlined brief framework shows that, even where the approach is somewhat similar, the dogmatic basis, the regulation of supervening unexpected events affecting the contract and their possible consequences could differ considerably among the different national legal systems, especially with regard to hardship.[100]

On this regard, no legal system prevents the parties from spontaneously re-negotiating the contract's content (and thus concluding a different contract, when the previous one is to be considered terminated), but in many of them there is no duty of doing so.[101] More over only few national laws contemplate the Court's power to adapt the contract as a consequence of the supervening event.

**48.** Therefore, parties seeking one of these solutions in case of unexpected supervening circumstances, should be very accurate in providing for it in the contract, for example through hardship clauses.

But, if the parties do not reach any agreement and they had not, for example, conferred the power of balancing the frustrated contract to a Court or to arbitrators or the law governing the contract does not provide for it, the contract itself shall be terminated according to the applicable law or the terms set by the parties.

**49.** In this sense, another important difference among the legal systems, especially between those of Common Law, from the one hand, and those of Civil Law, from the other, is the principle according to which the rules concerning supervening events are enforced: Common Law is mainly based on the principle of reasonableness, whereas

97 L Valle, 'Prospettive per la realizzazione di un diritto comune europeo dei contratti' [2000] Contratto e Impresa – EU 683; F P Traisci (2) 25 ff.

98 F P Traisci (2) 9.

99 *Introduction* to C von Bar, E Clive, H Schulte-Nölke, H Beale, J Herre, J Huet, M Storme, S Swann, P Varul, A Veneziano, F Zoll (Eds) (86) 4.

100 Notwithstanding these differences, some Authors observed that the actual final outcomes of supervening unexpected circumstances on the contract's sort are not very dissimilar [L Antoniolli (79) 49; Ph Delebecque (6) 283 ff. I would like to refer also to Prof Delebecque's lecture '*Foreseeability, flexibility and reasonableness in shipping contracts: a civil law approach*', on the 7th April 2014, as Visiting Professor at the Alma Mater Studiorum – University of Bologna, Italy].

101 Where Civil Law governs the contract, the re-negotiations must usually be conducted according to the principle of good faith.

Civil Law is mainly based on the principles of good faith and fair dealing, which do not exist in Common Law, even if many international forms concerning shipping contracts mention good faith in their clauses as the principle the parties must conform to and their behaviour must be assessed according to, for the issues those terms refer to.[102]

**50.** The above examined Soft Law instruments have adopted the principles of good faith and fair dealing as the main ones the parties' conduct must conform to.[103] The concept of good faith expressly extends to burdening the creditor with a duty to cooperate with the debtor in order to enable the latter to perform his obligation. This duty of co-operation, which is expressly provided for in the domestic law of some EU member States, is on the contrary unknown and in certain cases incompatible with the relevant law of other Countries, such as English law, according to which the main forms of the shipping sector are drafted and construed. Therefore, a problem of compatibility of the emerging EU Contract Law and the shipping contracts arises.[104] As it has been already mentioned above, often shipping contracts are governed by international conventions or by the contract clauses agreed by the parties, with the forms developed within their sector, and by national rules, when the latter are compulsory or for the aspects the parties did not provide for in their contract.[105]

**51.** DCFR and PECL could affect shipping contracts in two main manners: if they will be enacted as EU Hard Law or if they could apply according to a governing law clause, which could expressly choose one of them to govern the contract or refer to the 'principles developed in international law'.[106] In the first case, in other words if DCFR – or even PECL – will be enacted as EU Hard Law, according to my opinion, despite the specialty of Maritime Law, the incidence of a new European Contract or Private Law on shipping contracts should not be ruled out to the extent that it concerns mandatory principles and general duties of the contract parties, such as good faith and fair dealing and the subsequent duty of co-operation, or could complement contractual provisions, when the parties did not explicitly allocated contractual risks,[107] and does conform to the contract's construction.[108] However, their actual outcomes must be assessed with regard to each single case, also according to the contract's structure, framework and aim.

102 Ph Delebecque (6) 281 ff; *Davis Contractors Ltd v Fareham UDC* [1956] AC 696. For example, no obligation of good faith has the charterer when making a nomination [R Thomas, 'The evolving flexibility of voyage charterparties', in R. Thomas (Ed) (4) 9 ff].

103 Along with that of reasonableness for certain situations.

104 On this topic, also F Lorenzon (8) 137.

105 According to G Boi (8) 8, the reason is the absence of any need at the international level of superseding contractual autonomy and the rules provided for by the forms developed within trades.

106 In this case the issue is whether this clause can be interpreted as referring to the EU Contract Law, instead of the above-mentioned Unidroit Principles.

107 F P Traisci (2) 10.

108 For example, some German case-law, when deciding cases concerning contracts based on English-law forms, but providing for German law as the law governing the contract, applied English principles to the contract for ruling out some German law provisions.

**52.** It is my opinion that the specialty of Maritime Law, where it is admitted, could be preserved, first of all through contractual freedom, as nowadays happens: both international conventions and almost all national law admit contractual autonomy with ample extent even if within different limits, as PECL and DCFR do, probably because it can better govern the parties' relationship according to their intent.[109]

The room for Contract/Private Law would be limited to those aspects not explicitly or implicitly governed by international conventions, whose mandatory provisions, to be systematically interpreted according to their purposes, rule out any other different provision: therefore Private or Contract Law could complement the provisions of international conventions within such limits. In the case of commercial practices that fulfil the requirements for being considered as usages binding the contract's parties, including widely known practices regularly observed in international trade, they should supersede contrasting provisions of law, when the latter are not mandatory.

**53.** Already nowadays, in many national law, both of Civil Law and of Common Law, Contract/Private Law provisions are already the grounds for deciding matters not (entirely) governed by the contract or Maritime Law. In this case a problem of construction of the contract could emerge, insofar as the parties use forms based, for example, on English law, whose regulation of supervening unexpected events is funded on the principle of reasonableness instead of good faith. The same problem, i.e. construction of the contract, could arise when the parties choose for governing the contract a law that has principles unknown or even not compatible with the law according to which the form was drafted.

In order to avoid possible outcomes the parties did not desire, the contract should be as detailed as possible in regulating their commitments, rights and duties, but, according to my personal opinion, this risk could not be entirely avoided.[110]

109 G Boi (8) 2 f.; F Lorenzon (8) 156 f.

110 F Lorenzon (8) 157, similarly, evidenced this risk.

Belén García Álvarez*

# LIABILITY OF THE MARITIME CARRIER AND THE SHIPPER FOR OTHER PERSONS: UNIFORM MARITIME TRANSPORT RULES VS. EUROPEAN CONTRACT LAW**

## I. Introduction

1. Both the carrier and the shipper often entrust to another to perform any of its obligations under the contract of carriage. Consequently, these third parties are involved in the performance of the maritime carrier`s or the shipper`s obligations, and can cause damage to personal and/or property interests of the other party of the contract of carriage or third parties. Therefore, it is important to know if the carrier and shipper are responsible for actions or omissions of third persons, in other words, the extension of the liability of the principal for damages caused for other persons, so-called vicarious liability. For that purpose, we analyse not only maritime conventions, but also European Contract Law, in particular, the Draft Common Frame of Reference (DCFR) to discover if European Contract Law rules are similar or not to special maritime rules.

2. To this end, firstly we explain briefly the notion of auxiliary and classes. Secondly, it must be analysed the liability of the maritime carrier for other persons, as well as the liability of the shipper for other persons in maritime conventions. Then, it must be considered the liability of the debtor for other persons in European Contract Law. Finally, attention should be paid to a related and special issue, such as the liability of the debtor in case it is a third party who performs some of its obligations under the contract of carriage, or in case that the party not bound to perform the obligations give instructions to the debtor about these obligations.

* Assistant Professor of Commercial Law, University of Deusto (Spain).

** This paper is part of the Research Project "New legal solutions about documentation and liability faced with restructuring of transport market" (Ref. DER2012-37543-C03-02), funded by Ministry of Economy and Competitiveness. Also, in the Research Team "Public power and Enterprise in a multilevel and international context" (UD-R2010) funded by Government of Basque Country (IT607-13).

## II. Notion and Types of Auxiliaries

3. Third parties may intervene in the performance of any of the obligations of the carrier or of the shipper under the contract of carriage. In that case they will be his auxiliaries if the debtor freely has decided to include those third persons into the execution of the contract of carriage. These third persons must help the debtor in the fulfilment of his obligations under contract of carriage. In this regard, the relevant criterion for determining whether or not the third party is an auxiliary of the debtor is his function, if he collaborates with the principal and not the kind of relationship that binds third person, an auxiliary, with his principal, the debtor. Therefore, it will be auxiliary not only the person legally dependent on the principal, the debtor, but also everything the one that, somehow, collaborates or intervenes in the fulfilment of the obligation assumed by the debtor, even if there is no link of subordination, including even the substitute of the debtor.[1]

4. It must be referred to three categories of auxiliaries of the debtor, which are useful in particular in the regulation of carriage of goods. Firstly, it is common to distinguish between dependent and independent auxiliaries. Both are auxiliaries who collaborate in carrying out the duties of his principal on his own volition. The distinction between these classes of auxiliaries lies in the degree of autonomy in their acts. Dependent assistants or employees act in any case under the supervision or control of its principal in accordance with their instructions and, consequently, are in a relationship of subordination or hierarchical or functional dependence with his principal. Instead, independent auxiliaries act with greater autonomy in fulfilling the duties of his principal. However, this greater independence does not mean his principal cannot supervise their performance or provide specific instructions on performing the obligations. The scope of these powers of supervision will vary depending on the terms of the contract between the independent auxiliary and his principal, and in any case, be less compared to the supervision or control that are subject dependent auxiliaries.

5. In particular, maritime conventions distinguish between dependent and independent auxiliaries, but with other terms. The terms frequently used to name dependent auxiliaries are servants or employees in the English versions, and préposés in the French versions. With regard to independent auxiliaries, in some regulations reference is made to other people, whose services use the carrier or the shipper to fulfil some of its obligations under the contract of carriage. Also, it is possible the terms of independent contractors or subcontractors[2], the latter is used only with respect to the auxiliary of the shipper in Article 4.2 Rotterdam Rules.

1 Jordano Fraga, F., *La responsabilidad del deudor por los auxiliares que utiliza en el cumplimiento*, Civitas, Madrid, 1994, pp. 113–125.

2 Knöfel, S., *Die Haftung des Gütersbeforderes für Hilfspersonen*, Luchterhand, Neuwied, Kriftel, Berlin, 1994, pp. 36–37; Tetley, W., *Marine cargo claims*, 4th ed., Blais, Montreal, 2009, pp. 768–769.

**6.** In Rotterdam Rules it appears a new terminology used only to refer to the auxiliaries of the carrier, the concepts of performing party or non performing party (Article 1.6. and 1.7. Rotterdam Rules), which at the same time can be maritime or non-maritime. In general, the performing party is defined as a person other than the carrier that performs or undertakes to perform any of the carrier's obligations under the contract of carriage (Article 1.6.a) Rotterdam Rules). In particular, in this article it is listed a series of activities to carry out this performing party in connection with the receipt of the goods is listed, such as loading, handling, stowage, unloading, care and delivery. Also, it is necessary that this person acts directly or indirectly at the request of the carrier or under its supervision or control (Article 1.6.a) *in fine* Rotterdam Rules).[3] Thus remarks that this person should not only collaborate in the performance of the carrier's obligations, but also act at the request of the latter. That means they have been designated by the carrier itself, in other words, at his will and not at the will of other participants in the carriage of goods, or they must act under his control.

**7.** As a performing party is an auxiliary of the carrier, not of the shipper, is expressly rejects the possibility of a performing party is deemed to anyone directly or indirectly employed by the shipper, the documentary shipper, the controlling party (which in principle is the shipper or the consignee) or by the recipient, rather than the carrier (Article 1.6.b) Rotterdam Rules). However, the performing party as an auxiliary or representative of the carrier may be designated by the shipper or by the consignee, but in any case, this designation shall be expressly accepted by the carrier as it is prohibited that the performing party will be engaged directly or indirectly by such parties.

**8.** In addition, a maritime performing party performs or will agree to perform duties of the carrier that can only take place between the arrival of the goods at the port of loading of the ship and their departure from the port of discharge (Article 1.7. Rotterdam Rules). Moreover, it expressly states that an inland carrier shall be deemed maritime performing party performs or undertakes to perform its services exclusively within the port area (Article 1.7. *in fine* Rotterdam Rules).

**9.** Also, it is questionable whether or not they can be considered or included within this notion of performing party the people designating by the performing party itself, since the former can perform the carrier's obligations or undertaking to carry them out. The key is whether we can estimate that they have acted directly or indirectly to the carrier's request or under its supervision or control (Article 1.6.a) Rotterdam Rules). However, if it is an independent auxiliary, the supervision or control of the carrier will be more improbable, but we can interpret that they have acted indirectly to the carrier`s request. Therefore, we think that third parties designated by a performing party may be considered

3 Sturley, M.F., "Transport law: The Treatment of Performing Parties" in *CMI Yearbook 2003*, Antwerpen, Belgium, International Maritime Committee, 2003, 2, pp. 230–244.

in turn, as performing parties, provided they meet the requirements set for it (Article 1.6.a) Rotterdam Rules).[4]

**10.** Secondly, other type of auxiliary may intervene in the performance of the contract of carriage. For example, an auxiliary can address the issue of protests or notices by the consignee at the time of delivery of the goods to the carrier. Indeed, a third party can act at the risk of his principal, either the carrier or the shipper, and being, therefore, his representative in the performance of a particular duty. The representative has a power (legal or voluntary) to represent his principal. In maritime conventions the term commonly used is agent. This concept of agent corresponds to a person who has the power to bind another, the principal, on whose behalf he acts.

## III. Liability of the Maritime Carrier for Other Persons in Maritime Conventions

**11.** In the specific rules applicable to the maritime carriage of goods the primary object of attention is the liability of the carrier. It is liable in general for loss, damage and delay in delivery of the goods. In Hague-Visby Rules there is not mention about damages caused for delay in delivery of the goods, so the maritime carrier is not liable in this case. Note that this is a quantitatively limited liability, in other words, the carrier shall not compensate completely the damages incurred, unless there are particularly serious circumstances that determine the loss of his right under the maritime conventions. Although the liability of the carrier is the central issue in maritime conventions, his vicarious liability is not too much developed, except in the Rotterdam Rules.

**12.** In the Hague-Visby Rules we have Article 4.2.a), which states that "Neither the carrier nor the ship shall be responsible for loss or damage arising or resulting from: a) The acts, neglect or default of the master, mariner, pilot or the servants of the carrier in the navigation or in the management of the ship ", as well as Article 4.2.q) Hague-Visby Rules referred to any other cause arising from an act or omission of the carrier or its agents or employees of the carrier. Therefore, the carrier will be responsible for the acts of its employees, unless there is a ground for exemption from liability according to Article 4.2 Hague-Visby Rules.

**13.** Hamburg Rules is quite similar to Hague-Visby Rules on this issue, but the former are more detailed. Under the Hamburg Rules the carrier is liable for damages resulting from the loss, damage and delay in delivery of the goods if the event occurs

4 It must note that the Draft Convention contained in principle, the following statement within the definition of performing party "... includes subcontractors, employees and assistants or representatives of a performing party to the extent that also implement or undertake to perform any of the carrier's obligations under a contract of carriage...". Vid. Note 1 of the Draft Convention as set out in the UNCITRAL document A / CN.9 / WG.III / WP.101 of 14 November 2007.

during his period of liability, unless he proves that he, his employees or agents took all measures that could reasonably be required to avoid the occurrence and its consequences (Article 5.1 Hamburg Rules). Consequently, the carrier is liable for the acts or omissions of its employees and agents. This extension of liability is repeated in specific cases of liability of the carrier such as fire, transport of live animals, as well as in cases of contributory negligence or causes (Article 5.4.a and b, 5.5, and 5.7 Hamburg Rules).

**14.** Finally, Rotterdam Rules not only devote more attention to this aspect of the legal regime of maritime transport, but also significantly broaden the circumstances in which the carrier shall be liable for damages caused by the conduct of other persons. Rotterdam Rules contains a specific provision entitled "Carrier's liability for the actions of others" (Article 18 Rotterdam Rules). It is stated that the carrier is liable for the breach of its obligations caused by the acts or omissions of any performing party; Captain or any member of the crew of the ship; employee of the carrier or a performing party; or "any other person who performs or undertakes to perform any of the obligations of the carrier under the contract of carriage, to the extent that such person acts, directly or indirectly, at the carrier or under its supervision or control". In principle any case leaves out of this article. It thus includes dependent and independent auxiliaries of the maritime carrier, without distinguishing between maritime performing party and non-maritime performing party in the terminology of the Rotterdam Rules, representatives, and employees of the aforementioned persons. Furthermore, as a closing clause refers to anyone who performs or undertakes to perform the obligations of the carrier and acts under some kind of control on their part, so it includes dependent and independent auxiliaries of auxiliaries of the carrier. In this way it seems that the purpose is to avoid the possible intention of the carrier to liberate or disclaim his liability for the performance of its obligations by a third party with the use of different names or fictions when he signs a contract with a third person.

## IV. Liability of the Shipper for Other Persons in Maritime Conventions

**15.** The liability of the shipper is a secondary issue in international conventions on maritime carriage of goods, contrary to what happens with the carrier. The Hague-Visby Rules declares only that the shipper is not liable for any loss or damage sustained by the carrier or the ship that are not from the act or omission of the shipper, his agents or employees (Article 4.3. Hague-Visby Rules). So, it is the same rule that in the case of the carrier.

**16.** Hamburg Rules is quite similar too to Hague-Visby Rules on this issue, but the former are more detailed. In Article 12 Hamburg Rules it provides that the shipper is not liable for loss sustained by the carrier, or for damage to the ship, unless they have been caused by his fault or neglect, or by fault or neglect of its employees or agents. Therefore, it is not included within the scope of the shipper`s liability wilful or negligent acts or omissions that may have committed by its independent contractors or auxiliaries.

**17.** Meanwhile in the Rotterdam Rules there is an article about shipper's liability for the actions of others persons. According to Article 34 Rotterdam Rules, the shipper is responsible for the breach of its obligations caused by the acts or omissions of any person, "… including subcontractors, employees, representatives and assistants, who has entrusted the performance of any of its obligations". Of course, an exemption is established, as the shipper is not liable for the acts or omissions of the carrier or a maritime performing party acting on behalf of the carrier and to which the shipper has entrusted the fulfilment of its obligations. Although in these cases the carrier becomes *de facto* auxiliary of the shipper, the shipper is not liable because the person acts on behalf of the carrier and not on behalf of the shipper.

## V. Liability of the Debtor for Other Persons in European Contract Law

### *5.1. General rule*

**18.** Once exposed the regime under maritime conventions, we must examine the provisions of European Contract Law. The DFCR does not differ substantially from Principles of European Contract Law (PECL) on this issue.[5] We have to pay attention to Book III called Obligations and Corresponding rights, and particularly to Chapter 2 about Performance. Two options are contemplated: It may happen that the debtor itself performs his obligations, or entrusts its performance to another person. In the latter case, we must analyse, on one hand, the liability to the creditor, and, on the other hand, the liability to third persons or parties.

#### 5.1.1. Liability to the creditor

**19.** It may occur that the debtor of the obligation entrusted its performance to another, remaining the debtor logically as responsible for running to the creditor of the benefit (III.-2:106 DFCR). Also a third person may execute the obligation whenever it is not necessary that the debtor personally undertakes. In maritime transport frequently it is not necessary personal performance by the debtor of the obligations assumed under the contract of maritime carriage of goods.

**20.** In such a case, the creditor may not refuse the performance of the obligation for a third person if he acts with the consent of the debtor; or has a legitimate interest in the service is provided, or it is clear that the debtor does not execute the delivery in due time. Consequently the debtor itself will be liberated to perform the obligation. However, if the creditor accepts the performance of the service by a third party without happening any of the circumstances listed above, it is liable to the debtor for damages that such acceptance causes (III.-2:107 DFCR).

5 Bonell, M.J.; Peleggi, R., "UNIDROIT Principles of International Commercial Contracts and Draft Common Frame of Reference: a Synoptical Table", *Uniform Law Review*, vol. XIV, 2009, pp. 436–554.

### 5.1.2. Liability to third persons

21. In the field of tort it is established the liability of the person who employs others, that is, the debtor, for the damages caused to third persons. This rule only includes dependent auxiliaries or employees and representatives, excluding therefore independent auxiliaries. As has been shown in recent maritime conventions on carriage of goods, DFCR is more limited and restrictive. It is important to take into account that it is certainly more common in maritime transport to engage with independent contractors, because maritime carriage often involves the need to perform complex operations and not infrequently their execution requires a relevant degree of specialization.

22. In any case, two requirements must be met: first, the employee must have caused the damage in the exercise of their functions. This requirement is often required in the field of special regulation of transport, if auxiliary of the carrier wants to benefit of the grounds for exemption and limitations of liability applied in principle only to the carrier. That is, the auxiliary of the carrier must have acted within the scope of performance of the services that had been committed to and will have to demonstrate that subject to the duties assigned, since the application of the legal regime of liability of the carrier is more beneficial than the rules applicable to the auxiliary. If it is an employee or a representative, he will act within the scope of their duties ("scope of employment"), and if it is an independent auxiliary, he will act within the scope of the performance of the contract.

23. The interpretation of this requirement is not simple in some cases. Generally, it is estimated that there must be a link between the assigned functions and the harmful event whose occurrence should be assessed *ad hoc,* in other words, depending on the circumstances existing. But the problem arises when the auxiliary acts "in the exercise of their duties" but made no permitted behaviours such as theft or misuse of the goods or fail (binding) instructions of the carrier, his principal. In those cases, in which, during the performance of the assigned tasks, the auxiliary endangers the goods, it must be regarded as acts in the exercise of their functions, although it is not a proper behaviour. It must be interpreted in a broad sense this requirement, and thus, the auxiliary will continue to act in the exercise of their duties when they take advantage endangering goods.[6]

24. Second, the employee must have caused damages intentionally (VI.-3:101 DFCR) or negligently (VI.-3:102 DFCR), or otherwise be responsible for the damages. The latter hypothesis seems to accommodate cases in which it is legally established liability for

6 *Carver's on Bills of Lading*, 1ª ed. (by Treitel/Reynolds), Sweet & Maxwell, London, 2001, para. 9–205; Koller, I., *Transportrecht*, 7ª ed., C.H. Beck, Munich, 2010, Article 3 CMR, nm. 5; Martínez Sanz F., *La responsabilidad del porteador en el transporte internacional de mercancías por carretera – CMR –*, Comares, Granada, 2002, p. 611. On the contrary, Mankabady, S., "Comments on the Hamburg Rules", in *The Hamburg Rules on the carriage of goods by sea*, Mankabady (dir.), Leiden/Boston, 1978, p. 71, which estimated that in case of stolen goods, auxiliary does not act in the exercise of his functions.

damages in connection with a particular event or risk, that is to say, the liability is objective, for example, in the case of damages caused by defective products.

**25.** If these requirements met, the shipper and the carrier must have answered to third parties who may have suffered damage to their personal and/or economic interests. Anyway, as it can see, the DFCR is in general more restrictive than the maritime conventions, especially Rotterdam Rules that do not distinguish whether the damage occurred to a third party or to the creditor. Also, keep in mind that the application of the special regime of liability of the carrier to any action brought against him whether in contract, tort or based on any other cause (Article 4*bis*.1 Hague-Visby Rules; Article 7 Hamburg Rules; Article 4 Rotterdam Rules).

### *5.2. Special rule: The intervener*

**26.** It is possible another option though more exceptional and based on justice. It may occur that there is a benevolent intervention of a person in the affairs of another, the principal, or the performance of the obligations of another whose performance is due and urgent for reasons of public interest. This figure is regulated in Book V of the DFCR. The intervener is defined as the person who acts with the predominant intention to benefit another, the principal, and has a reasonable reason to act (not if the intervener will know or be found acting against the wishes of the principal), or the main approves such conduct by the harm that delaying action can cause to such intervener (V.-1:101 and 1:102 DFCR). Logically we cannot qualify as intervener to the person who is authorized to act pursuant to a contractual or other type of obligation (V.-1:103 DFCR).

**27.** The intervener must act diligently and must account for his performance (V.-2:101 and 2:103 DFCR). The intervener has to repair the damage caused by the breach of their duties of care, if their performance has caused the damage, or it has increased (V.-2:102 DFCR). However, the liability of the intervener can be reduced or even excluded in so far as this is fair and reasonable (V.-2:102 DFCR). So it depends on the circumstances, DFCR only mentions the reason for having acted on behalf of the principal or to have performed the service of another person without being obliged to do so (V.-2:102 *in fine* DFCR). But it could mention, among other circumstances, the degree of specialization of the intervener, the possibilities of adopting alternative measures, the behaviour is expected in reducing the damage, or the degree of negligence.

## VI. Special Situations. In particular, in Relation to Loading, Handling, Stowing, and Unloading of the Goods

### *6.1. Preliminary remarks*

**28.** It is possible to happen some special situations in relation to the performance of obligations under the contract of maritime carriage of goods. This type of situations may occur specially in relation to ancillary operations respect the carriage of the goods, such as loading, handling, stowing and unloading of the goods. It must distinguish two cases: Firstly, it is possible that a party of a contract of carriage performs an obligation of the other party, the debtor, which he has not to perform it. Secondly, it can occur that a party not bound to perform an obligation give instructions to the other party about its performance.

**29.** In such cases it must consider primarily the will of the parties concerned and their mode of action and if they act either on its own behalf or on behalf of another to determine the legal effect of the performance of the party is not bound to perform it.

### *6.2. Liability of the debtor in case it is the other party who performs some of the obligations*

**30.** If the other party performs some of the obligations of the debtor, it must determine the liability of the debtor and which rules have to apply.

**31.** If the debtor is the carrier, it must be solved whether is possible to apply the grounds for exemption of liability of the carrier. We have two options: We can take into account the formal aspect, that is, the contractual or legal assignment of the performance of these operations; or the factual aspect, in other words, the person who does materially these operations. The wording of the rules that collects these grounds for exemption refers to the loading and unloading of the goods have been "made" ("performs") by the shipper and/or the consignee (Article 17.3.i and k Rotterdam Rules). Consequently, the carrier may avail of these grounds for exemption if these operations have been made materially by the shipper and/or the consignee or their auxiliaries[7], irrespective of who would be legally or contractually required to carry them out.

**32.** However, this initial and simple solution to the problem does not take into account other factors that can come into these situations in which not match the person is required to perform these operations of loading and unloading the goods and who carried out effectively. If the carrier is not required to perform these operations of loading and unloading, but he or his auxiliaries carry them out, is a simplistic conclusion to state that in such a case, the carrier is liable for damages incurred in carrying out these operations, and the same in the opposite hypothesis.

**33.** In these anomalous cases in which the debtor not actually performs the loading and unloading of goods, it is important to know the will of the parties. It could be considered that the shipper and the carrier have agreed to validly modify the transport

7 Although in road transport, Koller, I., *Transportrecht, op. cit.*, Article CMR 17, nm. 46; Basedow, J., *Münchener Kommentar..., op. cit.*, Article CMR 17, nm. 65; Putzeys, J., *Le contrat de transport de marchandises routier*, Bruxelles, 1981, p. 263; Loewe, R., "Commentary on the Convention of 19 may 1956 on the contract for the international carriage of goods by road", *ETL*, 1976, p. 366; Martinez Sanz, *La responsabilidad del porteador..., op. cit.*, p. 267.

contract that binds them. That is, it would be a novation of the contract, in this case, its purpose, since the allocation of the benefits involved is changed. This amending agreement or contract between the parties does not require any special way, as the contract of carriage the content altered. Precisely the contract of carriage can be modified expressly or impliedly, that is, by conclusive facts of the parties, as may be the performance of the loading and unloading of whom no had originally committed to do it under the contract of carriage.[8] This approach is simple and overcomes the problems occurring in these anomalous cases. In particular it does not resolve the problem of mere supervision of the party not bound to it.

**34.** Also be assessed the way in which the other party acts, although he is not bound to do it, that is, if he has acted in his name and on his own behalf or on behalf of another, such as the debtor. In this sense, it can be proposed as a simple and general solution presumption that the party materially performs these operations, which corresponds to the other party, thus becomes *de facto* an auxiliary who is required to perform these operations under the contract of carriage. This approach has the advantage of offering a more or less only response to all cases that can be formulated. However, the interpretation of the will of the parties in this regard is questionable; at most, it could support a presumption should be rebuttable by the circumstances in each case. In particular, it should evaluate whether or not the obligation to perform these operations controls or supervises the execution of these tasks by the person making them effectively.

**35.** Therefore, due to the difficulty to implement and support this generic solution should be examined two principal hypotheses.

**36.** If the carrier performs the obligation although he is not obliged to do it. It is necessary to distinguish two possible situations: Firstly, the carrier may act on his own behalf when performs the obligation, so it produces the novation of the contract. Anyway, we must determine whether or not the carrier in such cases is within its period of responsibility, because if he performs these operations outside that period will not respond. In general, the liability of the carrier begins with the receipt of the goods by the carrier and ends with the delivery to the addressee or person entitled to receive them. So the carrier remains liable during the custody of the goods, in other words, during the period that the carrier may exercise control and supervision over the goods. For this reason, it should be understood that, if the carrier performs these operations effectively on its own behalf, he has already received the goods and has begun its period of responsibility.

8 It could understand that there has been such novation of the transport agreement regarding the obligation to make the loading and unloading, even if it is verified upon tacitly, for example, if the carrier makes this operation and then requires the corresponding remuneration for making it. Vid. Koller, I., *Transportrecht, op. cit.*, §412 HGB, nm. 11.

37. Secondly, the carrier can act too on behalf of the shipper and/or consignee. Thus, the carrier becomes *de facto* an auxiliary of the shipper and/or consignee. So the carrier would not have received the goods and would not have started their period of responsibility as a carrier. The shipper and the consignee respectively will still have the custody of the goods, in other words, the control over them. Therefore, the carrier will not be liable for damage or loss of the goods as a carrier. However, he will be liable under the general rules of civil liability against its principal, the shipper and/or the consignee, or against a holder of a legitimate interest in the goods through a tort claim.

38. This hypothesis provides expressly in Rotterdam Rules, especially in the case of exemption on the performance of the loading and unloading of the goods by the shipper, the documentary shipper or the consignee (Article 17.3.i Rotterdam Rules). It provides that if the carrier or his auxiliaries, that is, in terms of Rotterdam Rules, a performing party, make such operations on behalf of the shipper, the documentary shipper or consignee, may not plead this ground for exemption of liability. Meanwhile, in the case of the performance of the packaging operations and signalling and identification of the goods (Article 17.3.k Rotterdam Rules), it is required that these operations have not been carried out by the carrier or by someone on his behalf (Article 17.3.k *in fine* Rotterdam Rules). In sum, the carrier may not invoke these grounds for exemption, if such operations are carried himself even when performed by others. In connection with this provision, we note Article 34 of Rotterdam Rules, which states that the shipper is not responsible to the shipper has entrusted the performance of any of its obligations for the acts of the carrier or a performing party acting on behalf of the carrier (Article 34 *in fine* Rotterdam Rules).[9] Therefore, the shipper is liable for the acts of a performing party if he acts on shipper`s behalf, but in any case, for the acts of the carrier (and also of a performing party acting on behalf of carrier itself), even though the latter may have acted on behalf of the shipper, as auxiliary or a representative. This rule would create problems, especially if there is a negotiable document of transport and the holder is not the shipper, because if he exercises any right under the contract of carriage, he must assume the obligations stated on the contract of carriage, provided that these are reflected in the document of transport directly or indirectly (at least through an incorporation clause) (Article 58.2 Rotterdam Rules).[10]

39. In any case, if an auxiliary of the carrier is involved in the performance of these operations, the resolution of this issue is more complicated. In this respect we have to distinguish again two situations: Firstly, if the auxiliary of the carrier acts according to

9 It will happen more frequently that a performing party acts as auxiliary of the shipper and/or consignee than the carrier itself acts as auxiliary of the shipper and/or the consignee. Baatz/Debattista/Lorenzon/Serdy/Staniland/Tsimplis, *The Rotterdam Rules: A practical Annotation*, Informa, London, 2009, p. 96, par. 34.02.

10 This problem is highlighted in Baatz et al., *The Rotterdam Rule:...*, *op. cit.*, p. 96, par. 34.02 and pp. 176–179, pars. 58.01–58.10). Moreover, the holder of a document of transport in these cases is neither a shipper, nor a documentary shipper (Article 1.9 Rotterdam Rules), so he cannot benefit from the application of Article 4.2 Rotterdam Rules.

the decision of the carrier itself, it may be a case of transfer of labour. That is, the carrier facilitates the shipper and the consignee employees to perform these operations. However, in order to avoid fictions, the designation of the auxiliaries who actually perform the operations must be expressly accepted by the shipper and/or the consignee. And the latter should really have the ability to monitor and control the activity of these auxiliaries. Consequently, the auxiliary of the carrier will respond as auxiliary of the shipper and/or consignee for damage caused by performing these operations. The carrier may act too as an auxiliary of the shipper and/or consignee, and his auxiliaries become auxiliaries of auxiliaries of the shipper and/or the consignee.

**40.** Secondly, it may also happen that the auxiliary of the carrier acts on their own initiative. If the auxiliary of the carrier does these operations without the consent and knowledge of the carrier, the principal, the auxiliary becomes auxiliary of the shipper and/or the consignee at this moment.

**41.** If the shipper and/or consignee performs the obligation although they are not obliged to do it. It can distinguish two possible cases.

**42.** Firstly, the shipper and/or the consignee can act in their own name for themselves or through their auxiliary. In such a situation, the carrier in fact has not received the goods that remains in the custody of the shipper and therefore has not yet begun its period of responsibility. Also, the carrier has delivered the goods, which are in the custody of the consignee and therefore its liability period has ended. Therefore, the carrier is not liable for damages caused by the poor performance of these operations. In any event, even when it is considered that in these moments the carrier is within the period of responsibility, they may avail themselves of the grounds for exemption relating to the performance of the loading and unloading respectively. Anyway, in these scenarios many times it can easily estimate that the will of the parties in fact modify the contract of carriage and assigns the obligation to perform these operations for loading and unloading to the shipper and to the consignee respectively.

**43.** Secondly, the shipper and the consignee can act in their own or another name, but in any case, on behalf of the carrier. So the shipper and the consignee would act *de facto* as auxiliary of the carrier in the performance of the loading and unloading of goods. Consequently, the carrier could not claim the grounds for exemption relating to the performance of the loading and unloading, because the acts or the omissions of his auxiliaries, in that case the shipper and/or the consignee, will attribute to the carrier as their principal. However, the carrier may sue the shipper and the consignee as his auxiliaries, if they have been the cause of the damage and the carrier has previously had to compensate a third party, an owner with a legitimate interest in the goods.

**44.** Also, if the auxiliary of the shipper and/or the consignee carry out loading and unloading operations, can also be basically again two situations. These type of cases must be solved in a similar way that it explained regarding to the auxiliaries of the carrier.

45. In sum, we cannot give a comprehensive and unique solution to these anomalous cases in which the person that is required to perform the loading and unloading of the goods and the person making them effectively does not match. In any case, it should be investigated and interpreted the will of the parties and take into consideration all the circumstances.

### 6.3. *Liability of the party not bound to perform the obligations in case of giving instructions*

46. It is also appropriate to consider the impact it can have the fact that the party not bound to perform the obligation gives instructions to the debtor, and the latter follow the instructions and because of this occurs damages. Normally there are multiple causes in this type of cases. It must be applied as long as possible the same rules that we analyse in the previous heading.

47. In particular, in the case of the performance of the loading, handling, stowing or unloading of the goods, it can ask whether or not the carrier has a duty of supervision if the shipper and/or consignee must perform such operations. In other words, if is there an ancillary duty of the maritime carrier to supervise these operations in relation to the handling of the goods derived from the principle of good faith in the performance of contracts. In principle the answer can be affirmative, among other arguments due to the professional character of the carrier, but anyway it is a difficult question, except in case of stowing of the goods. Actually regarding the operation of stowing itself is estimated that the carrier has at least a duty to supervise the operation of stowing the goods on the ship, because their inadequate performance can affect the seaworthiness of the vessel. The carrier is bound to make and keep the ship seaworthy before, at the beginning of, and during the voyage by sea.

## VII. Conclusions

48. The vicarious liability according to European Contract Law presents relevant differences with uniform maritime transport rules. These dissimilarities are manifested particularly regarding Rotterdam Rules, which is the most recent uniform maritime transport regulation.

49. According to the DFCR the debtor would be liable for damages if the third persons have caused the damage in the course of the employment or engagement and, at least have acted negligently. However, in Maritime Transport Law it is often required only the first condition to entitle an employee or agent of the carrier to avail themselves of the defences, and especially the limits of liability applicable in principle only to the maritime carrier.

50. Moreover, the DFCR makes no mention of independent contractors. So the debtor, the principal, is not liable for damages caused by the independent contractors. In Hague-

Visby Rules it does not provide too the liability of the maritime carrier for acts or omissions of his independent auxiliaries. However, Hamburg Rules and Rotterdam Rules consider that the maritime carrier will be liable for damages caused not only by his employees and agents, but also for damages caused by his independent auxiliaries.

**51.** The DFCR does not resolve the special situations explained above, in particular in relation to loading, handling, stowing and unloading of the goods. Consequently, we must interpret the will of the parties involved and their mode of action, that is, if they act in his name and on his own behalf or not.

**52.** Finally, the DFCR provisions about vicarious liability are not adequate in maritime transport, because they do not take into consideration the frequency of subcontracting in maritime transport and the complexity of operations related to it. In fact, the implementation of the DFCR provisions in maritime transport would mean to continue in the way of the Hague-Visby Rules, which are in general much more beneficial for maritime carrier than for shippers and/or consignees.

Anastasiya Kozubovskaya Pellé*

# COULD THE DCFR BE AN ANSWER TO THE LACK OF HARMONIZATION IN THE FIELD OF FORWARDING LAW? – LEGAL QUALIFICATION

## I. Introduction

1. Who is the carrier in the line of sub-contractors involved in the carriage of goods by sea? Or let's put it in other words: "who is liable to pay damages when the cargo is lost or damaged?" Will the freight forwarders shipping under its own bills of lading be held liable and in what capacity? This is a major and classic question that faces cargo owner.

2. Although the law of carriage of goods is to a large extent harmonized by several international conventions[1] the attempts to harmonize the law of freight forwarding on international level have failed.[2] Consequently, the freight forwarders (legal qualification and liability) are still governed by national laws and therefore attract forum shopping attitude and uncertainty into the contractual relationship.

3. The Principles, Definitions and Model Rules of European Private Law, Draft Common Frame of Reference (DCFR) and Principles of European Contract Law (PECL) have been elaborated with the aim of providing European internal market with a uniform contract law. Various international and regional organisations, recognising that diverging contract law rules create obstacles to international trade, have been working to reduce such obstacles by providing uniform model rules.

* Project Officer for SAFEMED III European Maritime Safety Agency.
The views and opinions expressed in this article are solely those of the author. These views and opinions do not necessarily represent those of EMSA.

1 However, the carriage of goods is a victim of its success, as the existence of several international conventions (Hamburg Rules, Hague Rules, Hague-Visby Rules, Rotterdam Rules) prejudice the benefits of the said harmonization.

2 The UNIDROIT Draft Convention on Contract of Agency for Forwarding Agents relating to International Carriage of Goods was never submitted to a diplomatic conference.

4. Although the DCFR and PECL do not deal with contract of carriage[3], do not refer to the freight forwarding[4], and do not intend to apply to negotiable instruments[5], it contains some basic general principles, notably on contract interpretation and agency, that could be applied to a certain extent to the freight forwarding.

5. From legal qualification of a freight forwarder – intermediary or principal – will depend the liability he will be subject to. Legal qualification of the freight forwarder's function will usually vacillate between two contracts: agency and carriage of goods, and therefore between two legal qualifications: agent and carrier.

6. Whether the freight forwarder is an agent or a principal contractor depends on the facts of each case and on the law of the jurisdiction the case is brought to. Professor Tetley points out in this respect that "there are no hard rules for determining whether the freight forwarder is acting as agent or as principal contractor. The forwarder's role will depend on the facts of each case. There are, however, several useful criteria which can assist in making that determination".[6] To make it more complex, in a midway between the principle and contractor the French law places *commissionnaire de transport*-agent with a specific legal regime.

7. To summarise the freight forwarder may act as:

1) performing carrier – when he executes the carriage of goods;
2) contracting carrier – when, although he does not execute the carriage of goods, he assumes the liability and the legal capacity of the carrier (contractual carrier and *transporteur apparent* under the French law);
3) agent on behalf of the performing carrier.

8. The main challenge with regard to the legal qualification of the freight forwarder is mostly related to the last two situations. We will first analyse the case when the freight forwarder's activity is qualified as agency (II. Freight forwarder as an agent), and will then examine the situation when the freight forwarder is qualified as a carrier (I. Freight forwarder as a carrier). During this analysis we will refer to the provisions of the DCFR that might be applicable to the respective situations.

[3] The DCFR refer to the contract of carriage only in the light of the contract of sale which involves carriage of the goods; and they refer to the contract of carriage with a sole purpose to specify obligations of the parties to the contract of sale. Moreover the article 102 (Book II, Part C) of the Chapter II Rules applying to Service contracts in general clearly specifies that this part does not apply to contracts in so far as they are for transport.

[4] What could be easily understood bearing in mind different attempts in the past to harmonise the law governing freight forwarding; Ramberg, J. "Unification of the Law of International Freight Forwarding", *RDU* 1998–1, p. 5.

[5] Article I.-1:101 "Intended field of application" of the DCFR: §2 these rules "are not intended to be used, or used without modification or supplementation, ...in relation to [...] negotiable instruments". This is relevant when a negotiable Bill of lading is issued.

[6] Tetley W., *Marine Cargo Claims*, 4th ed., 2008, Chapter 33.

## II. Freight Forwarder as a Carrier

**9.** The freight forwarder will be qualified as a carrier in the following situations:

1) when he performs the carriage (performing carrier);
2) when, even though he does not execute the carriage of goods, he assumes the liability and the legal capacity of the carrier. We will call him "contractual carrier" in contrast to performing carrier. Here we will distinguish two different situations:
   a. when a freight forwarder expressly agreed to act as principal, thus subjecting him to carrier liability (express contractual intent);
   b. when there was only an implied agreement from the freight forwarder's statements or conduct. In the French courts it is not unusual to see the freight forwarder being held liable as a carrier – *transporteur apparent* – for the reason that he appeared in the eyes of the shipper as a carrier because of his attitude in the contractual relationship and mostly because of the documents issued and the statements such documents contain. The concept of *transporteur apparent* is wildly used by French courts especially when the transport documents are in the hands of a cargo owner (C) – third party to the initial relationship (when the transport documents have been circulated and the initial contract has been concluded between A and B).[7]

**10.** American law know the concept of contractual carrier, when the freight forwarder is to be held in the capacity of contractual carrier: the Non-Vessel-Operating Common Carriers (NVOCC). "The NVOCC acts in dual capacity: as a common carrier in relation to its shipper, and as a shipper (agent of the cargo owner) in relation to the underlying carriers". The NVOCC is described by the Ninth Circuit as "intermediary between the shipper of goods and the operator of the vessel that will carry the goods".[8]

**11.** Under the French law the freight forwarder acting as NVOCC is most likely to be qualified as *commissionnaire de transport*.[9] In certain cases, he could be qualified as *transporteur apparent* if the documents he issued made the shipper in good faith believing that he was dealing with a carrier and not with an intermediary.[10]

7 Kozubovskaya A., "La situation juridique du destinataire porteur au connaissement", mémoire sous la direction de Y. Tassel, 2004, CDMO, Université de Nantes; Cass.civ., 16 mars 2004, navire Alvis, JCP 2004 IV 1980; DMF 2004, p.423. For a divergent view see Cass.com., 8 October 2003 Sté Borsha Shipping Ltd, CJP, 19.10.2003, no. 47, IV 2 874.

8 Tetley W., *Marine Cargo Claims*, 4th Edition, 2008, Chapter 33.

9 Morinière J.-M., "Les "non-vessel-operating common carriers" (NVOCC) – essai sur le concept de transporteur maritime contractuel", 1997.

10 Kozubovskaya Pellé A., "De la qualité juridique de transporteur maritime de marchandises: notion et identification", *PUAM* 2011, p.160.

## III. Freight Forwarder as an Agent

**12.** Originally the freight forwarders were regarded as agents and the terminology used to define them was reflecting this, as they were called "freight forwarding agents". Progressively the word "agents" was dropped and problems of qualification arose due to the lack of uniform "agency" law and, consequently, due to the lack of uniformity in approaches of different national legal systems.

**13.** For example, in the French law, there are two kind of "agents": *commissionnaire de transport*[11] and *mandataire*. The main difference for the legal qualification between them is that even though both act on behalf of the principal, the *commissionnaire de transport* acts in his own name and the *mandataire* acts in the name of the principal.

The *commissionnaire de transport*, in midway between principle contractor and agent (*mandataire*), is unknown in Common law countries.

**14.** However, French law *commissionnaire de transport* is sometimes presented by English doctrine comparing him to the English law agent as "indirect agent".[12] If we draw a parallel, the *commissionnaire de transport* would be closer to English law undisclosed agency in which the existence of the principal is not revealed by the agent to a third party and the agent, as well as the *commissionnaire de transport*, is entitled and liable on the contract. The French law *mandataire* would be closer to a disclosed agency where the existence or the name of the principal is revealed to the third party by the agent and where the agent himself is not normally entitled to the benefit of, or be liable on, the contract.

**15.** Where under Common law a freight forwarder would be legally qualified as a principal contractor, i.e. a carrier, under French law he could still be qualified either as a carrier or as *commissionnaire de transport*. When under Common law freight forwarder is qualified as an agent, under French law the discussion will take place to determine if he is a *commissionnaire de transport* or *mandataire*. The legal qualification of an operator (*commissionnaire de transport* or *mandataire*) became a classic discussion in the transport hearings in the French courts. The operator's advocates will try to convince the judge that their client has been acting merely as a *mandataire* although the shipper's (or cargo owner's) advocates will make their best to show that the operator acted in capacity of *commissionnaire de transport* or in capacity of a carrier.

**16.** To resume, whether the freight forwarder is acting as an agent (*commissionnaire de transport* or *mandataire*) or as a principal contractor (carrier) depends on the facts of

11 For the definition of *commissionnaire de transport* in French law see Cour de cassation, 10 May 2005, *D.* 2005, no. 33, p. 2293; Cour de cassation, 16 February 1988, *BT* 1988, p.491.
For Standard Contract of *commission de transport* recently adopted see Décret n° 2013-293 du 5 avril 2013 portant approbation du contrat type de commission de transport, modified in May 2014.

12 Chuan J., *Law of International Trade*, 3rd Edition, London, 2005, p. 51-75.

each case and on the law of particular jurisdiction in question.[13] A proliferation of forum shopping attitude in the shipping claims is a consequence of this situation.

**17.** Regarding agency, the DCFR contains two chapters devoted to Representation (Book II, Part C, Chapter II) and Mandate contracts (Book IV, Part D). According to Article IV. D.–1:101 of the DCFR, the provisions related to the mandate apply "where the agent undertakes to act on behalf of, and in accordance with the instructions of the principal". They apply to contracts and other juridical acts under which a person, the agent, is authorised and instructed (mandated) by another person, the principal:

> "(a) to conclude a contract between the principal and a third party or otherwise directly affect the legal position of the principal in relation to a third party;
> (b) to conclude a contract with a third party, or do another juridical act in relation to a third party, on behalf of the principal but in such a way that the agent and not the principal is a party to the contract or other juridical act". To draw a parallel with French "agency" law, the first situation (described in (a)) would correspond to the French mandate contract, and the second one (described in (b)) would correspond to *commissionnaire de transport* contract.

**18.** The DCFR go further and explicitly lay down provisions with regard to the direct and indirect representation. According to Article IV. D.–1:102 of the DCFR,

> "(d) a mandate for direct representation is a mandate under which the agent is to act in the name of the principal, or otherwise in such a way as to indicate an intention to affect the principal's legal position;
> (e) a mandate for indirect representation is a mandate under which the agent is to act in the agent's own name or otherwise in such a way as not to indicate an intention to affect the principal's legal position".

**19.** The mandate rules laid down by the DCFR could be applicable in the shipping. As they clearly lay down the obligations of each party, they will contribute in the European internal market to an uniform interpretation of the contractual relationship between these two parties. As the DCFR clearly define direct and indirect representation, these rules will contribute avoiding divergent interpretation by different jurisdictions with regard to the parties to the prospective contract (principal or agent). As we have already mentioned before the denial of the existence of indirect representation (and therefore denial of being personally liable to the third party by virtue of the contract concluded on behalf of the principal) is frequent defence of the freight forwarders (*commissionnaire de transport*) in the French courts.

[13] Tetley W., *Marine Cargo Claims*, 4th ed., 2008, Chapter 33.
For an example of legal qualification operated by French court (qualifying as *commissionnaire de transport* and not as a sub-contracting carrier) see decision of the Court of appeal of Rennes, 2 October 2007.

## IV. Conclusion

20. Even though the DCFR do not apply to the transport contract, neither directly to the freight forwarding activity, the latter is concerned in so far the provisions addressing representation and mandate contracts could be applicable to freight forwarder and to the principle. Moreover, the DCFR general provisions on formation, validity, interpretation of the contracts, performance of obligations and on the remedies for the non-performance could be applicable to a certain extent to this relationship. We will not disagree with the commentators to the DCFR stating that "the DCFR may furnish the notion of a European private law with a new foundation which increases mutual understanding and promotes collective deliberation on private law in Europe".[14]

21. Indeed, the provisions on direct and indirect representation admitted on European level could be the way out from the forum shopping attitude related to the fact that some national legal systems do or do not recognise *commissionnaire de transport*.

22. The DCFR could be also a possible source of inspiration in the harmonization and modernisation process of national legislations. "The PECL, which the DCFR incorporates in a partly revised form, received the attention of many higher courts in Europe and numerous official bodies charged with preparing the modernisation of the relevant national law of contract. [...] If the content of the DCFR is convincing, it may contribute to a harmonious and informal Europeanisation of private law".[15] However, it should be kept in mind that freight forwarding and carriage of goods by sea go beyond European borders. Therefore, the question remains open with regard to the potential admission of these rules by non-European countries.

14 Comments to the DCFR, January 2009, Christian von Bar, Hugh Beale, Eric Clive, Hans Schulte-Nolke, §7.

15 *Ibid*, §8.

Wouter Verheyen

# HARMONISATION INSTRUMENTS: THE WAY FORWARD FOR FORWARDING LAW?

## I. Problem Statement

### *1.1. Uniform forwarding law is lacking*

1. Carriage law is one of the most unified fields of private law. Unification in this field started very early[1] and now for every mode of transportation, there is an international convention. An important limit to the unified law exists in the fact that unified law only applies to carriage contracts, contracts where a service provider agrees to carry the goods, leaving those contracts where the service provider agrees to arrange the carriage outside the scope of uniform law (hereinafter referred to as forwarding contracts). Not only is there no uniform law for forwarding contracts, moreover uniform principles underlying forwarding law in different states seem to be lacking. Both on the point of liability as on the point of qualification, there is an important divergence between forwarding laws in different countries.[2] The differences on the point of the qualification of the contract mainly exist with regards to the demarcation between carriage contract and freight forwarding contract.

2. The lack of uniformity on these points greatly impacts the degree of uniformity in carriage law: while in one country a contract might be considered as a carriage contract and thus as falling within the scope of uniform carriage law, in another country the same contract might be considered as a forwarding contract. Underlying reasons for this discrepancy are that on the hand judges in general have a wide discretionary power when qualifying the contract, as a wide variety of parameters can be taken into account when qualifying a contract as a carriage or forwarding contract, without there being a strict

1 The first convention on railway transportation already came into existence in 1890: the International Convention on the Carriage of Goods by Rail of 14 October 1890; unification in sea transportation followed in 1924 by the International Convention for the Unification of Certain Rules of Law relating to Bills of Lading ("Hague Rules"), and Protocol of Signature.
(Brussels, 25 August 1924).

2 See also on this problem: Jan Ramberg, "Unification of the law of international freight forwarding", (1998) *RDU* 5–14.

hierarchy between with multiple elements that are relevant for the qualification of the contract, without there being a strict hierarchy between these different elements. On the other hand, sometimes the same element is taken into account to support an opposite qualification. Moreover, in for example Holland and Germany, even if the service provider is qualified as a forwarder, sometimes he is held liable as a carrier, thus expanding the scope of carriage law beyond its natural habitat and increasing the differences in the scope of carriage law.

### *1.2. Can the harmonisation instruments unify forwarding law?*

3. Already in 1967 UNIDROIT proposed a draft Convention on Contracts of Agency for Forwarding Agents relating to International Carriage of Goods.[3] However, this convention was never adopted. As a uniform regime is not to be expected in the coming years, this research takes a step back, away from the sector-specific legislation and inquiries into the question whether harmonisation of forwarding law could benefit from harmonisation instruments in general civil law. The focus in this article lies on the question whether a contractual incorporation of DCFR,[4] PECL[5] or UNIDROIT principles 2010[6] could take away uncertainty with regards to the qualification of the same contract in different states.

4. In order for the harmonization instruments to be fit for this purpose, they should not only contain rules on contract interpretation, but it is required that these rules limit the discretionary power of national judges. If not, judges might continue to decide upon cases by interpreting these uniform rules from their own national perspective. Moreover, if the harmonisation instruments can take away uncertainties, in order for them to be useful today, a further question is in how far the mere contractual incorporation of one of these instrument can successfully lead to this result.

## II. Different Interpretations: Status Questionis

5. Even though liability consequences of a qualification as carrier or rather as a forwarder are very important, a uniform demarcation line between the two is currently lacking. A wide variety of parameters is taken into account to determine whether parties concluded a carriage contract or rather a forwarding contract. This gives judges a wide discretionary margin, but also leads to the unpredictability of a later qualification. Even though some praetorian and legislative interventions in different

3 Draft Convention on Contract of Agency for Forwarding Agents relating to International Carriage of Goods; *l'Unification du droit / Unification of Law 1967, YearBook 1966*, p. 413 and further (hereinafter referred to as Draft Convention on Contract of Agency for Forwarding Agents).

4 Von Bar Christian, Eric Clive and Hans Schulte-Nölke, *Principles, Definitions and Model Rules of European Private Law. Draft Common Frame of Reference (DCFR)* (Sellier, 2009).

5 Lando Ole, Hugh Beale, *The Principles Of European Contract Law 2002 (Parts I and II)* (Kluwer, 1999).

6 UNIDROIT Principles of International Commercial Contracts ("UNIDROIT Principles 2010") (Unidroit, 2010).

states created some hierarchy and made decisions more predictable, those interventions didn't take place in a uniform way in different states and thus the lack of uniformity increased even further.

## *2.1. Wide variety of parameters are taken into consideration: discretionary margin*

### 2.1.1. Contract interpretation based on broader context

6. Determining whether a contract is to be qualified as a carriage contract or as a forwarding contract, requires the judge to establish whether the service provider undertook to carry the goods (qualification as a carriage contract) or to arrange the carriage of the goods (qualification as a forwarding contract).[7] This is often a difficult job, as the judge can't limit himself to an analysis of the question whether the service provider performed part of the carriage himself: the carrier can subcontract (part of) the carriage, meaning that the lack of material performance of the contract in principle can't be considered as a relevant element pro qualification as forwarding contract.[8] On the other hand, forwarders often take up several accessory tasks and thus even if a service provider engaged to arrange the carriage, he might need to perform an accessory part of the

7 See f.ex.: Cass. be. 5 November 1936, (1938) TBH 42; See also for example Rb. Utrecht 27 February 2008, [2010] S&S 16 and Cass. fr. 15 June 2011, *J. D.* 2011-011797 (*"qu'entre les parties, la qualification de contrat de transport ne se présume pas mais se déduit de leur commune intention telle qu'elle s'exprime à travers les obligations souscrites par chacune d'elles"*); Kristiaan Bernauw, "Commissionnair-De commissionnair in de vervoersector", in Bernard Tilleman en Evelyne Terryn, *Ondernemingsrecht, liber amicorum Luc Ballon*, in *Beginselen van Belgisch privaatrecht, Handels- en economisch recht*, (Kluwer, 2011) 1053, 1061; Christophe Paulin, "Réflexions sur la distinction entre contrat de transport et contrat de commission de transport", in *études sur le droit de la concurrence et quelques thèmes fondamentaux, mélanges en l'honneur d'Yves Serra*, (Dalloz, 2006) 325, 326 (*"Lorsque l'expéditeur charge chronopost d'acheminer des marchandises en vingt-quatre heures, le prestataire s'oblige-t-il à déplacer celles-ci de façon à ce qu'elles arrivent dans les délais ou à organiser leur déplacement pour qu'elles arrivent dans les délais."*).

8 Netherlands: Maarten Claringbould, "De aansprakelijkheid van de expediteur, Over 'vervoer of expeditie' en gewoonte", (2008) NTHR55, France: Paris 17 May 1996, *BTL* 1996, 400; Com. Paris 14 March 1978, *ETL* 1978, 742 („*La qualité de commissionnaire de transport ne s'acquiert pas par le simple fait de la sous-traitance du transport; mais par l'acceptation expresse d'une prise de responsabilité de bout en bout"*); L. Guignard, *Sous-traitance et transport* (Litec, 2001) 436–461. Germany: §437 HGB; Hanno Merkt, "HGB §407 Frachtvertrag", in Klaus Hopt, Hanno Merkt, Markus Roth and Adolf Baumbach, *Handelsgesetzbuch*, 35th ed. (Beck, 2012) n° 18 („*Der Frachtführer kann sich mit selbstständigen Teilfrachtführern die Strecke teilen (dann erhält jeder seinen Auftrag vom Absender, dieser uU vertreten durch den Frachtführer) oder über die ganze Strecke weisungsgebundene Unterfrachtführer einschalten, letzteres ist dem Frachtführer grundsätzlich ohne weiteres erlaubt (aber Haftung des Hauptfrachtführers für diese, §428 Satz 2)* "); Beate Czerwenka, "HGB §407 Frachtvertrag ", in Beate Czerwenka en Ralf Herber (eds.), *Münchener Kommentar zum Handelsgesetzbuch: §§407–475h. Transportrecht*, 2nd ed. (Beck, 2009) n° 114. Belgium: Article 5 vervoerwet, Louis Fredericq, *Handboek van het Belgisch handelsrecht*, III (Larcier, 1980) 631; J. Loyens, *Handboek transportrecht*, (Intersentia, 2011) 379.

carriage himself.[9] Therefore in order to establish what obligation the service provider took up, judges need to interpret the contract. As Haak states in this regards: "*The problem does not lie so much in the question what obligations do each of the contracts give rise to but rather in the interpretation of the complex of facts that originates in essence in a factual interpretation problem.*"[10]

7. When interpreting or qualifying a contract, under civil law the judge can take into account all relevant elements from the contract, including contract negotiations and the way the contract was performed.[11] Even though the relevant context for contract interpretation is traditionally much narrower in English law (the so-called parole evidence rule)[12], especially after the case *Investors Compensation Scheme t. West Bromwich Building Society*[13] contract interpretation in English law has evolved towards contract interpretation in continental European countries.[14]

9 See for some examples in case law: Brussel 7 December 1977, (1878) *RGAR* n° 9952; Antwerpen 6 February 2012, 2011/AR/80, *n.p.*

10 Krijn Haak, *The liability of the carrier under the CMR*, (Stichting vervoeradres, 1986) 59. See also: Ellen Beukering-Rosmuller., *De expeditie-overeenkomst* (Gouda-Quint, 1992) 69; Johann Georg Helm, *Speditionsrecht* (De Gruyter) 1973, 8 and 77; Christophe Paulin, "Réflexions sur la distinction entre contrat de transport et contrat de commission de transport" in *Etudes sur le droit de la concurrence et quelques thèmes fondamentaux, mélanges en l'honneur d'Yves Serra* (Dalloz, 2006) 325, 327 ("*Il faut toutefois reconnaître que la volonté des parties n'est pas toujours exprimée de façon aussi simpliste et qu'il est rare que l'on demande expressément à une prestataire de transporter ou de faire transporter. La jurisprudence doit alors se livrer à des extrapolations hasardeuses.*").

11 See for example: HR 13 March 1981, *Haviltex*, *NJ* 1981, 635.

12 Hugh Beale, *Chitty on contracts, Volume I general principles*, 29th ed. (Sweet & Maxwell, 2004) 752 and further; Malcolm Clarke, "The interpretation of (transnational) commercial contracts according to English law", *NTHR* 2005, 114, 117. See also: Paul Bugden, *Freight forwarding and goods in transit* (Sweet and Maxwell, 1999) 49–50.

13 L.J. Hofmann in "Investors Compensation Scheme t. West Bromwich Building Society", *UKHL* 1997, 28; 1 *All ER* 1998, 98; 1 *WLR* 1998, 896. (Starting point for interpretation is now "*the ascertainment of the meaning which the document would convey to a reasonable person having all the background knowledge which would reasonably have been available to the parties in the situation in which they were at the time of the contract". Lord Hofmann defines background knowledge as "absolutely anything which would have affected the way in which the language of the document would have been understood by a reasonable man*".) See on this case: Paul Bugden, *Freight forwarding and goods in transit* (Sweet and Maxwell, 1999) 51–52; Gerard McMeel, "The rise of commercial construction in contract law", *LMCLQ* 1998, 382–393; Nicole Kornet, "The interpretation, implication and supplementation of contracts in England and the Netherlands" in Jan Smits en Sophie Stijns, *Inhoud en werking van de overeenkomst naar Belgisch en Nederlands recht*, (Intersentia, 2005) 47, 51–52 (Kornet makes a comparison between interpretation in Dutch and English law); M. Van Rossum, "Interpretation of Commercial Contracts", *EJCCL* 2011, (46) 47. According to Clarke: "*This statement opens the stable doors once formed by the parole evidence rule. The result has been a forensic gallop around the countryside in each case by barristers foraging for background material that might slant the often ordinary meaning of the contract in question in a way favorable to their client, but with modest success.*" (Malcolm Clarke, "The interpretation of (transnational) commercial contracts according to English law", *NTHR* 2005, 114, 117).

14 See however already in an earlier case: L.J. Diprock in HoL 1 januari 1980, Porter / National Union of Journalists [1980] *I.R.L.R.* 404 ("*I turn to the interpretation of the relevant rules, bearing in mind that their purpose is to inform the members of the N.U.J. of what rights they acquire and obligations they assume vis-à-vis the union and their fellow members, by becoming and remaining members of it. The*

### 2.1.2. Broad interpretation context creates wide discretionary power and unpredictable outcome disputes

**8.** This broad interpretation context leaves judges with a considerable margin of discretion. An example of how much different elements are sometimes taken into account, can be found in the Aqualon-case[15] where based on a study of existing case law,[16] five relevant elements are brought forward: "*a. the terms of the particular contract including the nature of the instructions given... b. any description used or adopted by the parties in relation to the contracting party's role... c. the course of any dealings, including the manner of performance at least in so far as it throws light on the way in which the parties understood their relationship... d. the nature and basis of charging... e. the nature and terms of any CMR note issued.*"[17] Even though in this case only the context prior to the conclusion of the contract is taken into account, already in *Jones v. European and General Express*[18] the way of performance of the contract was taken into account as a relevant element to determine the qualification.

**9.** The biggest problem with this wide variety of elements lies in the fact that often there is no strict hierarchy between the different elements. Thus it is often impossible for contract parties to predict the qualification that is to be given to the judge in a possible later conflict.

**10.** Even if the contract contains clear and unambiguous wordings, then still these don't necessarily have a decisive impact on the qualification of the contract. The contractual qualification of the contract is definitely taken into account in all jurisdictions[19] and is the starting point of the qualification question, but in none of them a decisive weight is adhered

*readership to which the rules are addressed consists of ordinary working journalists, not judges or lawyers versed in the semantic technicalities of statutory draftsmanship.*"). See also: Paul Bugden and Simone Lamont-Black, *Goods in transit and freight forwarding* (Sweet and Maxwell, 2010) 6; H.G. Beale, *Chitty on contracts, Volume I general principles*, 29e ed. (Sweet & Maxwell, 2004) 729 and further.

15 QB 17 november 1993 Aqualon (UK) Ltd / Vallana Shipping Corp [1994] 1, *Lloyd's Rep.*, 669.

16 Mance refers to the following cases: CA 13 January 1977, Ulster Swift Ltd. and Pigs Marketing Board / Taunton Meat Haulage Ltd. and Fransen Transport N.V., [1977] 1 W.L.R. 625; [1977] 3 All E.R. 641; [1977] 1, *Lloyd's Rep.*, 346; [1977] R.T.R. 475; (1977) 121 S.J. 169; QB 11 October 1984, Elektronska Industrija Oour Tva and another t. Transped Oour Kintinentalna Spedicna e.a., *Lloyd's Rep.* 1986, 49; QB 29 June 1990 Texas Instruments Ltd / Nason (Europe) Ltd., [1991] 1, *Lloyd's Rep.*, 146.

17 See for other cases where a wide variety of elements is taken into account: Rb. Amsterdam 23 April 2008, Kangus/Aerocar, [2010] S&S 43; Den Bosch 19 June 2000, [2001] S&S, 34; Rb. Rotterdam 14 April 2004, [2005] S&S103 (in this case no less than 9 elements were taken into account); Rb. Rotterdam 28 September 2011, Hydrospex Cylap / Tracotex, [2012] S&S,70. See also SDC New York 18 January 1980, Zima Corporation and Schweiter Corporation, Plaintiffs / M. V. Roman Pazinski, her boilers, etc., Polish Ocean Lines and Panalpina Welttransport Gmbh. Hamburg, 493 F. Supp. 268, 1980 A. M. C. 155.

18 KB 21 June 1920, Jones / European and General express [1920] 4, *Lloyd's Rep.*, 127.

19 See for example: Hof s Gravenhage 24 March 2009 [2010] S&S 18 ("*Een blik op de onderhavige opdracht leert evenwel dat het om een transportopdracht gaat. Zo luidt althans het opschrift, terwijl het daaronder verder gaat met het verzoek: 'gelieve voor ons te vervoeren' en daaraan gekoppeld de CMR-instructie. Dit duidt op een opdracht, respectievelijk verzoek tot vervoer en niet op één tot een doen vervoeren.*" And further "*... dat zegt de rechtsverhouding tussen partijen te regeren voor de gehele duur van het vervoer en dat Basamro aanwijst als 'transport company' en bijvoorbeeld niet als 'forwarder'.*").

to those wordings.[20] Particularly, the courts seem to be rather reluctant to rely on the contractual qualification if the wordings indicate a qualification as freight forwarder. The underlying reason for this is that first of all, these wordings are often multi-interpretable[21] and secondly, adding a decisive weight to these factors would create an incentive for evasion of the mandatory carriage law by including qualification clauses.[22] Exception to this limited role exists in France, where a more substantial role is given to those wordings because the line between carrier and *commissionnaire de transport* is so thin that sometimes only these wordings can be taken into account.[23]

### 2.1.3. Applying accessorium sequitur principale adds on to the uncertainty

**11.** Even though the performance of the contact is an element that is taken into account as an element pro qualification as a carrier, not all stretches of transport are taken into

[20] Cass. 3 January 1997, *Unilin N.V. v. Eagle N.V.* [1997] Arr.Cass. 8; [1997] Bull. 9; [1998] ETL, 820; [1997] Pas. I- 9; (1998–99) RW 681 (*"de feitenrechter de juridische aard van een overeenkomst kan bepalen op grond van de hem regelmatig voorgelegde gegevens binnen en buiten die overeenkomst, mits hij de bewijskracht hiervan niet miskent en geen bewijs aanneemt buiten en boven de inhoud van de akte in de gevallen waarin de wet zulks niet toelaat; Dat hij hierbij de gemeenschappelijke bedoeling van de contracterende partijen nagaat"*); Simone Lamont-Black, *Goods in transit and freight forwarding* ( Sweet and Maxwell, 2010) 11.

[21] QB 12 October 1979 (1984) ETL 411 (Parties agreed on "*to arrange carriage*", however, QB argues that: "*I think one has to be very careful not to attribute too much to a rather vague word such as 'arrange' used by a businessman in this context (...) I do not attach very much importance to it.*"). OLG München 12 April 1990 (1991) NJW-RR 230 ( "*Bei objektiver Auslegung der Erklärungen der Parteien gem. den §§BGB §133, BGB §157 BGB kann der Abschluß eines Speditionsvertrages auch nicht auf die Verwendung des Formulars mit der Aufschrift 'Versand-Auftrag' gestützt werden, denn sowohl der Begriff 'Auftrag' als auch der Begriff 'Versendung' ist mehrdeutig.*"); Hof 's Hertogenbosch 10 December 2002 [2004] S&S 95 ("laadopdracht" doesn't necessarily indicate a carriage contract); Kh. Brussel 23 November 1983 (1984) TBH 316 ("*weiterzuleiten*" doens't necessarily exclude a qualification as carriage contract); hof 's Hertogenbosch 8 June 2004 [2005] S&S 23; (2004) NJ 692 ("*Het hof stelt voorop, dat aan de taalkundige betekenis van de in de overeenkomst gebezigde woorden – of dat nu in het Nederlands, Engels of Duits is – geen doorslaggevende betekenis kan worden toegekend aangezien de termen vervoer(der) en expeditie/expediteur vaak willekeurig door elkaar worden gebruikt.*"); Rb. Rotterdam 26 January 2005 [2007] *S&S* 12.

[22] Frans Ponet, "Hoedanigheid commissionair-expediteur – commissionair-vervoerder" (1984) TBH 697 ("*Steeds opnieuw wordt door diegene die de kontraktuele wederpartij is van de goederenbelanghebbende i.v.m. een kontrakt van goederenvervoer en die zelf het vervoer niet verrichtte doch het in onderaanneming aan een effektief transporteur uitbesteedt, voorgehouden dat hij optreedt in de hoedanigheid van commissionair-verzender en niet van commissionair-vervoerder.*"); Jacques Libouton, "Le commissionnaire-expéditeur: un phénix?" in *Hommage à Jacques Heenen* (Bruylant 1994) 251, 254 ("*Il est certes parfaitement possible à celui qui veut bénéficier du statut de commissionnaire-expéditeur de le spécifier lors de la conclusion du contrat avec son commettant ou lors de la réception des instructions, souvent peu formalistes, du donneur d'ordre mais la vie des affaires n' incite guère les professionnels pour des raisons commerciales ou psychologiques évidentes, à refroidir la confiance du donneur d'ordre en soulignant à son intention que ses instructions ne acceptées et ne seront executes que comme un mandataire sans représentation*").

[23] Delphine Bazin-Beust and Jocelyne Vallansan, "Commission de transport", *J.Cl.Trans.*, Fasc. 612, nr. 22–23; Cass. fr. 2 February 1988, (1988) BT 490; C. Paulin, "Réflexions sur la distinction entre contrat de transport et contrat de commission de transport", in *études sur le droit de la concurrence et quelques thèmes fondamentaux, mélanges en l'honneur d'Yves Serra* (Dalloz, 2006) 325, 336. (According to Paulin the carrier and the *commissionnaire de transport* are "*des notions identiques mais engendrant des régimes différents*").

account in this way. in such cases the principle *accessorium sequitur principale* is applied.[24] This means that insofar the carriage is accessory to the freight forwarding activities, the service provider will remain liable as freight forwarder for the entire contract. Applying this principle widens even more the discretionary power of individual judges: even if a predominant weight is adhered to the material performance of the carriage (see next title), then still individual judges can refuse to adhere such weight to a specific stretch of carriage, due to the accessory nature of it. The possible application of this principle further adds on to uncertainty. This is evidenced by some examples from Belgian case law where application of this principle sought.

12. This case law clearly evidences that the length of the accessory transportation cannot be upheld as a relevant parameter. The qualification as forwarder was not only upheld in case of an accessory transportation from Brussels to Ternat (16.9 km)[25], but also from Zaventem to Houthalen (82.9 km)[26] and even from Antwerpen to Kaulille.[27] On the other hand in another case the accessory character was not upheld in case of a transport from Zaventem to Brussels (12.5 km).[28]

### 2.2. *Predominant weight specific elements and different division burden of proof create diverging qualifications*

13. As in most countries no decisive role comes to the wordings of the contract, the negative impact of the wide discretionary power can only erode if praetorian or legislative rules come into existence that create a hierarchy between the different parameters. In some countries indeed it has become stare case law that a bigger weight is to be attributed to specific elements. Especially in France, praetorian rules have been developed on this point. In other countries, such as Germany and Holland, the legislator intervened and developed rules holding the forwarder liable as a carrier. In these situations, in fact the role of all other elements is disregarded, as the presence of this one element is sufficient to trigger carrier liability. Finally, in all countries but France, case law developed rules on the division of the burden of proof, creating a soft information duty for the forwarder.

24 See for example: Antwerp 20 October 2003, (2005) RHA 111 ("*zelfs in de veronderstelling dat appelante was gelast met de overbrenging van de goederen van Merksem naar kaai 242 in de haven van Antwerpen, dient te worden aangenomen... dat deze overbrenging een accessorium uitmaakt van de hoofdverbintenis, nl. een expeditieopdracht en dat deze bijkomende werkzaamheid geen afzonderlijke overeenkomst uitmaakt.*").

25 Brussel 7 December 1977, (1978) RGAR nr. 9952.

26 Kh. Brussels 8 March 1989, RG 7324, not published, in J. Libouton, "Le commissionnaire-expéditeur: un phénix?" in *Hommage à Jacques Heenen* (Bruylant, 1994), (251) 261. In Appeal the court found that in this case the transportation was not accessory to the carriage (Brussel 26 juni 1991, AR 1907/89, not published., in J. Libouton, "Le commissionnaire-expéditeur: un phénix?" in *Hommage à Jacques Heenen (* Bruylant, 1994), (251) 261.

27 Antwerp 6 February 2012, 2011/AR/80, *not published.*

28 Kh. Brussel 3 October 1983, (1984) TBH 310.

**14.** The downside to these praetorian and legislative developments is that these developments didn't take place in a uniform way in different countries. Consequently, these developments increase the gap between the different national law interpretation standards. This is even true to such an extent that an identical argument might be taken into account to support a qualification as carrier in one country, while the same element is taken into account to support a qualification as forwarder in another country.

### 2.2.1. Dominant weight specific elements in case law

**15.** The important influence of case law on the lack of uniformity in forwarding law, is best illustrated by the position of the subcontracting carrier in French law.[29] In most jurisdictions only the actual performance of the transport by the transport operator is taken into account as an argument pro qualification as a carrier. The lack of performance of the carriage is not taken into account as a relevant element pro qualification as a freight forwarder due to the fact that a carrier can also undertake to carry but subcontract the carriage. Even all international conventions for this reason assimilate the subcontracting carrier with the performing carrier.[30] In France however, even though the right of the carrier to subcontract is accepted likewise, still the non-performance of the carriage is taken into account as an important factor contra a qualification as carrier and pro a qualification as *commissionnaire de transport*.[31] Over the years the weight of this element lost some importance, as first the duty to give notice of the *possibility* to subcontract was introduced and second in case the qualification as carrier was contractually agreed upon, this qualification was upheld in case the carriage was subcontracted.[32] However, the introduction of the *code des transport* strengthens the role of the non-performance of the contract in the qualification question again (see next title).

**16.** Apart from this difference on the point of the subcontracting of the carriage, there are also two other points where French case law differs from the case law in other countries: both the consolidation[33] of the cargo and a lump sum compensation are

29 See the sources referred to in footnote 31.

30 See Article 3 CMR; Article 40 COTIF-CIM '99; Article 17 CMNI and Article 4 2) q) HV.

31 See for examples where this principle was applied: Cass. fr. 17 November 1965, n 61–10. 968 (1966) BT 38. Cass. fr. 22 January 2002, n° 98–18. 975; Cass. fr. 5 februari 2002, n° 00–12. 045; Paris, 28 March 1977 (1977) BT 348; Parijs 22 juni 1978, *BT* 1978, 484; Parijs 4 December 1978, *BT* 1979, 20; Colmar 10 September 1982, (1982) BT, 538; Aix-en-Provence13 January 2004, n 00/07876., *Lamyline*. See also Laurent Guignard, *Sous-traitance et transport* (Litec, 2001) 444; Delphine Bazin-Beust and Jocelyne Vallansan, "Commission de transport", *J. Cl. Trans.*, Fasc. 612, n°. 23; Philippe Delbecque, Cass. 8 november 2004, *RTD Com*, 2005, 871 (note).

32 A first condition that was introduced was the duty to give notice of the *possibility* to subcontract, a second evolution was that in case the qualification as carrier was contractually agreed upon, this qualification was upheld in case the carriage was subcontracted (See eg Paris, 27 January 1986, no K. 14841, *Lamyline* (this contractual qualification was here even derived from the clause "*camion direct Istanbul*"); Bernadette Kerguelen-Neyrolles, *Lamy transport tome 2, commission de transport, mer, fer, air, commerce extérieur* (Lamy, 2013) 7.

33 Delphine Bazin-Beust and Jocelyne Vallansan, "Commission de transport", *J.Cl.Trans.*, Fasc. 612, 14–15.

considered as elements pro qualification as a *commissionnaire*. However, these elements[34] are referred to in other countries to support a qualification as a carrier.[35] In spite of the fact that the weight given to these elements is not substantial,[36] still the difference is relevant for some contracts such as the growing market of parcel distribution contracts.

### 2.2.2. Legislative development: liability as carrier

**17.** In some countries legislative interventions have adhered a specific importance to some of the parameters that are also taken into account in other countries. This is done by imposing the carrier's or *commissionare de transport*'s liability on the service provider if the specific parameter is present in the contract. Mainly in German law, there are several separate grounds that impose the liability as a carrier. That is the actual performance of the carriage (*Selbsteintritt*), which is also a ground for liability as carrier in the Netherlands,[37] the billing of a lump sum compensation (*Fixkostenspedition*)[38] and the consolidation of cargo (*Sammelladungsspedition*).[39]

34 See for Belgium: Antwerpen 19 December 1990 (1992) RHA 39; Gent 7 October 1993, (1994) ETL 207; Gent 5 November 2003 (2006–07) RW 177; Gent 5 January 2004 (2005) TBH 528; Gent 6 September 2004 (2005) DAOR 113; for the Netherlands: Hof 's Hertogenbosch 10 December 2002 [2004] S&S 95; Den Bosch 8 June 2004 [2005] S&S 23; Rb. Rotterdam 17 January 2007, *LJN* AZ 8549; Rb. 's Hertogenbosch 30 December 2009 [2010] S&S 103; Krijn Haak and Richard Zwitser, *Opdracht aan hulppersonen over logistieke dienstverlening in het vervoer* (Kluwer, 2003) 462. See for *UK*: KB 5 Oktober 1921 *Colley v. Brewer's wharf & Transport*, [1921] *Lloyd's Rep* 5; QB 17 November 1993 *Aqualon (UK) Ltd v. Vallana Shipping* Corp [1994] 1 *Lloyd's Rep.* 669; QB 12 Oktober 1979 (1984) ETL 411.

35 See with regards to cargo consolidation: for Germany:§460 HGB; Hanno Merkt, "§460 Sammelladung" in Klaus Hopt, Hanno Merkt, Markus Roth and Adolf Baumbach (eds.), *Handelsgesetzbuch: mit GmbH & Co., Handelsklauseln, Bank- und Börsenrecht, Transportrecht (ohne Seerecht)* (Beck, 2012) 1; A. Rinkler, "§460 Sammelladung" in C.T. Ebenroth, E. Boujong, D. Joost en L. Strohn (eds), *Handelsgesetzbuch* (2th ed., Beck, 2009); J. Ramberg, "Unification of the law of international freight forwarding", (1998) RDU 5, 8; see for Belgium: Kh. Brussel 23 November 1983 (1984) TBH 316.

36 See contra a decisive weight of the consolidation activities: Paris 17 May 1996 (1996) BTL 400; see however pro such role: Versailles 6 March 1997 (1997) BTL 668.

37 Hof Den Haag 18 July 1996 (1997) S&S 106; Maarten. H. Claringbould, "De aansprakelijkheid van de expediteur. Over 'vervoer of expeditie' en gewoonte" (2008) NTHR 55; Hanno Merkt, "§461 Haftung des Spediteurs" in in Klaus Hopt, Hanno Merkt, Markus Roth and Adolf Baumbach (eds.), *Handelsgesetzbuch: mit GmbH & Co., Handelsklauseln, Bank- und Börsenrecht, Transportrecht (ohne Seerecht)* (Beck, 2012) 2–4.

38 See Article 459 BGH; BGH 14 February 2008, I ZR 183/05 (2008) MDR 1168 ("*Die Fixkostenspedition unterfällt dem Geltungsbereich der CMR, unabhängig davon, ob dies in nationalen (unvereinheitlichten) Rechtsvorschriften ausdrücklich bestimmt ist oder auf nationalen Grundsätzen über die Behandlung gemischter Verträge beruht. Maßgeblich hierfür ist die gebotene autonome, vom ergänzend anwendbaren nationalen Recht losgelöste Auslegung der CMR*"); W. Bayer, "Die Haftung des Fixkostenspediteurs gegenüber dem Versender für Ladungsschäden bei Seetransport" (1985) VersR. 1110; P. Bydlinsk, "Spedition zu festen kosten" in B. Czerwenka and R. Herber (eds.), *Münchener Kommentar zum Handelsgesetzbuch: §§407–475h. Transportrecht* (2e ed., Beck, 2009) §459.

39 §460 HGB; Hanno Merkt, "§460 Sammelladung" in Klaus Hopt, Hanno Merkt, Markus Roth and Adolf Baumbach (eds), *Handelsgesetzbuch: mit GmbH & Co., Handelsklauseln, Bank- und Börsenrecht, Transportrecht (ohne Seerecht)* (Beck, 2012) 1.

**18.** Despite the fact that those elements can also play a role in other countries, for example billing a lump sum will in other countries mostly not be sufficient for a qualification as a carrier.[40] What is important here is that if a German court is seized in a case of *Fixkostenspedition*, it might accept jurisdiction based on article 31 CMR that applies because of the liability as a carrier of the *Fixkostenspediteur*, in spite of a jurisdiction clause referring to another country, regardless of the contract being governed by a law that does not contain a *fixkostenspedition*-concept.[41]

**19.** With regards to *Selbsteintritt*, it was mentioned above that in case of accessory transportation, judges can apply the principle *accessorium sequitur principale*. However, in Germany and Holland, the forwarder will anyway be held liable as a carrier for the stretches during which he performance the carriage, irrespective of the length of such stretch. Even for the period that the cargo is merely held in custody of the forwarder, without there being an actual carriage, he is liable as a carrier.[42] This adds on to the diverging qualifications. This is even more so because also in situations where the forwarder performs a substantial part of the carriage himself, he will only be held liable as a carrier for this stretch, while he will be held liable as a forwarder for the remainder of the contract.[43] In Belgium,[44] France[45] and the UK,[46] the service provider would in general be held liable as a carrier for the entire contract.

**20.** Contrary to the liability as a carrier in Germany and Holland, in France the Code des Transports installed the liability of the carrier as *commissionnaire de transport*. The road carrier is liable as *commissionnaire* in case he subcontracts the carriage.[47] While the lack of material performance of the carriage doesn't have any weight in other countries, in France the lack of material performance in itself is sufficient for the service provider to be liable as *commissionnaire*.

40 See explicit: MvT en bijlage bij de vaststelling van boek 8, eerste stuk van het nieuw Burgerlijk Wetboek, met uitzondering van de afdelingen 1 en 3 van titel 4, afdeling 3 van titel 5, de afdelingen 1 en 3 van titel 9 en de afdelingen 3 en 4 van titel 10, Tweede Kamer, 1975–76, 14049, 3–4, 30–31; Parl. Gesch. Boek 8, p. 113.

41 BGH, 14 February 2008, Az. I ZR 183/05. Personally I don't agree with this, because this contract doesn't fall within the scope of CMR and the convention is here only applicable because of the reference by the German national law. I believe therefore, that Brussels I should have priority in such a case.

42 See for example Hanno Merkt, "§461 Haftung des Spediteurs" in Klaus Hopt, Hanno Merkt, Markus Roth and Adolf Baumbach (eds), *Handelsgesetzbuch: mit GmbH & Co., Handelsklauseln, Bank- und Börsenrecht, Transportrecht (ohne Seerecht)* (Beck, 2012), 2–4.

43 See for example in Holland: MvT, Kamerstukken II 1975–76, 14 049, no. 3–4, p. 31 ("*De expediteur wordt slechts als vervoerder beschouwd voor zover hij als zodanig optreedt. Vervoert hij slechts op een gedeelte van het vervoer of vervoert hij zelf slechts een gedeelte der goederen, dan is hij derhalve slechts over dat traject of voor die goederen als vervoerder aansprakelijk.*"); Parl. Gesch. Boek 8, blz. 114.

44 See the above mentioned case law, no. 11 and 12.

45 Cass. com. fr. 17 November 1965, (1966) *BT* 38.

46 KB 21 juni 1920, Jones / European and General express [1920] 4, *Loyd's Rep.*, 127.

47 L 3224–1CTF ("*Les responsabilités du transporteur routier qui recourt à la sous-traitance sont celles prévues par le Code de Commerce pour les commissionnaires*"); Bernadette Kerguelen-Neyrolles, *Lamy transport tome 2, commission de transport, mer, fer, air, commerce extérieur* ( Lamy, 2013) 11.

### 2.2.3. Praetorian presumption: qualification as carrier

21. Often it is impossible to assess the qualification of the contract, even when taking into account all possibly relevant elements. As a qualification as freight forwarder is in general more favourable, in most of the countries, case law applies the *contra proferentem* rule in case of uncertainty with regards to the qualification. Consequently the logistics service provider will be qualified as carrier.[48] However, such a presumption is not omnipresent. In French law the general rule *actori incumbit probatio* is applied. Here, if the cargo interest claims that the service provider contracted as a carrier, the burden of proof rests upon him.[49] Moreover, also in other countries, the way this rule is applied differs. In most cases the *contra proferentem rule* is applied only as to divide the burden of proof: the service provider is held liable as carrier, unless he establishes that he contracted as a freight forwarder.[50] In some cases, however, the lack of clear disclosure of the capacity of freight forwarder is considered sufficient to qualify a service provider as a

[48] See for example: Kh. Antwerpen 23 November 1983 (1984) TBH 316 ( "*dat geen stukken worden neergelegd waaruit blijkt dat Milchsack in tempore non suspecto aan haar medecontractant A.G. Ciba Geigy (Duitsland) te kennen gaf, uitsluitend als commissionair-expediteur te zullen optreden.*"); Brussel 11 Oktober 1990 (1992) RGAR 11962 ("*qui ne fait pas clairement savoir qu'il n'intervient que comme simle intermédiaire sans assurer auncune obligation de transport doit être considéré comme transporteur ou comme commissionnaire de transport*".); Hof Hertogenbosch 7 April 2009, *Van Aar v. Compagnie Europeene de Contruction Stone* [2011] S&S 35 ("*Indien een opdrachtnemer uitsluitend als expediteur wenst op te treden en niet als vervoerder, dient hij zich bij het aangaan van de overeenkomst duidelijk als expediteur aan zijn wederpartij te presenteren, bij gebreke waarvan er in beginsel van moet worden uitgegaan dat een vervoerovereenkomst tot stand is gekomen.*"); QB 17 November 1993 *Aqualon (UK) Ltd / Vallana Shipping Corp* [1994] 1, Lloyd's Rep., 669): ("*I would accept that it must be possible for a contractor to undertake an intermediate role ... This does not mean that such a role is either likely or lightly to be inferred. It represents an intermediate position between the responsibility of a carrier and an agent... I consider that it could not infrequently conflict with the expectations of a goodsowner consigning goods from one part of Europe to another. A finding that a contracting party was intended to fulfil an intermediate role of this nature would require in my view to be supported by evidence demonstrating clearly that this was the intention*").

[49] Cass. fr. 27 November 2007 (2008) *D.* 11 (In this case the service provider invoked the capacity of carrier, in order to enjoy limited liability.); Paris 15 December 2000, nr. 1999/24035 (2001) BTL 115; Chambéry 8 January 2002, nr. 2001/01514 (2002) BTL 307; Rouen 20 January 2005, nr. 03/02093 (2005) BTL 161; Laurent Guignard, *Sous-traitance et transport* (Litec, 2001) 447; Bernadette Kerguelen-Neyrolles (ed.), *Lamy transport*, t2 (Kluwer, 2012) 5–6; Xavier Delpech, "Transport: qualification du contrat, faute lourde du transporteur" 2008 D., 11, 12 ("*Dès lors que le demandeur invoque à son profit la qualité de transporteur, c'est à lui de prouver l'existence d'un contrat de transport, conformément à l'article 1315, alinéa 1er, du Code civil.*").

[50] See for example: Hof 's Hertogenbosch 7 April 2009, *Van Aar / Compagnie Europeene de Contruction Stone* [2011] *S&S* 2011, 35; Hof 's Hertogenbosch 10 December 2002 [2004] S&S 95 ("*Rooskens verwijst voorts naar de vrachtbrieven, die zij na belading naar LVC stuurde en waarop zij niet als afzender zou zijn vermeld. Deze vrachtbrieven zijn echter niet in het geding gebracht. Anders dan Rooskens stelt is het hof van oordeel dat het op haar weg had gelegen, nu zij zich er op beroept als expediteur te hebben gecontracteerd, de vrachtbrieven over te leggen.*"); Liege 17 March 2005, 2004RG647 ("*Il faut rappeler qu'en cas d'imprécision quant à l'étendue exacte de la mission impartie, la personne chargée d'un transport doit être qualifiée de transporteur.*").

carrier.[51] Because of the vague terms of many contracts, the question whether the *contra proferentem* rule will be applied and to what extent, can greatly influence the qualification of the contract and thus the applicability of CMR.

### 2.2.4. Conclusion

22. The main difference between the countries with a freight forwarder-figure, lies in the fact that in Germany and Holland in some situations the forwarder will be held liable as a carrier, even if the overall picture doesn't support a qualification as carrier. However, the difference between freight forwarding-countries and France is much bigger: first, a bigger weight is attached to party qualifications, secondly several points that support a qualification as *commissionnaire de transport*, would in other countries be considered as neutral elements (for example lack of material performance of the carriage) or even support a qualification as carrier (groupage and lump sum compensation). Moreover, the division of the burden of proof in French law makes a qualification as *commissionnaire de transport* likely in case of uncertainty, while the application of the *contra proferentem rule* in other countries would in this case rather give rise to a qualification as carrier.

## III. Can the Harmonisation Instruments Eliminate Different Interpretations of the Same Contract?

23. In the previous chapter, four causes of the lack of uniformity were identified: 1) the wide catalogue of parameters that are taken into account to qualify the contract, leaving the judge with a wide discretionary power, 2) the lack of strict hierarchy between the different parameters and the often very limited role of the wording of the contract, 3) the different weight that is attributed to specific elements and 4) the lack of uniform rules on the division of the burden of proof. Even though the harmonisation instruments install uniform interpretation rules, the harmonisation instruments will not be able to succeed in harmonising case law: the rules of the harmonisation instruments to a large extent merely confirm today's practise and anyway leave the judge with such a wide margin of discretion as to allow him to continue today's practise. In fact the only point where harmonisation instruments can contribute to a harmonisation, is on the point of the division of the burden of proof. The harmonisation instruments all incorporate the *contra proferentem* rule, consequently on this point the distinction between France and the other countries could disappear.

### 3.1.1. Wide catalogue with open rules inappropriate for unification of case law

24. Even though the wording of the contract is definitely relevant for the qualification of the contract, none of the harmonisation instruments adheres a decisive weight to this wording. Just like it is held today in case law, he literal meaning of the wordings is not

51 Brussel 11 October 1990 (1992) *RGAR* 11962.

decisive[52] and that the wording has to be interpreted taking into account the relevant context.[53]

25. All harmonisation instruments contain a catalogue that enumerates elements from the broader context that can be taken into account. Even though such list is missing in national legislation, this list codifies the elements that are today taken into account in national case law. DCFR refers among others to the circumstances in which it was concluded;[54] the conduct of the parties, even subsequent to the conclusion of the contract,[55] the meaning commonly given to such terms or expressions in the branch of activity concerned and the usages.[56] As the scope of the context outlined as relevant in the different harmonisation instruments is similar to that of the context taken into account today, here no unification is to be expected. For third parties and assignees there could however be some improvement here: for example DCFR states that for them reference to the circumstances before and after the contract and prior interpretations may only be taken into account if this party, who in good faith relied on these terms, was aware of, or could reasonably be expected to be aware of, these circumstances.[57]

26. In addition to the fact that there is a wide catalogue, an additional problem is that for example article 8:102 DCFR merely gives an option to the judge to take these elements into account. As is illustrated in the previous footnotes, all of the parameters mentioned in DCFR are currently considered in some case law, but for all of these parameters there are also cases where judges refuse to attach such weight to this specific element. As article 8:102 DCFR clearly states that "regard *may* be had, in particular, to...", judges still possess of the same wide margin of discretion to decide whether they will take into

52 See for example: Article 8:101 (1) DCFR; Article 5:101 (1) PECL.

53 Article 8:105 DCFR; Article 4.4 UNIDROIT principles 2010 and Article 5:105 PECL.

54 See for example for this element in current case law: previous contracts: QB 11 oktober 1984, Elektronska Industrija Oour Tva and another t. Transped Oour Kintinentalna Spedicna e.a.,(1986) *Lloyd's Rep.* 49 (*"It is admitted in the present case that the defendants sometimes act as principal carriers and themselves perform activities in relation to goods."*); Rb. Rotterdam 23 February 2005, [2006] S&S 103; Rb. Rotterdam 10 November 1970, [1971]S&S, 61; Kh. Antwerpen 28 June 1971, (1971)RHA 162. See however: Hong Kong Hua Guang Industrial Co. t. Midway International Ltd. [2000] 2 HKC 348 (*"Obviously, a person who usually acts as a forwarding agent, pure and simple, can act as a carrier and vice-versa."*). Name: Liège 17 March 2005, 2004RG647 (*"L'appelante persiste à soutenir qu'aux termes du contrat verbal intervenu fin 1998 avec l'intimée son obligation était d'organiser le transport des marchandises litigieuses et non d'en assurer elle-même le transport... Elle fait état de ses informations publicitaires sur internet. Cependant, outre que celles-ci comportent aussi des activités de transporteur, elle n'établit pas que ses activités de commissaire-expéditeur existaient en 1998 et surtout qu'elles auraient une quelconque force contractuelle."*); CA Antwerpen 20 April 1983, (1983–84)RHA 264. See however: Rb. Rotterdam 10 November 2010, Basamro-Shipping / NMT Projects International, [2011]S&S and Rb. 's Hertogenbosch 30 December 2009, [2010]S&S 103.

55 The higher mentioned (lack of) material performance of the contract and cargo consolidation (groupage) that are considered by (part of) today's case law, qualify under this point.

56 See Article 8:102 (1) DCFR, Article 5:102 PECL and Article 4.3 UNIDROIT principles. See further on this DCFR-provision: Christian von Bar and Eric Clive (eds.), *Principles, definitions and model rules of European Private law, Draft Common Frame of Reference (DCFR) Full edition* (Sellier 2009) 561.

57 See Article 8:102 (2) DCFR.

account a specific element. Moreover, the words "In particular", indicate that this list is not exhaustive and that judges can still take into account other elements.

**27.** Finally a last shortcoming is that creating a uniform catalogue can anyway not be sufficient to create uniform interpretations in practise. By stating what parts of the context can be relevant, the harmonisation instruments don't state what qualification is supported by a specific element. For example, also if DCFR is contractually incorporated Belgian, German and French judges will just like today all take into account the fact that cargo was consolidated, as this element qualifies under Article 8:102 (I) (b) DCFR. However, even though they will take into account the same parameter, they can still support opposite qualifications/ impose a different liability regime by doing this.

### 3.1.2. *Accessorium sequitur principale* rule inappropriate to solve discrepancies

**28.** A second problem that was identified above, lies in the fact that the principle *accessorium sequitur principale* is not uniformly applied in the different countries. First of all, there is a wide discretionary margin for individual judges. Moreover, there is a strong difference between Belgian, French and UK case law, where this principle is applied, and the situation in Germany and Holland where the forwarder is held liable as a carrier for all stretches of transport and even for the periods during which the goods are held in custody by the forwarder. Again however, harmonisation instruments seem to be incapable in solving these divergences.

**29.** In for example the DCFR the rule on mixed contracts can be found in article II 1:107 DCFR. In general, in such situations the combination theory is to be applied. If however one part of a mixed contract is in fact so predominant that it would be unreasonable not to regard the contract as falling primarily within one category, the principle *accessorium sequitur principale* is to be applied. This rule still leaves the judge with the same discretionary power and can't solve the first mentioned problem.

**30.** Moreover, as *accessorium sequitur principale* should only be applied here insofar the application of any mandatory rules is not prevented by it. Consequently also for the discrepancy between Belgian, French and UK law on the one hand and German and Dutch law on the other hand, this can't bring any changes, as carrier liability applies mandatorily in such situations.

### 3.1.3. *Contra proferentem* rule can avoid some discrepancies

**31.** When it comes to the burden of proof, the harmonisation instruments do contribute to uniformity. All mentioned instruments provide that in case of doubt with regards to the meaning of a term, the interpretation against the party that provided this term or that had a dominant influence in establishing this term is to be preferred.[58] Consequently,

[58] See Article 8:103 DCFR, Article 5:103 PECL; and Article 4.6 UNIDROIT principles 2010.

as the general conditions of the logistic service provider are often applicable, in case of doubt these provisions have to be interpreted against the logistic service provider. However, again a great margin of discretion is left to the judge. Not only will the judge have to take the factual decision whether there is any ambiguity, but moreover the harmonisation instruments don't oblige him to apply the *contra proferentem* rule if there is such ambiguity. For example Article 8:103 DCFR merely states that this interpretation "*is to be preferred*" in such a case.[59] In countries where currently the *contra proferentem* rule is applied (the freight forwarder countries) it is to be expected that courts will also do so if for example DCFR is contractually incorporated. The question is however, whether this formulation is strong enough to take a French judge away from applying the traditional rule *actori incumbit probation.*

### 3.1.4. Technical hindrance to substantial role harmonisation instruments

32. Also on the points where the harmonisation instruments could play a role in harmonising forwarding law, there is a Technical hindrance that stands in the way to a great role for the harmonisation instruments on the present day. In order for the harmonisation instruments to be a practical solution today, it is required that they are contractually incorporated in the contract. However, as a primary choice of law for soft law is not governed by Rome I,[60] this choice for the harmonisation instruments can only be made as a secondary choice of law,[61] insofar as the rules of the harmonisation instruments don't conflict with the national law rules of a mandatory nature. To a large extend forwarding law is only supplementary law and here the lack of a primary choice of law for harmonisation instruments is no obstacle. However, on two points this can constitute an obstacle.

33. First of all, courts might still find that a specific contract, that should according to the rules of such harmonisation instrument be qualified as a forwarding contract, should fall within the scope of one of the carriage conventions and that parties in fact try to

59 In the comments it is explicitly stated that this is only a preference. (Christian von Bar and Eric Clive (eds.), *Principles, definitions and model rules of European Private law, Draft Common Frame of Reference (DCFR) Full edition* (Sellier 2009), 565). See also article 4.6 UNIDROIT principles 2010. Here, the comment (art 4.6 UNIDROIT principles 2010, 144) gives some clarification on the meaning of "preferred": *("...if contract terms supplied by one party are unclear, there is a preference for their interpretation against that party. The extend to which this rule applies will depend on the circumstances of the case; the less the contract term in question was the subject of further negotiations between the parties, the greater the justification for interpreting it against the party who included it in the contract.").* See on *contra proferentem* in the sense of Article 3 (2) DCFR, meaning in contracts that were individually negotiated: Olaf Munthorst, "Contract interpretation under the German BGB and under the DCFR", in Bettina Heiderhoff and Grzegorz Zmij (eds.), *Interpretation in Polish, German and European Private law* (Sellier 2011), 55.

60 See for example: Paul Lagarde en Andrew Tenenbaum, "De la convention de Rome au règlement Rome I", (2008) RCDIP 727, n° 9.

61 See for the difference between a primary and a secondary choice of law: Luc Strikwerda, *de overeenkomst in het IPR,* 3th ed. (Maklu 2010) 111.

evade mandatory carriage law. In such case, courts could still qualify the contract as a carriage contract and thus apply carriage law.[62]

**34.** A second problem is that in situations where the forwarder is held liable as a carrier in German or Dutch law, this carrier liability mandatorily applies.[63] Therefore, uniformity could only result from a contractual incorporation of the harmonisation instruments, insofar as the chosen instrument is on the relevant points identical to this German regime.

## IV. Conclusion: Harmonisation Instruments cannot Eliminate Different Interpretations of the Same Contract

**35.** Even though the harmonisation instruments contain uniform interpretation rules, still they cannot induce a unification in practise. It is even questionable whether unification of general private law can achieve the goal of uniform interpretation in practise.

**36.** First of all, except if only a very narrow context is taken into account (just like in English law before case *Investors Compensation Scheme v. West Bromwich Building Society*[64]), in order to create uniform interpretations in practise, specific guidance is to be given not only with regard to the elements that are to be taken into account, but also with regards to the qualification they are to support.

**37.** Secondly, contract interpretation depends strongly on the factual circumstances of the specific case. Therefore an open catalogue, again can't create uniformity,[65] as

62 Article 12, 2 Code de Procédure Civile (Fr.); Cass.Be. 14 April 2005, AR C.03.0148.F, www.cass.be; Cass. 16 march 2006, AR C.04.0267.N,; Paul Bugden and Simone Lamont-Black, *Goods in transit and freight forwarding*, London, Sweet and Maxwell, 2010, 9.

63 Hanno Merkt, "§458 Selbsteintritt" in in Klaus Hopt, Hanno Merkt, Markus Roth and Adolf Baumbach (eds), *Handelsgesetzbuch: mit GmbH & Co., Handelsklauseln, Bank- und Börsenrecht, Transportrecht (ohne Seerecht)* (Beck, 2012), 1 (*"Nach §§458–460 hat der Spediteur in drei für den Versender besonders kritischen Fällen von Gesetzes wegen die Rechte und Pflichten eines Frachtführers oder Verfrachters: bei Selbsteintritt, bei Fixkostenspedition und bei Sammelladung. Mit dieser Regelung bezweckt der Gesetzgeber, dass sich der Spediteur nicht den kundenschützenden Vorschriften des Frachtrechts entziehen kann."*). For case law, see for example:. BGH 21 November 1975, I ZR 74/75, (65) BGHZ 340; (1976 ) NJW 433; BGH 24 June 1987, I ZR 127/85, (101) BGHZ 172; (1988) NJW 640; (1987) *TranspR.* 447; BGH 6 February 1997, I ZR 202/94, (1997) *TranspR* 335; BGH 20 January 2005, I ZR 95/01, (2005) *TranspR* 311; BGH 14 February 2008, I ZR 183/05.

64 L.J. Hofmann in "Investors Compensation Scheme t. West Bromwich Building Society", [1997]UKHL 28; 1 *All ER* 1998, 98; [1998]1 *WLR* 896. According to Robert Hardy ("the DCFR rules on contract interpretation: efficient defaults?", in Vincent Sagaert, Matthias Storme and Evelyne Terryn (eds.), *The draft common frame of reference: national and comparative perspectives* ( Intersentia 2012), 203, 215) a more textualist approach would also have been more suitable for an instrument such as DCFR.

65 See with the same critique: Robert Hardy ("the DCFR rules on contract interpretation: efficient defaults?", in Vincent Sagaert, Matthias Storme and Evelyne Terryn (eds.), *The draft common frame of reference: national and comparative perspectives* ( Intersentia 2012), 203, 215–216.

different judges might estimate other elements higher. Even with uniform rules that indicate the qualification that is to be supported by this specific element, this problem will not necessarily cease to exist.

**38.** The same is true for the *accessorium sequitur principale rule,* as individual judges can still appreciate whether a specific stretch of transportation is accessory to the forwarding activities.

**39.** Therefore, in order to create real uniformity, a system like the German system seems to be the only real way to achieve uniformity: if the presence of a specific characteristic automatically leads to qualification (or liability) A or B, this process is predictable and judges in different states will be able to apply the same liability rules by just *observing* the case, without having to engage in *interpretation.* This was exactly what the UNIDROIT draft convention envisaged. According to this draft convention, just like in current German law, the freight forwarder is to be held liable as a carrier if he bills a lump sum compensation (Article 23 Draft Convention) and when cargo is consolidated (Article 24 Draft Convention). In addition, the freight forwarder is held liable as carrier if he issues an "international forwarding note" (Article 25 Draft Convention). Thus, instead of a choice for the harmonisation instruments, a contractual incorporation of the draft convention seems advisable.

**40.** A second problem is that the harmonisation instruments can only be a practical solution today insofar there are no mandatory rules in national legislations that deviate from these principles. As a primary choice of law for soft law is not governed by Rome I, such choice can only be made as a secondary choice of law, that is insofar national law allows for such reference., However, for example the liability as a carrier in Dutch or German law is mandatory. On this point a contractual incorporation of the draft convention faces the same problems as an incorporation of one of the harmonisation instruments. Even though it hasn't been proven successful before, the only way to uniformity therefore seems to go through a convention for transport intermediaries.[66]

[66] Ramberg is not very much in favour of this and advocates self regulation (Jan Ramberg, "Unification of the law of international freight forwarding", (1998) RDU 5, 14).

Simone
Lamont-Black

# COULD THE DCFR CHANGE SHIPPING LAW? THE POTENTIAL IMPACT OF THE DCFR ON THIRD PARTY RIGHTS UNDER SHIPPING DOCUMENTS – A UK PERSPECTIVE*

## I. Introduction

1. Could the Draft Common Frame of Reference (DCFR)[1] change shipping law? Although only soft law at present, what would be the impact of implementing its rules on third party rights under transport documents in the laws of EU Member States? Would this result in a true change in UK shipping law regarding third party rights? After setting out the UK framework, this chapter will discuss the DCFR rules and compare and contrast them with the current provisions in the UK. As will be shown, the situation in the UK is far from straightforward. Analysing the impact of the DCFR rules against this framework, it will be argued that implementation of the DCFR third party rules throughout, including the whole of shipping and transport law, would have potential for welcome simplification.

2. It is generally accepted that a bill of lading in the appropriate form is able to function as a document of title and that the holder of the bill of lading can claim delivery of the goods enshrined therein from the carrier.[2] How the third party obtains this right to

* Dr. Simone Lamont-Black, Assessorin (iur.) (= 1st and 2nd State Examination in Law in Germany), Dr (iur.), Lecturer in International Trade Law at the University of Edinburgh. This chapter is based on a conference paper presented at the 8th European Colloquium on Maritime Law Research on the conference theme "Common core, PECL and DCFR: Could they change shipping law?". My gratitude goes to my colleagues at the 8th ECLMR conference of September 2014 for their feedback and to Ms Kathryn Hunt, Morton Fraser LLP, for her comments. Any mistakes that may still have found their way into the work are obviously my own.

1 C. Von Bar and E. Clive (eds), *Principles, Definitions and Model Rules of European Private Law: Draft Common Frame of Reference (DCFR)* (Sellier, European Law Publishers, 2010).

2 See *Scrutton on Charterparties and Bills of Lading* (22nd edn, Sweet & Maxwell, 2011) (hereafter Scrutton), chs 2 & 10 esp. paras 2-008 and 10-001 & 10-005; Girvin, *Carriage of Goods by Sea* (2nd edn, Oxford University Press, 2011) (hereafter Girvin), ch 8; G. Treitel and F. Reynolds, *Carver on Bills of Lading* (3rd edn, Sweet & Maxwell, 2011) (hereafter Carver), chs 5 & 6; F Stevens, "Third Party Rights under Bills of Lading", [2012] EJCCL 54, 56 and see also F. Smeele, "The bill of lading contracts under European national laws (civil law approaches to explaining the legal position of the consignee under bills of lading)" in Thomas, *The Evolving Law and Practice of Voyage Charterparties* (Informa, 2009) 251, 253.

delivery has been explained in different ways by different legal systems. Many theories seem to point to a contractual solution, even if there are also some approaches which are non-contractual, mainly the statutory solution in the UK or views that the holder's position should be categorised as *sui generis.*[3]

**3.** Continental Europe seems to generally favour the contractual approach and see the contract of carriage as a contract for the benefit of a third party or as a three-party contract.[4] This seems to be confirmed by the stipulations in favour of the third party consignee in transport conventions which were heavily influenced by continental thinking,[5] such as the CMR,[6] COTIF-CIM[7] and the CMNI,[8] but also the Warsaw and Montreal Conventions.[9] The Principles of European Contract Law (PECL)[10] and the DCFR also seem to understand in the transport conventions a specific codification of the general third party rule.[11]

3 See F. Stevens, "Third Party Rights under Bills of Lading", [2012] EJCCL 54, listing the UK Carriage of Goods by See Act 1992 (hereafter CoGSA 1992) and some Belgian case-law as examples of the non-contractual category and concluding in agreement with DeWitt in favour of a *sui generis* classification.

4 See Law Commission, *Privity of Contract: Contract for the Benefit of Third Parties* (Law Com No LC242, 1996), para 3.8 and F. Smeele, "The bill of lading contracts", op cit, at p 251 et seq. with reference to The Netherlands and Germany, by the doctrine of a contract in favour of third parties ("Derdenbeding" or "*Vertrag zugunsten Dritter*" respectively) and in France as a three-party contract (*contrat à trois personnes*); and more generally M. Sturley, T. Fujita, J. Van Der Ziel, *The Rotterdam Rules, The UN Convention on Contracts for the International Carriage of Goods wholly or Partly by Sea*, (Sweet & Maxwell, London 2010) (hereafter Sturley et al) at para 10.002 and see O. Lando and H. Beale (eds), *Principles of European Contract Law, Part I: Performance, Non-performance and Remedies, Combined and Revise* (Kluwer Law International, 2000), Art 6:110 and Notes.

5 F. Smeele, "The bill of lading contracts", op cit, at 258.

6 The United Nations Convention on International Carriage of Goods by Road 1956 (CMR); see CMR, art 13.

7 CIM stands for Uniform Rules Concerning the Contract of International Carriage of Goods by Rail, being Appendix B to the Convention concerning International Carriage by Rail 1980 in the version of the Protocol of Modification of June 3, 1999 (COTIF); see CIM, art 17.

8 Budapest Convention on the Contract for the Carriage of Goods by Inland Waterways (CMNI) (2001), see CMNI, Articles 10, 13 & 14.

9 Convention for the Unification of Certain Rules Relating to International Carriage by Air (Warsaw) 1929 (WC) (and its versions as amended respectively by the Hague Protocol 1955, and/or the Additional Protocols agreed at Montreal in 1975, Nos 1, 2 and 4, and supplemented by the Guadalajara Convention 1961) and Convention for the Unification of Certain Rules for International Carriage by Air (Montreal) 1999 (MC); see WC, art 13 and MC, art 13.

10 O. Lando and H. Beale (eds), *Principles of European Contract Law, Parts I and II (Combined and Revised), prepared by the Commission of European Contract Law* (Kluwer Law International, 2000).

11 See DCFR Commentary to II.–9:301 at E and PECL Commentary to Article 6:110 H.

## II. The Fragmented Position in the UK

### 2.1. *The framework in the UK*

4. In the UK different rules on and approaches to the position of third parties[12] pertain depending on the type of contract and the legal system involved, that is, that of either England & Wales, Northern Ireland or Scotland. The core rule in the law of England & Wales was strict privity of contract, meaning that the contract was a relationship exclusive to the parties who made it and who, in turn, were the only ones able to enforce it. This principle was eroded bit-by-bit by case-law and statutory amendment, such as the former Bill of Lading Act 1855, replaced by the current Carriage of Goods by Sea Act 1992 (CoGSA 1992), but also by the much broader Contracts (Rights of Third Parties) Act 1999 (TPA 1999), the latter being only applicable in England & Wales and Northern Ireland. In contrast, Scotland, like most other European jurisdictions recognised rights of third parties in certain situations already for centuries. The principle, known as the "*jus quaesitum tertio*" was founded in case-law, on the basis that the privity rule yields to the even more fundamental principle of freedom of contract, thus taking account of the intention of the parties, who may contract to confer a benefit on a third party.

### 2.2. *Scottish reform discussions*

5. However, whilst the principle of *jus quaesitum tertio* is recognised, its details and boundaries are far from clear. The Scottish Law Commission emphasised the need for its modernisation: "much of the case-law is very old, and it is neither clear nor comprehensive. What may once have been satisfactory for resolving disputes is no longer suitable for today's citizens and business people, who rightly demand that contract law should be certain, robust and clear, yet also flexible."[13] For example, a major problem under Scots law is the requirement of irrevocability for the constitution of the right of the third party. Difficulties also arise in identifying the remedies available to the third party due to lack of clarity over the legal basis of the third party right. In particular, it is subject to doubt whether the third party has a right to claim damages, nor is it clear whether the third party can rely on a limitation or exclusion clause.[14]

12 I.e. contractual and statutory or *sui generis*.

13 Discussion Paper 157 – Review of Contract Law: Third Party Rights in Contract, News Release "Two's a Party; Three's a Crowd?" available at: www.scotlawcom.gov.uk/publications/discussion-papers-and-consultative-memoranda/2010-present/ (last accessed on 06.01.2015).

14 See Discussion Paper No. 157 of the Scottish Law Commission of March 2014: "Discussion Paper on Third Party Rights in Contract", available at www.scotlawcom.gov.uk/law-reform-projects/contract-law-in-light-of-the-draft-common-frame-of-reference-dcf/ (last accessed 06.01.2015) (Scot Law Com DP 157), paras 2.57 ff & 3.2, paras 2.82 f, and 2.84 ff. and L. Macgregor *Report on the Draft Common Frame of Reference: a report prepared for the Scottish Government by Laura Macgregor, University of Edinburgh, on the document known as 'Principles, Definitions and Model Rules on European Private Law'* (26/09/08), Appendix, 5.2.1.

6. A driving factor towards reform[15] is also the introduction of statutory third party rights in the laws of England & Wales for the first time.[16] The reform consideration preceding the English TPA 1999 also influenced the Scottish Law Commission's thinking. The Scottish Law Commission suggests close modelling on the principles developed by the DCFR,[17] by the UNIDROIT Principles of International Commercial Contracts (PICC)[18] and by the Proposal for a Regulation on a Common European Sales Law (CESL),[19] bearing in mind the TPA 1999 which was generally on the same lines.[20]

## 2.3. *Excluding shipping law?*

7. Similarly to the English 1999 Act, the Scottish reform discussions consider whether to only implement reform of the general rules and to leave unaffected the specific matters governed by statutory or common law rules which tended to be recognised for particular spheres of activity. These considerations were partly due to subject matter considerations and partly due to constitutional constraints.[21] The relevant specific statutory solutions for our purposes are the CoGSA 1992 and the implementations into UK law of the various road, rail and air transport conventions. Both the CoGSA 1992 and the Acts and statutoryinstrumentsimplementingtheCMR,COTIF-CIM,andtheWarsaw,Guadalajara[22]

15 See Scot Law Com DP 157, in particular see chapters (chs) 1, 9 and 10.

16 See the TPA 1999 of England & Wales and Northern Ireland, but see also other examples of codification of third party rights in common law jurisdictions such as the Contracts (Privity) Act 1982 of New Zealand, and the Contracts (Rights of Third Parties) Act 2001 of Singapore and the Draft Contracts (Rights of Third Parties) Bill 2013 of Hong Kong (see the Consultation Paper at www.doj.gov.hk/eng/public/pdf/2012/consulte.pdf (last accessed 06.01.2015). See also a further discussion of the developments of third party rights and the privity principle are set out in the Discussion Paper No. 157 of the Scottish Law Commission of March 2014: "Discussion Paper on Third Party Rights in Contract" at para. 1.15, available at www.scotlawcom.gov.uk/law-reform-projects/contract-law-in-light-of-the-draft-common-frame-of-reference-dcf/ (last accessed 06.01.2015) (Scot Law Com DP 157).

17 C. Von Bar and E. Clive (eds), *Principles, Definitions and Model Rules of European Private Law: Draft Common Frame of Reference (DCFR)* (Sellier, European Law Publishers, 2010), Model Rules II.-9:301 – II.-9:303.

18 UNIDROIT Principles of International Commercial Contracts (PICC) (3rd edn, 2010), Articles 5.2.1 – 5.2.6, available at: www.unidroit.org/english/principles/contracts/principles2010/integralversionprinciples2010-e.pdf (last accessed 06.01.2015).

19 Proposal for a Regulation on a Common European Sales Law (CESL), COM(2011) 635 final, Article. 78, available at: http://eur-lex.europa.eu/LexUriServ/LexUriServ.do?uri=COM:2011:0635:FIN:en:PDF (last accessed 06.01.2015).

20 Scot Law Com DP 157, paras 1.16 – 1.19.

21 See Scot Law Com DP 157, ch. 8 and see Scotland Act 1998, sections 28 & 29 and Sched 5 regarding the limited legislative competence of the Scottish Parliament.

22 The Convention Supplementary to the Warsaw Convention for the Unification of Certain Rules to International Carriage by Air Performed by a Person other than the Contracting Carrier (Guadalajara) 1961. It works in conjunction with the Warsaw Conventions insofar as the actual carrier is not the contractual one.

and Montreal Conventions are applicable throughout the whole of the UK, thus also binding Scotland.[23]

**8.** Already during the reform discussion preceding the 1999 Act, the (English) Law Commission decided to leave the existing provisions on carriage of goods[24] undisturbed, so as not to risk causing unacceptable commercial uncertainty by changing these rules and not to interfere with the different underlying policy considerations in this area since the regulation of carriage of goods was underpinned by a different legal model. Under the CoGSA 1992 a type of statutory assignment was effected maintaining a relationship between benefit and burden, by transferring rights but also effecting a corresponding burden on the third party. Under the 1992 Act, the transfer of the bill of lading led to the loss of the right in the hands of the initial party and only a limited type of third party may avail himself of rights under the contract. Commercial uncertainty was to be avoided by keeping to a system that worked, rather than reforming it in the interest of uniformity with general principles.[25] Similar considerations also applied to the exclusion of contracts for the carriage of goods by road, rail or air under international conventions, where rights and burdens were connected, only limited third parties were entitled to benefit from the 'transfer' and where at least in some of the conventions enforcement rights were only to be exercised by either the consignor or the consignee.[26]

**9.** The Scottish Law Commission also leaned towards leaving carriage of goods, amongst other specific matters, untouched. It noted that such an approach of codifying general rules while leaving specific rules intact would be in line with domestic linguistic canons of statutory interpretation, that the specific rule prevails over the general,[27] and would also echo a similar provision of both the DCFR and CESL.[28]

23 The CMR is given statutory force by the Carriage of Goods by Road Act 1965, COTIF-CIM by the Railways (Convention on International Carriage by Rail) Regulations 2005 (SI 2005/2092), made under s 103 of the Railways and Transport Safety Act 2003, and for carriage by air, the Warsaw Convention in its different versions according to the amending protocols, the Hague Protocol of 1955 and 1975 Montreal Protocols Nos 1,2 and 4, the 1961 Guadalajara and 1999 Montreal Conventions, applied in UK law via the Carriage by Air Act 1961, the Carriage by Air (Supplementary Provisions) Act 1962, the Carriage by Air Acts (Application of Provisions) Order 2004, SI 2004/1899, and see also European Union legislation on air carrier liability.

24 Equally, legislation on contracts contained in bills of exchange, promissory notes and other negotiable instruments was to remain unchanged. Further, any reform of the Third Parties (Rights against Insures) Act 1930 and, if at all, also of the Married Women's Property Act 1882 was to be done separately (Law Com No LC242, 1996, Part XII). The former reform has now been undertaken with the enactment of the Third Parties (Rights against Insurers) Act 2010.

25 Law Com No LC242, 1996, paras 12.7 – 12.11.

26 Law Com No LC242, 1996, paras 12.12 – 12.15.

27 See Scot Law Com DP 157, para. 8.8 with further references to O. Jones and F. A. R. Bennion, *Bennion on Statutory Interpretation*, ($6^{th}$ edn, Lexis Nexis, 2013), p.1038.

28 See both DCFR, I.-1:102(5) and CESL, Article 4(3): "Where there is a general rule and a specific rues applying to a particular situation within the scope of the general rule, the specific rule prevails in any case of conflict."

### 2.4. *The fragmented UK position under transport documents*

10. But is it really necessary to regulate third party rights in the carriage of goods separately and, in particular, to distinguish between the specified documents in carriage of goods by sea and other forms of carriage, domestic and international and apply different regimes? Since their boundaries are not always clear, the multiplicity of instruments with their different rules adds further complexity. Resulting is the following piecemeal situation as is applicable in the UK at present:

11. a) For **carriage of goods by sea using bills of lading, sea waybills or ship's delivery orders** the CoGSA 1992 applies to these specified documents, irrespective of whether the carriage is domestic or international.[29] However, while the 1992 Act makes provision for regulations to be made to enable the use of electronic documents and document transfer, this power has not yet been used, so that it seems that the Act does **not** cater for electronic bills of lading or waybills.[30]

12. b) For **carriage of goods by sea under other documents and domestic carriage of goods by land and air** the TPA 1999 applies in England & Wales and Northern Ireland, whereas in Scotland, the principle of *jus quaesitum tertio* (JQT) with its related case-law applies or alternatively any new legislation that may arise from the current reform discussions.

13. c) If, instead, **carriage is international carriage of goods by land or air and where the carriage falls within the application range of the relevant international transport convention**, such as the CMR, CIM or of the Montreal or one of the Warsaw Conventions in its relevant amendment, the pertinent transport convention as implemented into the law of the UK applies.

14. d) Yet where the **carriage falls outside of the land or air conventions' application range** the relevant domestic third party rules apply. For England & Wales and Northern Ireland, these are the TPA 1999[31] and for Scotland, the principle of *jus quaesitum tertio* or any new law that may be enacted. While the above domestic instruments allow a third party in appropriate circumstances to avail himself of an exclusion or

29 See CoGSA 1992, s1(1).

30 See CoGSA 1992, s1(5)-(6) and see P Bugden, S Lamont-Black, *Goods in Transit* (3rd edn, Sweet & Maxwell, 2013) (hereafter Bugden) para 5–017; Beale and Griffiths, "Electronic commerce: formal requirements in commercial transactions" [2002] LMCLQ 467, 477; M. Clarke, "Transport documents: their transferability as document of title; electronic documents" [2002] LMCLQ 356, 359 and more generally on electronic bills of lading, including their application under the Rotterdam Rules; See Gaskell, "Bills of Lading in an Electronic Age" [2010] LMCLQ 233, 269 ff.

31 See TPA 1999, s 6(5).

limitation of liability of a contract between others,[32] this is not free from doubt for Scots law.[33]

15. e) In case of **carriage of goods under multimodal transport documents** we have to distinguish whether the multimodal carriage includes sea carriage or not. In case sea carriage is included the question arises whether the CoGSA 1992 is applicable to such transport documents,[34] or whether otherwise the fall-back positions of the respective applicable domestic law, the TPA 1999 or the Scots law solution will apply, unless the damage is localised which may cause a unimodal transport convention to take priority.[35] Where the multimodal transport does not contain a sea-leg the choice is only between the relevant domestic law, the TPA 1999 or the Scots law solution, or a unimodal transport convention in case the damage is localised.

## *2.5. An artificial or necessary distinction?*

16. The discussion in the UK on the position of electronic bills of lading and whether multimodal bills of lading can fall within the CoGSA 1992, whereas road and rail consignment notes and airway bills are covered by the TPA 1999 (unless they are excluded from the 1999 Act due to their inclusion in international transport conventions) seems to reveal an artificial distinction between the different modes of transport and their documents, unless the difference can be adequately explained by the bill of lading's function of a document of title or by sea transport being so substantially different from other modes as to require different treatment in the dealings with third parties.

32 See TPA 1999, s 6(5) where this is explicitly set out for clarification. See also the relevant third party provisions enshrined in the transport conventions: CMR, Article 28.2; CIM, Article 41.2; MC, Article 43; and the Guadalajara Convention for air transport under the Warsaw Convention. For sea carriage see the International Convention for the Unification of Certain Rules of Law Relating to Bills of Lading signed at Brussels on 25th August 1924 as amended by the Protocol signed at Brussels on 23rd February 1968 (Hague-Visby Rules (HVR)), Article IVbis; the United Nations Convention on the Carriage of Goods by Sea, Hamburg, 1978 (Hamburg Rules (HambR)), Articles 7.2 and 10.2; the United Nations Convention on Contracts for the International Carriage of Goods Wholly or Partly by Sea, 2008, opened for signature at Rotterdam; not (yet) in force (Rotterdam Rules (RR)), Article 4; and for carriage by inland waterways the CMNI, Article 17.3.

33 L. Macgregor, *Report on the Draft Common Frame of Reference*, op cit, Appendix, 5.2.1.

34 For a discussion of third party rights under multimodal transport documents see S. Lamont-Black, "Third Party Rights and Multimodal Transport Documents" in F. Lorenzon, *Third Parties' Rights and Bills of Lading* (Informa, 2015, forthcoming); R. D. Thomas, "International Sale Contracts and Multimodal Transport Documents: Two Issues of Significance", in Soyer and Tettenborn (eds), *Carriage of Goods by Sea, Land and Air: Unimodal and Multimodal Transport in the 21st Century* (Informa Law, 2014), 145, 158; A Tettenborn, "Bills of Lading, Multimodal Transport Documents, and Other Things" in Soyer and Tettenborn (eds), op cit, 126, 138; and M. Ozdel "Multimodal Transport Documents in International Sale of Goods" [2012] ICCLR 238, 246–247; cf. Bridge, *Benjamin's Sale of Goods* (8th edn, Sweet & Maxwell, 2010), (hereafter *Benjamin),* para 21–083 and *Carver*, paras 8–084 – 8–092.

35 See *Quantum Corporation Inc v Plane Trucking* [2002] EWCA Civ 350, [2002] 1 WLR 2678, [2002] 2 Lloyd's Rep 25, where the CMR was held applicable to the road leg of a multimodal transport enshrined in a master air waybill.

**17.** This paper seeks to identify whether the DCFR rules on third parties rights would be appropriate to regulate the whole area of carriage irrespective of the mode and nature of the transport and the transport document used and, if so, which changes this would bring as regards to the current position in English law. While the areas outside sea carriage have already, with the enactment of the English TPA 1999[36] and any potential future Scottish Third Parties Act, been heavily influenced by the DCFR,[37] any changes effected by the DCFR would be limited unless the specific (sea) carriage rules would also be included in the amended regime.

**18.** While the DCFR was not intended, at least without further modification or supplementation, for matters of bills of exchange, cheques and promissory notes and other negotiable instruments[38] – and one may return to the discussion whether a bill of lading falls under the definition of other negotiable instruments[39] – the commentary explains that this is only meant as a warning, alerting to the fact that the rules were not developed with the listed matters in mind.[40] Thus, one does not need to limit the DCFR rules to an application on consignment notes alone, but is free to consider whether they are also apt to be applied to bills of lading.

**19.** If, after careful evaluation, it was still felt that third party rules on the carriage of goods (by sea) ought to be specialised and set apart from the general rule and that the third party bill of lading rules could not be classified satisfactorily as provisions for a conferral of rights on a third party but instead were *sui generis* or other, then it may indeed warrant a separate stipulation, which would yet have to be modelled under the DCFR.[41]

36 With reference to the then (1995) Principles of European Contract Law; see Law Commission, *Privity of Contract: Contract for the Benefit of Third Parties* (Law Com No LC242, 1996), para 3.8.

37 Since the start in PECL, Article 6:110 as forerunner, the DCFR has developed third party rights much more comprehensively the focus of the discussion will be on the latter.

38 I.-1:101(2) "They are not intended to be used, or used without modification or supplementation, in relation to rights and obligations of a public law nature or, except where otherwise provided, in relation to: …(d) bills of exchange, cheques and promissory notes and other negotiable instruments".

39 Which under English law it would not be (see Guest, *Benjamin's Sale of Goods* (8th edn, Sweet & Maxwell, 2010) at para 26-088 and Fawcett, Harris, Bridge, *International Sale of Goods in the Conflict of Laws* (OUP, 2005) at paras 14.03 et seq.), but see also Recital (9) of the Regulation (EC) No 593/2008 of the European Parliament and of the Council of 17 June 2008 on the law applicable to contractual obligations (Rome I): "Obligations under bills of exchange, cheques and promissory notes and other negotiable instruments should also cover bills of lading to the extent that the obligations under the bill of lading arise out of its negotiable character.".

40 Commentary to I.-1:101(2): "Paragraph (2) lists certain matters in relation to which the rules are not intended to be used, or used without modification or supplementation. Paragraph (2) does not mean that particular rules or concepts or terms could not be used in relation to the listed matters. The use to be made of the rules depends entirely on those using them. The paragraph just serves as a warning that the rules have not, except in a few places, been drafted with the listed matters in mind."

41 While the DCFR contains rules on the transfer of a (full) contractual position under the DCFR (see III.-5:301 – III.-5:302 on transfer of contractual position by agreement), it is unlikely that these would be deemed suitable. The carrier would not normally wish to replace his contracting party completely with an unknown third party. It thus seems unlikely that his consent to such a transfer of position could be implied merely by the act of issuing a transport document. Equally it is not usually intended that the

20. Could the third party rights provisions of the DCFR thus change shipping law? Should the same rules be applied to bills of lading and other transport documents alike? Could therefore such harmonised rules of the DCFR unify the approach to third parties involved in shipping transactions, whether within the UK or throughout the EU Member States?

## III. Comparative Analysis of the Different Regimes

21. From a UK perspective what would the changes be? To evaluate the impact of such a change the differences in requirements and effects of the CoGSA 1992, the TPA 1999 and the third party rights provisions of the DCFR will be contrasted before asking whether the DCFR is capable of providing an appropriate solution. The effectiveness of the DCFR rules are measured against the following test scenario:

> 22. *A consignment of 25 bales of new lamb's wool are transported alternatively either 1) intra UK between Stornoway on the Isle of Lewis in Scotland and St Ives in Cornwall, England or 2) internationally between Stornoway and Rotterdam, Holland. The contractual carrier is alternatively a) an English freight forwarder who insists on incorporation of an English law and arbitration clause, or b) a Scottish freight forwarder who in turn uses a Scots law and arbitration clause. The contract requires the goods to be shipped in March, to be kept dry and at 10 degrees Celsius. 25 bales are to be shipped, 3 of which are showing moisture damage. The transport document, once issued, states that 25 bales of new lamb's wool were shipped in good order and condition on 2nd April. It includes no information or promises as to temperature or storage. The transport document issued is freight forwarder's document and alternatively aa) an ocean bill of lading, bb) a multimodal bill of lading, cc) an electronic bill of lading or dd) a road consignment note. The terms of the transport document include the relevant law and arbitration clause, an exclusion of liability for transhipment, a limitation of liability to the amounts under the Hague-Visby Rules, a 9 months' time bar and a Himalaya clause. While still in possession of the transport document, the shipper changes the named consignee from B1 to B2. Once transfer has been made, the document is further transferred from B2 to B3. The goods are carried by an actual, non-contracting, carrier. During transhipment one bale of wool is lost and a further one is damaged due to bad stowage. During the transit an infestation of the wool with beetles spreads to other cargo.*
>
> 23. *The cargo receiver wishes to claim damages from the freight forwarder under the transport document. The freight forwarder in turn seeks compensation for all damage resulting from the contamination of the cargo. The actual carrier, if sued by the cargo receiver, wants to rely on the limitations and exclusions of liability as stated in the freight forwarder's transport document. What solutions to the relevant third party rights issues would the DCFR rules provide?*

entire contractual position is transferred but rather that limited rights (and potentially also the duties) arising from the bill of lading can be vested in the third party – which is pointing again towards a third party rights solution.

### 3.1. *Scope*

24. Alongside the specialised CoGSA 1992, the TPA 1999 creates a further and broad statutory exemption from the strict English privity rules. Whereas the CoGSA 1992 is only available to lawful holders of bills of lading[42] and the persons designated to receive the goods under a sea waybill or a ship's delivery order, and gives only the rights and duties specified in the CoGSA, the 1999 Act gives any third party a direct right to claim under a contract made between others if the contracting parties intended him to have such right. It is up to the contracting parties to decide what right is to be bestowed on the third party. The 1999 Act gives the third party either a positive right to enforce a contractual provision in his favour, such as in claiming delivery of goods consigned to him under a local road consignment note,[43] or a negative right in that he can avail himself of an exclusion or limitation clause provided in the contract; for example where a non-contracting performing carrier or other independent contractor of the carrier wishes to rely on a Himalaya type protection clause in the contract of carriage.[44] To similar effect, the DCFR provides broadly that parties can confer a right or other benefit on a third party,[45] which can also be the benefit of an exclusion or limitation of the third party's liability.[46] In contrast, the CoGSA 1992 focuses only on the cargo receiver as third party and does not extend to non-contracting carriers or other independent contractors; so that other constructs and principles such as agency were required to ensure Himalaya clauses were effective to protect the non-contracting carrier or other independent contractors of the carrier. The 1999 Act now supplements the CoGSA 1992 to close this gap, yet the DCFR is capable of effectively dealing with both benefits, positive and negative, at the same time. The 1999 Act and the DCFR confer benefits only, whereas the 1992 Act vests rights of suit and liabilities in the third party holder, consignee or deliveree.

### 3.2. *Requirements*

25. The conferral of rights under the DCFR is done by means of the contract and it is the contract that determines the nature and content of the third party's right or benefit.[47] Whether or not a right was conferred will depend on the intention of the parties as express or implied in the contract.[48] The third party does not need to be identified at the time of the conclusion of the contract nor does he need to be in existence at that time.[49] The requirements are defined somewhat narrower under the 1999 Act. For the third party

42 See CoGSA 1992, s 2(1) and s 5(2)–(3).
43 TPA 1999, s 1(1); note that international road carriage would usually be covered by the CMR, so that the 1999 Act would not apply (s 6(5)(b)).
44 TPA 1999, s 1 (6).
45 DCFR, II.–9:301(1).
46 DCFR, II.–9:301(3).
47 DCFR, II.–9:301(2).
48 See DCFR Commentary to II.–9:301 at E.
49 DCFR, II.–9:301(1).

under the 1999 Act to have a right of his own to enforce a term of the contract, one of two alternatives must be fulfilled. The contract must either a) expressly provide for such a right of the third party or b) the contract term must purport to confer a benefit on the third party, unless on proper construction of the contract it appears that the contracting parties had not intended the term to be enforceable by the third party.[50] Similarly to the DCFR, the third party needs not be in existence at the time of the conclusion of the contract, yet under the 1999 Act the third party must be identified in some way, whether by name, as a member of a class, or as answering a particular description.[51]

**26.** Potentially any third party can qualify under the 1999 Act or the DCFR, whereas only the lawful holder of a bill of lading, the consignee under a sea waybill or the deliveree under a ship's delivery order can avail himself of rights of suit under the CoGSA 1992 which the Act vests in the third party. The contracting parties have no choice whether they wish or intend to effect a transfer of rights and duties under the 1992 Act; the transfer is automatic, whereas under the 1999 Act or the DCFR the parties can chose by means of their contract terms, express and implied, whether a conferral of a benefit – and of a benefit only – is to take place. The DCFR thus allows overall most flexibility to cater for the needs and fulfil the intentions of the parties.

> 27. *Both types of third parties in our scenario, the cargo receiver and the non-contractual actual carrier, can claim third party benefits under the DCFR, whether for damages or for limitation of liability, respectively. For the application of the DCFR it is irrelevant what type of transport document was issued, what matters is the express or implied intention of the parties as to the conferral of rights. Here, however, the type of transport document and the usages commonly associated with such a document will be relevant in interpreting which rights and remedies have been implied by the usage of such a document.*

### *3.3. Remedies provided for third parties*

**28.** Under CoGSA 1992, the qualifying third party has "transferred to and vested in him all rights of suit under the contract of carriage as if he had been a party to the contract",[52] although this is limited where a bill of lading no longer gives a right to possession of the goods as against the carrier.[53] To enforce a term of the contract in his favour under the 1999 Act, the third party can avail himself of any remedy that would have been available to him, had he been a party to the contract, with rules relating to damages, injunctions, specific performance and other relief applying accordingly.[54] The DCFR here provides a slightly different approach, giving the third party only the same rights and remedies as if the contracting party was bound to render the performance under a binding unilateral

50 TPA 1999, s 1(1),(2). The burden of proof that the intention was not to confer a benefit is thus on the contracting party.
51 TPA 1999, s 1(3).
52 CoGSA 1992, s 2(1).
53 See CoGSA 1992, s 2(2).
54 TPA 1999, s 1(5).

undertaking in favour of the third party.[55] This is to take account of the fact that some of the remedies under a contract depend on mutuality; therefore not all remedies under the contract are capable of being used by the third party.[56] The DCFR thus clarifies that the position of the third party is as provided for him by the contracting parties and not necessarily the same as between the contracting parties under the contract.

**29.** How would this play out in a bill of lading context? The contract of carriage is almost invariably made before the bill of lading is issued and may contain differing or additional provision to those of the bill, particularly where bills of lading are issued under charterparties.[57] Under the flexibility of the DCFR rules, where a bill of lading is issued one may take account of trade usage and, for example, imply that the parties to the contract of carriage giving rise to the bill were intending to confer on the holder of the bill of lading the rights to delivery and corresponding rights to damages for loss of or damage to the goods. Depending on whether the bill of lading is a straight consigned, an order or a bearer bill, the rights would be intended to be with the named consignee, the consignee to whom the goods are ordered to be delivered or to the bearer of the bill, as the case may be, as the appropriate third party.

**30.** On the basis of the receipt and evidence function of the bill of lading, the parties surely would be taken to have intended these rights to be based on the statements on and terms of the bill of lading itself. One may even go further and imply that due to the importance of the receipt function, particularly where the bill of lading acts as a document of title or symbol of the goods,[58] the bill of lading in the hands of the third party is meant to be conclusive evidence and thus the contracting party, here the carrier, had undertaken towards the third party holder that the statements and terms of the bill of lading are accurately represented,[59] even where the contract itself may have included amendments or other stipulations. Any express contractual provisions to the contrary to invalidate the statements or terms of the bill of lading would be falling foul of the principles of good faith and fair dealing under the DCFR and may also possibly constitute unfair terms.[60] That the

55 DCFR, II.9:302(a).

56 DCFR Commentary to II.9:302(a).

57 See Bugden, para 7–020.

58 Given to the bill of lading by the custom of merchants; see *Lickbarrow v Mason* (1794) 5 TR 683; R Aikens, R Lord and M Bools, *Bills of Lading* (Informa, 2006) paras 1.28 – 1.45; G Treitel and F Reynolds, *Carver on Bills of Lading* (3rd edn, Sweet & Maxwell, 2011), para 6–002 and Girvin, *Carriage of Goods by Sea* (2nd edn, Oxford University Press, 2011), paras 8.02 ff. See also HGB, §519, stipulating this effect for the new German Maritime Law.

59 See also Girvin paras 6.03, 6.06, 6.19 & 6.23 on relevant English case-law using estoppel by representation to similar effect and see insofar also the new German Maritime Law, HGB, §§517 and 522(2) on the evidentiary effect of the bill of lading.

60 See DCFR, Principles, Nos 17 (contractual security: main ingredients), 23 (contractual security: good faith and fair dealing), 25 (contractual security: inconsistent behaviour), 42 (contract: not allowing people to rely on their own unlawful, dishonest or unreasonable conduct), 48 (non-contractual obligations: not allowing people to gain an advantage from their own unlawful, dishonest or unreasonable conduct) and Model Rules, Book I General Provisions I.-1:102(3): Interpretation and Development; I.-1:103(2): good faith and fair dealing; Book II Contracts and other juridical acts, II. –

statements in the bill of lading as to goods shipped and their condition should be irrefutable evidence between the third party and the contracting party is also backed by most sea carriage conventions, that is, the Hague-Visby Rules, Hamburg and Rotterdam Rules.[61]

31. The CoGSA 1992 also relies heavily on the principles developed by the common law as it does not define whether and which bill of lading statements can be relied upon by a third party. Other than treating a representation in a bill of lading that goods had been shipped or received for shipment, as the case may be, as conclusive evidence, the 1992 Act does not deal with other representations, such as to weight, quantity or condition.[62] It is therefore submitted that the DCFR is just as capable of tackling the situation presented by the bill of lading's document of title, receipt and evidence functions. Both the DCFR and the CoGSA 1992 allow a focus on the document and its clauses, rather than referring back to the original contract of carriage, as in the TPA 1999, which would not be appropriate here.

32. *The holder of the ocean bill of lading, the electronic or multimodal bill of lading could thus rely on his position as holder – depending on meeting the particular requirements of the bill – to claim damages against the freight forwarder, based on the stipulations of the contract that the goods were received in good order and condition. The fact that 3 bales were already received in a wet condition was not included in the bill and can therefore not be relied upon by the carrier against the third party holder, although it could be used against the initial party to the contract of carriage. The content of the original contract regarding time of shipment and the storage conditions (dry and 10 degrees Celsius) cannot be relied on by the third party cargo claimant, as these were not included in the bill, although he can rely on appropriate cargo care. The role of a CMR consignment note would not be as prominent and its contents would only be treated as prima facie evidence of the goods shipped, so here proof to the contrary and thus the details of the contract would be relevant.*

33. *Against any cargo claims the freight forwarder can rely on the terms of his transport document insofar as acceptable when measured against the mandatory requirements of any applicable transport conventions. The actual carrier in turn, based on the third party rules, is able to rely on the limitation and exclusion clauses provided in the bill, insofar as they are valid. Accordingly the limitation provisions, time bar and exclusion of liability for transhipment damage of the 2 bales could be relied on, insofar as valid.*

3:301: Negotiations contrary to good faith and fair dealing, II. -9:402: Duty of transparency of terms not individually negotiated, II. -9:405: Meaning of "unfair" in contracts between businesses; Book III Obligations and Corresponding Rights, III. – 1:103: Good faith and fair dealing.

61 See HVR, Article III r 4, HambR, Article 16.3(b) and RR, Article 41.2. Although for bills of lading under the Hague Rules and for consignment notes under other forms of transport, such statements would only be prima facie evidence, see HR, Article III r4; CMR, Article 9; CIM, Article 12 and MC, Article 11 and WC, Article 11 and see Bugden, ch 6 and Smeele, 251, 254 f.

62 See CoGSA 1992, s 4(1), enacted to amend the common law rule in *Grant v Norway* (1851) 10 CB 665 that a master had no apparent authority to sign bills of lading for goods not actually shipped. However, s 4 only deals with bills of lading, so the old common law rule remains in force for sea waybills and ship's delivery orders. For other representations recourse to the principles of estoppel are needed. See also Bugden, paras 6–009 ff and 6–014 and Girvin paras 6.03, 6.06, 6.19 & 6.23.

### 3.4. *Conditions and limitations on conferred benefit*

**34.** As in the CoGSA 1992,[63] the rights available to the third party under the 1999 Act[64] as well as those under the DCFR[65] are not limitless, but are curtailed to the content and terms of the contract and thus subject to any conditions or other limitations under the contract. Thus, for example, where the right to claim damages under the contract is limited to a certain monetary ceiling the third party will only be able claim damages up to such amount, as the contractual limitation clause will also be valid as against him.[66] The Commentary to the DCFR specifically highlights that the rules of the DCFR are consistent with the stipulations of transport conventions regarding the right of disposal of the consignor and the conditions under which the consignee may claim delivery of the goods.[67] The right to delivery of the goods may thus be conditional upon payment of freight or expenses due under the transport document.

> **35.** *For example, any freight charges due under the transport document would have to be paid by the cargo receiver as a condition to the benefit. The carrier could withhold delivery until such payment was made.*

**36.** How clear the charges and expenses or other connected conditions have to be and whether any terms imposing payments or duties from other documents or the underlying contract of carriage, such as standard terms or charterparties, are validly incorporated may be a matter of determination by the courts.[68] Alongside the rules of interpretation the courts may also refer to the DCFR provisions on unfair terms and transparency of terms and in a business context the alignment of terms with good commercial practice.[69] Equally the CoGSA does not regulate the question of clarity of and incorporation of terms, but relies on common law to provide appropriate solutions.

**37.** Under the DCFR one could argue that, as the basis is a transfer of rights rather than that of liabilities, the third party ought to be able to determine the conditions and

63 CoGSA 1992, s 2(1) – "as if he had been a party to that contract".

64 TPA 1999, s 1(4) and s 8.

65 DCFR, II.–9:301(2).

66 Although subject to the framework of mandatory rules, which may impose higher limits or a longer limitation period. See also G Treitel, "The Contracts (Rights of Third Parties) Act 1999 and the Law of Carriage of Goods by Sea" in Rose (ed), *LEX MERCATORIA: Essays on International Commercial Law in Honour of Francis Reynolds*, (LLP Professional Publishing, 2000), 345, 346.

67 DCFR Commentary to II.–9:301 at E.

68 For interpretation of the DCFR provisions see Book I General Provisions I.-1:102(3): Interpretation and Development, which requires autonomous interpretation and the promotion of uniformity of application and II.–8:101 ff. on interpretation of contracts. For the current German solution under the HGB, §522(1), (3): objections of the carrier are limited to the statements made in the bill of lading; moreover an agreement that is merely referred to in the bill of lading is not incorporated in the bill. Contrast this solution to the broad ability under English law to incorporate charterparty terms (see *Carver* at paras 3–014 ff., Eder et al, *Scrutton on Charterparties and Bills of Lading* (22nd edn, Sweet & Maxwell, 2011) at paras 6–012 ff.).

69 See DCFR, II.-9.402(1) and II.-9.405.

connected burdens to his right at the time of claiming delivery, so that he can decide whether to make use of the right or not.[70] As long as overall there is a transfer of rights, rather than a net transfer of burdens or liabilities, the DCFR seems to allow the attachment of conditions to the conferral of rights. Liabilities can thus, it is submitted, only be incurred by the third party up to the value of the right and no further. This would be a departure of the solution as enshrined in the CoGSA 1992, which allows the imposition of burdens on the third party holder of the bill of lading once he has made use of his rights.[71] The impact may, however, it is submitted, be slighter than it seems at first, as the courts have been reluctant to impose severe burdens.[72]

### 3.5. *Jurisdiction and arbitration clauses as a condition on the conferred benefit*

**38.** Another question of importance in the context of carriage is whether any jurisdiction and arbitration clauses included in the contract or in a transport document can be validly imposed on the third party, as well as relied upon by him. The question as to whether a jurisdiction clause could bind a third party was addressed by the European Court of Justice (ECJ)[73] in Case 71/83 *Tilly Russ*[74] and Case C-387/98 *Coreck Maritime*[75], which set out that one had to look at the fulfilment of the formal requirements of the prorogation provision of the Brussels I jurisdiction regime[76] as between the initial parties to the agreement.[77] If those requirements were met, whether the jurisdiction clause could bind the third party depended on (a) whether under the applicable national law the third

70 See for example the new German Maritime Law, German Commercial Code (Handelsgesetzbuch (HGB)), §494 (2) and (3) where a consignee who is using his rights of demanding delivery or claiming against the carrier under the contract of carriage, is charged with the duty to pay outstanding freight, insofar as it is determinable from the transport document or, where no reference is made, according to the contract of carriage insofar as not unreasonable, and also certain delay charges, but only where the amount was notified to the consignee on delivery of the goods. In a similar vein of being able to determine the cost related to the goods, a receiver of cargo transported under a voyage charter must only pay load-port demurrage where the amount has been notified to him on delivery of the goods, although demurrage accumulating at the port of discharge is borne by the consignee without such notification; see HGB, §§530 (3) 2 and 535 (1) 2.

71 See CoGSA 1992, s 3(1).

72 See further below at "Obligations".

73 As it was called then; now the Court of Justice of the European Union (CJEU).

74 Case 71/83 *Partenreederei ms Tilly Russ and Ernest Russ v NV Haven- & Vervoerbedrijf Nova and NV Goeminne Hout* [1984] ECR 2417.

75 Case C-387/98, *Coreck Maritime GmbH v Handelsveem BV and Others,* [2000] ECR I-9337.

76 Which is, as of 10 January 2015, the Regulation (EU) No 1215/2012 of the European Parliament and of the Council of 12 December 2012 on jurisdiction and the recognition and enforcement of judgments in civil and commercial matters (recast) (OJ L351, 20.12.2012, p 1, also referred to as the Brussels I Recast Regulation), Article 25, and was at the time of the decision the Brussels Convention on jurisdiction and the recognition and enforcement of judgments in civil and commercial matters of 1968, Article 17.

77 Here difficulties may arise in particular for charterparty bills of lading, in case of alleged incorporation of jurisdiction clauses. See *The Varenna* [1983] 2 Lloyd's Rep 592 and *Sibioti v BP France* [2003] 2 Lloyd's Rep 364, with respect to the requirement under English law that for an incorporation of a charterparty choice of jurisdiction or law clause to be valid, an explicit reference to the incorporation of such

party succeeded to the shipper's rights and obligations when he acquired the bill of lading, in which case the clause was binding, or (b) if that was not the case, whether the third party had agreed to the jurisdiction clause, for example by claiming against the carrier in the forum stipulated in the bill. Under the CoGSA 1992[78] the bill of lading holder "has transferred and vested in him all rights of suit under the contract of carriage as if he had been a party to that contract" and conversely becomes[79] "subject to the same liabilities under that contract as if he had been a party" to it. Therefore, in accordance with the jurisprudence of the ECJ, the lawful holder succeeds in the rights and obligations of the contracting party and thus is bound by the jurisdiction clause.

**39.** Whether one could go so far as to apply a similar argument to the conditional benefit approach of the TPA 1999[80] is questionable. The English High Court held in *Nisshin* that under the 1999 Act, the right, at least insofar as it is a positive right, was transferred together with the method of enforcement; the contract has provided for arbitration.[81] The court saw in the working of the Act an analogy to a statutory assignment and held therefore that the general arbitration clause in the contract was also binding on the third party enforcing a positive right or indemnity.[82] It might, however, be too far to see this as a succession to the shipper's rights and duties, as indeed it is only the right, with its related conditions, that is vested in the third party. It seems here that the 1999 Act does not fulfil the ECJ standards, equally as it is suggested that the DCFR solution does not. While the ECJ decision is relevant for matters on court jurisdiction only, and not on arbitration clauses,[83] the problem in the latter context is also that to resort to arbitration usually requires a valid arbitration agreement by the parties that are to be subjected to arbitration. An agreement by the contracting party for the third party may not be sufficient in the absence of a later ratification by the third party. A solution to this problem of the third party not being party to the arbitration agreement has been attempted by the 1999 Act in its section 8.[84]

arbitration or jurisdiction and applicable law clause must have been made in the bill of lading. A general statement of 'all rights and duties as per charterparty' would be insufficient to achieve this result.

78 CoGSA 1992, s2(1).

79 After acts showing his intention to take up these rights, such as demanding delivery or making a claim; see CoGSA 1992, s3(1).

80 See TPA 1999, ss 1(4),(5) and 8.

81 *Nisshin Shipping Co Ltd Co Ltd v Cleaves & Co Ltd* [2003] EWHC 2602 (Comm); [2004] 1 Lloyd's Rep 38 for direct claims of a chartering broker under charterparties; the broker availing himself of the third party right in this contract also had to use the remedy of suing in arbitration as provided for in the contract. See *Fortress Value Recovery Fund I LLC v Blue Skye Special Opportunities Fund LP* [2013] EWCA Civ 367; [2013] 1 W.L.R. 3466; [2013] 1 Lloyd's Rep. 606, [24, 29] approving of *Nissin*.

82 *Nisshin Shipping Co Ltd Co Ltd v Cleaves & Co Ltd* [2003] EWHC 2602 (Comm); [2004] 1 Lloyd's Rep 38 with reference to the Explanatory Notes to the Act and *Schiffahrtsgesellschaft Detlev Von Appen GmbH v Weiner Allianz Versicherungs AG (The Jay Bola)* [1997] CLC 993 (concerning the status of the insurers of cargo subrogated to the rights of action of the cargo owner).

83 Arbitration being excluded from the scope of the Brussels I regime, see Brussels I Recast Regulation, Article 1(2) (d).

84 TPA 1999, s8:
"(1) Where – (a) a right under section 1 to enforce a term ('the substantive term') is subject to a term providing for the submission of disputes to arbitration ('the arbitration agreement'), and (b) the arbitration

**40.** What would the solution be under the DCFR? The DCFR provision on remedies[85] may suggest that a third party claiming against the contracting party can only do so as provided by the contract, yet as if the right to performance was provided by a binding unilateral undertaking. This undertaking could be subject to arbitration or a forum clause. This suggests that it would have to be clear from the contract whether a dispute resolution clause was intended to also cover the third party position or was only intended to govern the contracting parties.[86] Where the rights were enshrined in a bill of lading one may deem it to be clear that the dispute resolution provision was also intended for the third party, but where the dispute resolution mechanism was only provided as part of the contract as a whole, it may be more difficult to discern an intention to also bind the third party to this method. For example, for the validity of charterparty arbitration clauses on third parties, one would need to seek guidance from the rules of incorporation as to whether the clause was also meant for the third party relationship. Although, it might be useful to remember that a similar analysis is also necessary under the CoGSA1992, as the third party is taken to have transferred to him the rights as enshrined in the bill of lading, sea waybill or ship's delivery order, even if this was not the relevant contract of carriage as between the initial parties, for example, because they were operating under a charterparty.

**41.** For the purpose of an arbitration agreement or to satisfy the ECJ requirement on jurisdiction agreements, the unilateral undertaking according to the DCFR could thus be seen as including an offer to arbitrate or to litigate in a particular forum, which may be accepted by the third party using the rights conferred on him.[87] While the DCFR

agreement is an agreement in writing for the purposes of Part I of the Arbitration Act 1996, the third party shall be treated for the purposes of that Act as a party to the arbitration agreement as regards disputes between himself and the promisor relating to the enforcement of the substantive term by the third party. "(2) Where – (a) a third party has a right under section 1 to enforce a term providing for one or more descriptions of dispute between the third party and the promisor to be submitted to arbitration ('the arbitration agreement'), (b) the arbitration agreement is an agreement in writing for the purposes of Part I of the Arbitration Act 1996, and (c) the third party does not fall to be treated under subsection (1) as a party to the arbitration agreement, the third party shall, if he exercises the right, be treated for the purposes of that Act as a party to the arbitration agreement in relation to the matter with respect to which the right is exercised, and be treated as having been so immediately before the exercise of the right."

85 DCFR, II.-9:302(a).

86 C Ambrose, p 422 ff.

87 There is good argument that the requirements of Article 25.1(c) of the Brussels I Recast Regulation of a jurisdiction agreement in the form of trade usage are fulfilled. For references to the acceptance of jurisdiction agreements under third party beneficiary concepts see N Carette, "Third Party Beneficiary in Commercial Law: A Comparative Analysis of Belgian, Dutch, English and French law", [2012] EJCCL 21, 29 f. See also TPA 1999, Explanatory Notes, paras 8, 33 – 35 to s 1(4) and s 8, but see *Law Com No LC242, 1996,* paras 14.14–14.19 on the difficulties in providing for jurisdiction and arbitration clauses in the third parties legislation, recommending to exclude the matter from the reform; yet rules to cover arbitration agreements were inserted by Government amendment at the Report Stage in the House of Commons (see C Ambrose, "When can a third party enforce an arbitration clause?" [2001] JBL 415, 419 f. and A Burrows, "The Contracts (Rights of Third Parties) Act 1999 and its implications for commercial contracts" [2000] LMCLQ 540, 511 f.) and see also *Fortress Value Recovery Fund I LLC v Blue Skye Special Opportunities Fund LP* [2013] EWCA Civ 367; [2013] 1 W.L.R. 3466; [2013] 1 Lloyd's Rep. 606, [1, 29, 36] on arbitration agreements and their potential application on third parties via the TPA 1999.

generally does not require acceptance of the right for it to be validly conferred, acceptance would seem to be of importance regarding the reach of a dispute resolution clause.

**42.** However, where the contracting party wanted to sue the third party, it seems that in the absence of an act that would be taken as an acceptance of the dispute resolution clause, the ordinary rules of allocating jurisdiction may have to be used. This may cause difficulties where the conferred benefit was that of a limitation clause so that no positive enforcement of rights would take place. That the reference to a benefit arising from a limitation clause would be sufficient as to constitute an acceptance of the offer for agreement to litigate in the particular forum or to arbitrate is unlikely, even more so, if such reliance only took place at litigation stage.[88] If the use of the exclusion or limitation clause was only possible in the forum as agreed by the contracting parties, one would in effect require the third party to take the burden of submitting to a forum which he had not chosen and to proceedings which he had not initiated. This would then indeed impose a burden on the third party, not acceptable under the DCFR.

This is not comparable to the situation where a substantive benefit, such as a claim for an indemnity, is subject to a procedural condition. In contrast, if a forum clause in the main contract had the effect of giving the designated forum exclusive jurisdiction over the question of availability of the defence to the third party, the third party would have to submit to jurisdiction of this forum. Yet, if disputes were not to be fragmented, this forum would also decide the claim against the third party as a whole, even where it was decided that the defence was not available. Thus, the benefit of the (negative) limitation or exclusion could in the end create a serious burden instead. In the words of Tomlinson LJ, in a case where this question arose under the TPA 1999, this would be "a striking outcome". He rejected such a result, even though section 8 of the TPA 1999[89] had been specifically introduced in the Act so as to facilitate the reach of arbitration agreements.[90]

It is thus submitted that a third party's avail of a contractual limitation or exclusion clause bestowed on him in a contract between others, cannot be interpreted as having the effect of accepting the arbitration or jurisdiction clause of the contract. Such a benefit could not outweigh the burden that would otherwise be imposed and would fall foul of the conditional benefit approach of the DCFR. Where a positive right enshrined in a transport document is concerned however, the acceptance or use of the transport document by the third party may lead a court to conclude that the documents' forum clause was also agreed or ratified. One may argue that a buyer who would not wish to accept a bill of lading with a particular dispute resolution clause could have instructed his seller accordingly and thus had a choice whether or not to "agree" to the clause.

88 See C Ambrose, "When can a third party enforce an arbitration clause?" [2001] JBL 415, 419 f.

89 See *Fortress Value Recovery Fund I LLC v Blue Skye Special Opportunities Fund LP* [2013] EWCA Civ 367; [2013] 1 W.L.R. 3466; [2013] 1 Lloyd's Rep. 606, [29, 36]. The case concerned an application to stay court proceedings in favour of arbitration by asset managers as third party beneficiaries of an exclusion clause in a partnership deed. Suit was brought against them in tort for dishonest mismanagement. The third parties wanted to rely on the arbitration clause as binding upon proceedings against them. Both the High Court and the court of Appeal refused the application to stay proceedings, although with partly different reasoning. See TPA 1999, Explanatory Notes para 34 last sentence.

90 See TPA 1999, Explanatory Notes paras 33–35.

**43.** While a more straightforward solution and better clarity as to the validity of arbitration and jurisdiction clauses on third parties is achieved by means of the CoGSA 1992, the DCFR seems capable of solving a good deal of the issues via its conditional benefit approach. The reach and boundaries will however have to be determined by the courts, although one could try to help a uniform approach by inserting a paragraph into the DCFR specifically accepting forum clauses as means of enforcing positive benefits conferred upon the third party. It may be of interest to remember here that the case of negative enforcement of a limitation clause is not covered by the CoGSA 1992 either, due to the Act's narrow scope, thus remaining to be considered under a conditional benefit approach. However, even it was not possible to guarantee the validity of jurisdiction and arbitration clauses, should this be a major sticking point?

Consent of the third party seems to be the status quo under the Brussels I jurisdiction regime and the jurisprudence of the ECJ. The ECJ's argumentation referring to the applicable law for determining the consequences of a jurisdiction clause under the Brussels I jurisdiction regime and whether under this law the third party could be seen as stepping into the shoes of the contracting party, has been held to be unique to the bill of lading context, mostly due to the fact that bills of lading in most Member States were seen as a negotiable instrument.[91] In general however, the ECJ, now the CJEU, held that the concept of a jurisdiction clause must be interpreted as an independent concept, giving full effect to the principle of freedom of choice. While "the conditions and forms under which a third party to the contract may be regarded as having given his consent to a jurisdiction clause may vary in accordance with the nature of the initial contract",[92] consent of the third party is generally needed for the third party to be able to rely on or be bound by the provisions of a jurisdiction agreement.[93] Consent would thus be required where the transport document was not a bill of lading but a consignment note.

**44.** Furthermore, is it essential that jurisdiction and arbitration clauses are upheld in the relationship between carrier and third party holder of the bill of lading? While such clauses allow the contracting parties to calculate their exposure, it is submitted that the reliance on the allocation of exclusive fora may no longer be the status quo. The more recent sea carriage conventions, the Hamburg and Rotterdam Rules, similarly to the road, rail and air transport conventions contain rules on jurisdiction and arbitration which do not allow for exclusive jurisdiction according to an agreement, but contain a number of choices in favour of the claimant as to where he can bring suit, the place agreed being only one of them.[94] Giving the claimant the choice of forum, while possibly leading to a race to the courts to forum shop, may also encourage performance to a

91 *Case C-543/10 Refcomp SpA v Axa Corporate Solutions Assurance SA and others* at [24-41, esp. 34 ff.]. In particular, it was not transferrable to the context of a buyer and sub-buyer's relationship to a manufacturer of goods which whom he had made no direct contract, but only obtained the goods from his seller, the initial buyer.

92 Ibid at [30].

93 *Case C-543/10 Refcomp SpA v Axa Corporate Solutions Assurance SA and others* at [40].

94 See HambR, Articles 21, 22; RR, chs 14 and 15; CMR Articles 31, 33; CIM Article 46; cf. MC, Article 33 (without scope for a jurisdiction agreement) and 34.

higher standard, particularly where certain performance duties have received different treatment in the courts of different countries, such as the question of whether certain contractual provisions fall foul of mandatory rules or what constitutes wilful misconduct under the CMR or other transport conventions. To keep to several different third party regimes merely to ensure validity of jurisdiction and arbitration clauses on third parties in certain circumstances in sea transport[95] may thus no longer seem such an important end in itself – although from a UK perspective it is certainly a key advantage to be able to provide certainty for the industry and to ensure the validity of clauses in favour of UK courts or arbitration proceedings seated in the UK.

Overall it seems that the DCFR via acceptance of the forum clause can solve many of the forum problems. Where there is no consent or ratification the forum clause however cannot be used against the third party. So for example where a carrier wanted to sue the third party bill of lading holder, even where the holder had not taken any steps of using his rights, which in turn may be interpreted as acceptance of the rights enshrined in the bill together with the forum clause, such a claim would have to be filed according to the normal rules of jurisdiction. However such a claim could not be filed in the forum as per contractual agreement under the CoGSA 1992 either, as in order to become liable under the bill the third party must have taken steps to assert his rights.[96] Equally the ordinary jurisdiction rules would have to be used where a third party was sued who may be able to claim a benefit of a limitation or exclusion clause only – again leading to no change of the status quo.

> **45.** *The third party cargo claimant would have to sue the freight forwarder in the forum as agreed in the contract between the original parties only insofar as this provision was validly included in the transport document handed to him; otherwise only if it was clear that the original parties intended the third party to be bound by their forum clause and the third party could be taken to have accepted it. The actual carrier however would not be bound by any forum clauses between the original parties to the contract simply to be able to rely on an exclusion or limitation clause.*

### 3.6. Time of transfer/conferral; modification and revocation of benefit

**46.** The CoGSA 1992 only vests rights on the bill of lading holder once and so long as the bill of lading is transferred to him and has not been passed further down the line.[97] Before the bill of lading has been transferred no rights vest in a third party and the contracting parties are free to alter or amend it. The 1999 Act contains rules on variation and rescission of the contract by the parties to protect a third party who is relying on a clause in his favour.[98] Once the third party has communicated his assent to the promisor,

95 I.e. where the CoGSA 1992 requirements are fulfilled and no Hamburg or Rotterdam Rules apply, although the latter are not (yet) in force.

96 CoGSA 1992, s 3(1).

97 See CoGSA 1992, s 2(1), (5) and *Borealis AB v Stargas Ltd (The Berge Sisar)* [2001] UKHL 17, [2002] 2 AC 205.

98 TPA 1999, s 2.

the promisor is aware that the third party has relied on the term in his favour or, where this can reasonably be expected to be foreseen by the promisor and the third party has in fact relied on the term, the contract can no longer be rescinded or the term varied, unless there is an express provision to the contrary[99] or the third party consents.[100] Under the DCFR the rules on modification and revocation are both broader and narrower. Unless the benefit was communicated to the third party it can be freely removed or modified, as it has not yet been conferred. After conferral, it depends on whether the right or benefit is irrevocable and whether this is the case is determined by the contract. If the right is irrevocable it is irrelevant whether the third party has relied on it or not.[101] Reliance is however determinative even where the right is revocable or subject to modification, where the parties have let the third party believe that the right could not be modified or revoked.[102]

47. Relevant in a shipping context is that the original contract may differ from the one enshrined in the transport document and amendments to the contract and documents are generally possible. While this may give rise to difficulties under the rules of the 1999 Act,[103] it seems that the DCFR provides sufficient flexibility to allow modification of the rights. However, where rights are enshrined in transport documents, reliance would seem to be the norm, in particular where the document was transferred or handed over to the third party according to the usual rules for such a document. Further, the benefit could be lost by the third party where he transferred the bill of lading to a fourth party or where he exercised his right of disposal available under a consignment note. The contract would seem to imply that the right moves to the fourth party and the new consignee and thus no longer vests in the original third party.

**48.** *Where in our scenario the shipper changed the name of the consignee of the transport document before transfer, no rights had been established with the third party, B1, allowing a change freely. After the amendment to B2 however the document was transferred to B2, so B2 obtained rights under the document as third party and, depending on the type of document could transfer it on to another party, B3. Any particular trade usages pertaining to the type of document used and any convention rules applicable should be implied accordingly as part of the original contract. In case of a bill of lading the implied intention would be that the right transfers with the document. On transfer to B3 B2 loses his third party rights under the bill of lading while B3 obtains them. In case of a CMR consignment note, the rules as in the CMR on transfer of rights and control would be implied.*

99 TPA 1999, s2 (1)–(3).

100 TPA 1999, s2 (1), (4)–(5).

101 DCFR Commentary to II.9:303 at B. This would be counter to the solution that the third party has the rights to performance and remedies for non-performance under a unilateral juridical act, as set out it II.-9:302(a).

102 DCFR, II.9:303(3).

103 See also Treitel, "The Contracts (Rights of Third Parties) Act 1999 and the Law of Carriage of Goods by Sea" in Rose (ed), *LEX MERCATORIA: Essays on International Commercial Law in Honour of Francis Reynolds*, (LLP Professional Publishing, 2000), 345, 353–354.

### 3.7. *Performance rights of the contracting party (promisee)*

**49.** Under the TPA 1999, the third party's right of enforcement of the term does not prevent the promisee to enforce any term of the contract,[104] although the promisor is protected from double liability.[105] In contrast, under the CoGSA 1992, once rights of suit are transferred to the lawful holder of a bill of lading, the original party's rights are extinguished.[106] The DCFR does not provide any particular rule in this context, but it seems in line with the rules of contract law that the contracting party can require performance by his counterpart to the third party, unless the contract provides otherwise.[107]

### 3.8. *Defences*

**50.** Provision is made in the TPA 1999 to allow the promisor to use certain matters as a defence or set-off against the claim by the third party, to ensure that he is not worse off than if the promisee had enforced the contract or if the third party had been party to the contract.[108] If this was applied, for example in a multimodal bill of lading context,[109] the carrier could rely as against the third party on contractual variations[110] that were never included into the bill of lading, which would run counter to the current status quo in sea carriage where the terms of the bill of lading are conclusive as against the third party holder.[111] The DCFR has however a much more pliable solution. It sets out that the right to assert defences against the third party which the contracting party could assert against the other party to the contract is subject to contrary provision in the contract.[112] The commentary clarifies that availability of the defences of the contracting party is a default rule only and that any provision to the contrary may be made, express or by implication.[113] This therefore allows the implication, if not already expressly included, implied by the contract or imposed by mandatory rules,[114] that at least a transport document which is treated as a document of title is conclusive in the hands of the third party. The contracting parties therefore cannot hold any variations against the third party. This will be of crucial

[104] TPA 1999, s4. It is suggested that therefore the rule of *Dunlop v Lambert* as interpreted by Lord Diplock in *The Albazero* ([1977] AC 774 (HL)) is hardly necessary, since the promise can enforce also the terms of the contract in favour of the third party (Treitel, op cit, 348 and 372–375 and see Bugden, op cit, 14–026).

[105] TPA 1999, s 5.

[106] CoGSA 1992, s 2(5).

[107] See DCFR, II.–9:301(2) and see also DCFR Commentary to II.–9:302(b).

[108] TPA 1999, s 3.

[109] If one argued that this bill would not fall under the 1992 CoGSA; see above n. 34 on this discussion.

[110] Agreed between the parties before the bill of lading was issued.

[111] See TPA 1999, s 3(2) (a): "The promisor shall have available to him by way of defence or set-off any matter that (a) arises form or in connection with the contract and is relevant to the term, and (b) would have been available to him by way of defence or set-off if the proceedings had been brought by the promise." And see Treitel, "The Contracts (Rights of Third Parties) Act 1999 and the Law of Carriage of Goods by Sea" in Rose (ed), *LEX MERCATORIA: Essays on International Commercial Law in Honour of Francis Reynolds*, (LLP Professional Publishing, 2000), 345, 352.

[112] DCFR, II.–9:302(b).

[113] DCFR Commentary to II.–9:302 on rule(b).

[114] See Hague Visby Rules, Article III r4.

importance particularly where the contracting parties knowingly misstated the goods or the goods' condition in the transport document.

> 51. *The damage to the 3 bales of wool prior to takeover of the goods by the freight forwarder cannot be held against the bill of lading holder, irrespective of any agreement between the initial parties to the contract. Had the freight forwarder not wished to incur such a liability he could have noted the damage in the bill issued by him. Yet it would be a different matter under a CMR consignment note.*

## 3.9. *Transfer of obligations*

52. The TPA 1999 does not envisage, create or allow enforcement of contractual rights by any contracting party *against* the third party, so that above and beyond any claims arising from defences or set-off available to the promisor, the third party is not liable, whether for freight, expenses or for damages caused by the cargo or else.[115] This should mean that a carrier could use his lien to withhold delivery, but once delivered could not claim any outstanding freight from the third party. Such claims would however be possible if the CoGSA 1992 applied.[116] However, the 1999 Act does not oust rights or remedies of a third party apart from the Act and therefore does not abolish the common law solutions of implied or collateral contracts.[117] Such implied contract might also be argued by the carrier to sue the consignee for freight and other expenses.

53. If the DCFR was to apply, similarly to the TPA 1999, the third party could not be burdened with obligations or duties as only rights or benefits could be conferred. However the rights or benefits could be subject to any conditions or limitations under the contract, so that freight and other charges may be payable against delivery of the goods to the third party. The benefit may thus reduce, yet no burden greater than the benefit could be imposed. The position of a plegee or of an intermediate holder of a bill of lading would thus also be appropriately secured. The plegee of the bill would be holder of the bill of lading, but once he indorsed and transferred the bill to another the rights (and any connected 'conditions') would pass with it, as for any other intermediate holder. Such result was also achieved under the CoGSA 1992 by case-law of (what was then) the House of Lords.[118]

54. It is suggested that this is a sufficiently appropriate distribution of rights and obligations. The parties to the contract of carriage have their respective rights and obligations. To impose duties or liabilities on the third party over and beyond the benefit conferred, such as the value of the cargo, seems not necessary or appropriate. The shipper

115 See TPA 1999, s 3 and Treitel, "The Contracts (Rights of Third Parties) Act 1999 and the Law of Carriage of Goods by Sea" in Rose (ed), *LEX MERCATORIA: Essays on International Commercial Law in Honour of Francis Reynolds*, (LLP Professional Publishing, 2000), 345, 346, 360.

116 CoGSA 1992, s 3.

117 See Treitel, op cit, 358 and above at 2.2.

118 *Borealis AB v Stargas Ltd (The Berge Sisar)* [2001] UKHL 17, [2002] 2 AC 205.

and carrier remain under contractual obligations of their own.[119] Even though the CoGSA 1992 allows the lawful holder of a bill of lading to be burdened with liabilities, whether below, up to, or beyond the value of the cargo, the courts have been reluctant to impose serious burdens, such as the liability for dangerous cargo, and tended to interpret the requirements of the CoGSA restrictively, so as not to impose the burden on the third party.[120]

**55.** *The third party cargo receiver would not be liable for damages for the shipment of dangerous cargo, due to the infestation of the wool. If transportation was under the CMR, the cargo receiver would only have to pay the charges shown to be due under the consignment note,*[121] *and even where a bill of lading included liability of the third party for dangerous cargo, if domestic law or the HVR applied, such liability could only be incurred up to the level of the benefit obtained, if at all.*

## IV. Conclusion

**56.** The DCFR provides for sufficient flexibility to allow the parties of a contract of carriage to vest rights in a third party holder, consignee or consignor, as the case may be. It is capable of applying to the various transport modes and documents and could thus unify the fragmented UK position. This in turn could help to avoid putting too much emphasis on the selection of the instrument depending on the use of transport mode(s) and document. Where transport conventions apply, their rules also fit within the framework of the third party rights rules, so that an overall unified and harmonious approach is achieved. Overall no drastic change needs to be feared, although some adjustment and rethinking would be required from a UK perspective. The detailed application of the principles will need to be clarified and moulded by their application in the courts. In so doing, courts should however be careful to consider the autonomous character of the DCFR and the spirit of the DCFR rules as a whole – rather than leaning too closely to any case-law developed under the previous instruments – so as to enable progress towards true harmonisation.

119 See also DCFR Commentary to II.9:302 as to the independence of the rights of the contracting parties according to ordinary rules of contract law.

120 See the speech of Lord Hobhouse in *Borealis AB v Stargas* Ltd [2001] UKHL 17; [2002] 2 AC 205 at para 33: "From the context in the Act and the purpose underlying section 3(1), it is clear that section 3 must be understood in a way which reflects the potentially important consequences of the choice or election which the bill of lading holder is making. The liabilities, particularly when alleged dangerous goods are involved, may be disproportionate to the value of the goods; the liabilities may not be covered by insurance; the endorsee may not be fully aware of what the liabilities are." And see *Borealis AB v Stargas Ltd (The Berge Sisar)* [2001] UKHL 17, [2002] 2 AC 205 and *Primetrade AG v Ythan Ltd (The Ythan)* [2005] EWHC 2399 (Comm), [2006] 1 Lloyd's Rep. 457. And see also *Miramar Maritime Corp v Holborn Oil Trading (The Miramar)*, HL [1984] 2 Lloyd's Rep 129 at p 132, Lord Diplock, although not directly on the CoGSA 1992 but on the undesirable effects of charterparty incorporation clauses in bills of lading if accepted to readily, it being unlikely that the consignee would want to accept "blindfold a potential liability to pay an unknown and wholly unpredictable sum for demurrage… [and where] that sum may actually exceed the delivered value of the goods to which the bill of lading gives title".

121 CMR, Article 13.2.

Cinzia Ingratoci

# THE EFFECTS OF PRINCIPLES OF EUROPEAN LAW ON NON-CONTRACTUAL LIABILITY OF CLASSIFICATION SOCIETIES

## I. Introduction

1. A ship's classification consists of a commercial service intended to provide a professional, independent assessment of the construction qualities and hardness of a ship at the time of the survey. Classification societies are bodies of ancient tradition, specialized in technical surveys on structures and on-board systems (including materials, equipment and testing).[1] This service is provided following a "classification contract" between the ship-owners (or the shipyards) and the classification society. Substantive obligations arising from the contract consist of carrying out inspections, at scheduled dates, and assigning a class to the vessel. Following the surveys, a class certificate[2] is issued (or renewed) which documents the level of compliance of parts inspected with the standards of quality (rules) developed and implemented by the same classification society, with particular reference to the design, structure and mechanical and electrical systems on board.

2. While not constituting proof of seaworthiness, a class certificate is perceived as a fundamental index of quality in the shipping market: it attests the suitability of the vessel for a particular use or service and determines the value of reference of the ship in commercial transactions; it is essential for the issuance of insurance certificates and is important for obtaining safety certifications. Thus, it has a considerable impact on shipping trade[3], although it is not mandatory under international law.

1 Lux J., *Classification Societies*, LLP, London, 1993, 25 ff.

2 Under Reg. EC 391/2009, a "class certificate" is "a document issued by a recognized organization certifying the fitness of a ship for a particular use or service in accordance with the rules and procedures laid down and made public by that recognized organization" (Article 2, §1. *i*).

3 Any contract related to ship and shipping trade normally has a clause concerning the class of the vessel. P & I Clubs, as well as underwriters, require that the vessel remains in class throughout the period of coverage. If the ship does not comply with all the rules, recommendations and requirements of the society, it will no longer be insured and the insurance company is exempt from liability: see Lagoni N., *The liability of Classification Societies*, Springer, Hamburg, 2007, 14.

3. Because of their professionalism and world-class credibility, classification societies (members of the International Association of Classification Societies, IACS)[4] are requested to carry out technical surveys on ships, also as delegates of the Flag States, which are obliged, under international law, to verify and certify the safety conditions of their ships before permitting them to sail.[5]

4. There is a legal relationship between a ship's compliance with the requirements of class, laid down in the rules of the classification societies, and the issue of statutory certificates[6] on behalf of the Flag State Authority: according to SOLAS '74[7], Regulation 3–1, Chapter II-1, Part A-1, on Structural, mechanical and electrical requirements for ships, States must ensure "that, in addition to the requirements contained elsewhere in the present regulations, ships be designed, constructed and maintained in compliance with the structural, mechanical and electrical requirements of a classification society which is recognized by the Administration [...] or with applicable national standards of the Administration which provide an equivalent level of safety".[8]

5. The liability of classification societies in the area of public service certification purposes is subject to numerous international soft law acts[9], regulations and EU directives that provide a framework of appropriate regulations also on financial consequences of negligent conduct of the surveyors[10]; classification services, on the contrary, are

4 The International Association of Classification Societies (IACS) was founded in 1968 by seven leading societies (ABS, BV, GL, LR, NV, DNV, RINA) to develop standardization of classifications rules and improve the quality of classification services. Today, it is composed of thirteen members and has acquired a consultative status to the International Maritime Organization (IMO).

5 Article 94 of the United Nation Convention on the Law of the Sea.

6 According to Article 2, §1, *g*, of EC reg. N. 391/2009 on common rules and standards for ship inspection and survey organizations, "statutory certificate means a certificate issued by or on behalf of a flag State in accordance with the international conventions". We can find the same definition under Article 3, §1, *d*, of Directive 2009/21/EC on compliance with flag State requirements.

7 International Convention for the Safety of Life at Sea, (SOLAS) of 1 November 1974, in force from 25 May 1980.

8 This relationship is strengthened within the framework of European Union law where it is stipulated that Member States, in their capacity as Flag Administrations, must ensure that ships are constructed and maintained in accordance with the rules established by a recognized organization.

9 See IMO Res. A.739/1993 (18) on "Guidelines for the Authorization of Organizations Acting on Behalf of the Administration"; this resolution became mandatory since inclusion in Regulation 1, Chapter XI-1, of the SOLAS Convention. See also IMO Res. A.789/1995 on "Specification on the Survey and Certification Functions of Recognized Organizations acting on behalf of the Administration", and IMO Res. A.847/1997 (19) on "Guidelines to Assist Flag States in the Implementation of IMO Instruments". In 1992, the Comité Maritime International (CMI) set up a Joint Working Group on Issues of Classification Societies whose task was, among other things, to address the issue of liability of classification societies. In this framework, the CMI has developed principles of conduct and Model Clauses recommended to recognized organizations. It is therein suggested that contracts contain a limitation of liability equal to the higher amount between 10 times the rate charged, or the total amount of $ 4 million.

10 See Directive 2009/15/EC on common rules and standards for ship inspection and survey organizations and for the relevant activities of maritime administrations. In this argument, see Ingratoci C., Sicurezza

essentially governed by the contract[11] between societies and ship-owners, according to the standard form furnished by the contracting society. As a rule, this form provides clauses for limitation of liability for any claims for damages made by third parties.[12]

6. Despite the fact that the contract is binding only between the parties, it is clear that negligence in carrying out inspections on board, or an incorrect representation of a ship's defects in the class certificate (misrepresentation), is not only a breach of the duties toward ship-owner; this type of conduct could expose all involved in the shipping sector to risk, along with the wider group of those who could suffer injuries or loss as a result of accidents at sea. This is a matter of growing concern, with the increase in transport of dangerous and pollutant goods.[13] In addition, a misrepresentation may damage the economic interests of those who, trusting in the class, conclude contracts on a vessel not in compliance with requirements of the rules.[14]

7. In the absence of International[15] or European legislation, the aim of this paper is to verify if and what general principles on non-contractual liability it is possible to infer

e certificazione navale: considerazioni in tema di responsabilità degli organismi riconosciuti, in La Torre U., Sia A.M., *La sicurezza nel trasporto e nelle infrastrutture della navigazione marittima ed aerea*, Soveria Mannelli, 2011, 115 ff.; Lagoni N., cit., 234 ff.; Pulido Begines J.L., "The EU Law on Classification Societies: Scope and Liability Issues", (2005) 38, *J. Mar. L. & Com.*, 487.

11 With a classification contract, the society is committed to providing a professional and independent assessment on the quality of the ship, following the implementation of various services, that include visit and classify the ship in accordance with the rules laid down by the same company; monitor the structural characteristics of the vessel, informing the owner on any defects found, if they are not obvious or known to him. In the event of damage to the hull, the classification societies will carry out a more thorough inspection (special visit) to see if the ship still has all the requirements related to the class assigned and, if not, will indicate any repairs necessary to bring the vehicle into compliance or proceed to its declassification. The most important obligations of the owner under the contract are maintaining the ship in line with conditions laid down by class, between one inspection and the next, and notify the inspector of the classification society immediately in the case of grounding or other damage to the hull, both in the main parts (engines) and to those accessories which relate or could relate to the class. For further considerations see Boisson P., *Politiques et droit de la sécurité maritime*, Paris, 1999, 129.

12 The contracts often include clauses limiting liability, such as "hold harmless" clause, for which the contractor agrees to indemnify the society for any damage that this has to bear as a result of claims brought by injured third parties. See Antapassis A., "Liability of Classification Societies" (2007), *Electronic Journal of Comparative Law*, 11, 3, 22 ff.

13 An example of this new approach is the suit against ABS which had classified the "Prestige". On this subject, see United States Court of Appeal, 29 August 2012, *il Diritto marittimo*, 2013, 1 ff.

14 On this subject see Antapassis A., *Liability of Classification Societies*, cit., 25; Lagoni N., T*he Liability of Classification Societies*, cit., *passim*; Micciché L., "In tema di responsabilità extracontrattuale delle società di classificazione", *il Diritto Marittimo*, 2006, 1335; Basedow J., Wurmnest W., *Third-Party Liability of Classification Societies*, Springer, Berlin, 2005; Comenale Pinto M.M., "La responsabilità delle società di classificazione", *il Diritto Marittimo*, 2003, 32 ff.; Lopez de Gonzalo M., "La responsabilità delle società di classifica", *Diritto del commercio internazionale*, 1997, 651 ff.; Miller M.A, "Liability of Classification Societies from the perspective of United States Law" (1997), *Tulane Maritime Law Journal*, 22, 3.

15 CMI, Joint Working Group on a Study of Issues re-Classification Societies, *Yearbook 1996*, London, 1997, 328–342.

from the legal systems of selected Member States, applying them to classification societies in the event of damage to third parties caused by non-performance, or poor performance on the part of classification services.

**8.** With this purpose, we will refer to the jurisprudence on tort liability of classification societies according to the leading cases decided by the national Courts in the European Union, both in civil and common law. We will then try to frame the decisions under the common principles of European Civil Law, fixed in the Draft Common Frame of Reference (DCFR) on Principles, Definitions and Model Rules of European Private Law, to obtain a more systematic legal basis of non-contractual liability of classification societies.

## II. Case Law of the European Courts of Common and Civil Law

**9.** Despite the differences among the EU legal systems of civil and common law, all national Courts are similar in being reluctant to recognize the liability of classification societies for damage caused by structural defects of a vessel; the legal basis of non-liability decisions is the principle of non-delegable duty of ship-owners to guarantee seaworthiness of vessels, before and at the beginning of a voyage.

**10.** Nonetheless, more recently, the Courts' position regarding classification societies has been affected by political consideration, in particular on justice in proper allocation of risks, and by public opinion, which is evermore intolerant of failure of maritime professionals that may cause enormous damage to the global commons and individuals.

**11.** According to common law, liability of classification societies toward third parties arises under the principle of "tort of negligence" in carrying out surveys, or "tort of negligent misrepresentation" in issuing certificates. In particular, under English law the tort of negligence requires: [1)] a duty of care which is owned by the defendant to the claimant, due to a statutory rule aimed to protect the damaged party; [2)] an act or enunciation that could be regarded as a breach of such a duty; [3)] a damage proved by claimant; and [4)] a causal link between the fault of the surveyor and the damage suffered by the third party.[16] As clarified in the Morning Watch case[17], the existence of a duty of care, on a case by case basis, depends on the following criteria: foresee ability of damage; proximity between claimant and defendant; respect of principles of justice and reasonableness.[18]

**12.** According to the proximity criterion, in the Nicholas H case[19], the House of Lord concludes that classification societies do not have a duty of care towards cargo owners, as

16 Lagoni N., cit., 106.

17 Queen's Bench Division, Mariola Marine Corporation v. Lloyd's Register of Shipping, the "Morning Watch" (1990) 1, *Lloyd's Law Report*, 547.

18 Basedow J., Wurmnest W, cit., 16.

19 Marc Rich & Co.A.G. v. Bishop rock Marine Co Ltd, (1992), *Lloyd's Law Report*, 481.

the purpose of classification is to further safety at sea rather than protecting the commercial interest of third parties. In addition, classification societies cannot have the ship under their control after the surveys: thus, cargo owners are entitled to be indemnified for the loss suffered by the ship-owner, under his non-delegable duty to guarantee seaworthiness.

13. On the contrary, German Courts have recognized the liability of classification societies for damages to third parties arising from an accident of navigation, referring to the figure of the contract in favor of third parties[20]: for this purpose, it is requested that damaged party be in proximity of performance and the contracting party have an objective interest to protect the third party.

14. The implications of general interest relating to the safety of navigation are central in the judgments of the French courts: in the Elodie II case[21], the Court of Appeal of Versailles (in a situation similar to that of the Morning Watch case, where the English court decided in favour of the surveyor) recognized the liability of classification society owing to negligence in surveying and misrepresentation of the conditions of the vessel; this behaviour was qualified as a serious fault for a professional entrusted with a public interest service.[22]

15. In the *Wellborn* case[23], Bureau Veritas was held liable on the basis of the violation of a non-contractual general duty of care and diligence, which was shown by the fact that it allowed a ship to sail in conditions of high risk, seriously endangering the crew, the marine environment and, more generally, the safety of navigation.

20 According to Article 823 of BGB, a person who, through his activities, creates a hazardous condition is liable to injured third parties if he has acted negligently, or deliberately operates a violation of the law and, in particular, a violation of a provision aimed to protect the interests of third parties or public interests. This provision (tort law) protects only an enumerated number of rights and interests, but it does not include a protection of pure economic loss. In the presence of issuance of a class certificate that confirms the class of a ship, the buyer may be included in the scope of protection offered by the contract between the seller and the classification society. On this subject see Kareman T.A., "Comparative Study on the Liability of Classification Societies to third Party Purchaser with reference to Turkish, Swiss, German and US Law", (2011) *Journal of Maritime Law §Commerce*, 42, 1, 134 ff.; Grellet L., "Fondement et limites de la responsabilité des sociétés de classification: Rigueur de l'analyse outre Rhin", *Droit Maritime Français*, 1998, 451 ff.

21 21 March 1996, *il Diritto Marittimo*, 1998, 861, ff.

22 In the judgment, the Court said that "en raison de ses manquements importants [...] manifestés par des négligences répétées qui touchent à l'essence même de sa mission générale et qui l'ont conduit, faute d'avoir décelé les vices qui affectaient le navire, à maintenir une classe qui ne se justifiait pas, constituent une faute lourde". According to art. 1382 of the French Civil Code, damages incurred as a result of incorrect information may be pursued in tort under French principles of tort liability. Also in Spanish and Greek law "the aggrieved party must demonstrate negligence, damage, a causal link between the negligent act and the damage and [...] the unlawfulness of the negligent act": Kareman T.A., cit., 129.

23 Court d'Appel di Versaillex, 9 December 2004, confirmed by Court de Cassation, 27 marzo 2007, *il Diritto Marittimo*, 2008, 237 ff.

**16.** The fault of the inspector in ascertaining the conditions of the vessel is considered a direct cause of the damage (loss load) when, in the absence of renewal of the certificate, the ship would not have been able to sail and, therefore, the accident would not have occurred. Thus, with regard to causation, the French Court recognizes the liability of classification societies, apparently overcoming the considerations which led the English Courts to exclude the liability of classification society in the Nicholas H case.[24]

**17.** For the purpose of protecting safety at sea, the French "Court de Cassation, Chambre Criminelle", was more precise in identifying a chain of responsibility, beyond the ship owner himself, in its judgment of 25 September 2012, Erika case. Here RINA was found guilty of recklessness in renewing the class certificate by virtue of an inspection that was carried out below the requested standards of care.[25] In doing so, RINA did not comply with the professional care required by its role, deliberately threatening the safety of navigation and the rights of third parties as a result of the creation of an unreasonable danger.[26]

**18.** The Court of Genoa, in the *Redwood* case[27], recognized the liability of Lloyd's Register of Shipping on the basis of negligent behaviour in contrast with safety regulations and classification standards. In the view of the judge, according to the specific social-economic purpose of classification contracts, the obligation of workmanlike performance is aimed to protect both, the commercial interest of the ship-owner (and his contractors) and public interest in safety of navigation.

**19.** In summary, as a general rule the question regarding liability of classification societies is related to the fault of a person, who holds a qualified position in relation to the protection of the damaged parties, having to act professionally – albeit through a market service – to keep the risks of dangerous activity to acceptable levels.

24 Cour de Cass., 1ere Ch. Civ., 27 March 2007, ship "Wellborn", *il Diritto Marittimo* (2008), with the comment of Lopez de Gonzalo M., "Osservazioni in tema di responsabilità extracontrattuale degli istituti di classifica", 238 ff.

25 In detail, the Court judges that "En renouvelant […] le certificat de classe dans la précipitation et […] sous la pression de contraintes commerciales, avec la seule réserve d'une nouvelle inspection avant fin janvier 2000 […] alors que les zones suspectes de corrosion substantielle qu'il avait observées tout juste quinze mois après la visite spéciale quinquennale étaient, pour un professionnel, le signe manifeste de l'état préoccupant des structures […] l'inspecteur de la société a commis une faute d'imprudence".

26 For comments on the Court of Cassation's judgment see Delebecque P., Aspects civile de la décision Erika, Droit Maritime Français (2012), 1003; Bonassies P., "L'arrêt Erika", *il Diritto Marittimo* (2012), 1278.

27 The Court of Appeal of Genoa, 24 February 2010, *il Diritto Marittimo*, 2013, 1 ff., states that the performance of Lloyd's Register of Shipping was in contrast "con le regole tecniche e precauzionali circa i presupposti nei quali rilasciare le necessarie certificazioni contrattuali e quelle discendenti dalle Convenzioni; certificazioni le quali, oltre agli immediati interessi della committenza pubblica e armatoriale, tutelano in chiave preventiva i non meno primari interessi della sicurezza per l'incolumità di chi viaggia e lavora per mare, nonché degli utilizzatori commerciali della nave e del comparto assicurativo".

**20.** In this context, under English law, in the case of physically loss[28] classification societies owe a duty of care to the victim if proximity can be proven. As explained in the Morning Watch judgment, in the case of economic loss liability of classification societies also requires that the imposition of a duty of care on the surveyor be fair, just and reasonable.[29] The criterion of proximity, which is required to compensate personal or property damages suffered by a third party, translates to a strict requirement of near privities[30] in the case of pure economic loss: according to the theory of voluntary assumption of responsibility, a duty of care can be proven when the information provided by classification society is "plaintiff specific", "purpose specific" and "transaction specific".[31]

**21.** Also German Courts require a qualified proximity with the activity provided by the classification society, a sort of "relationship of confidence"[32] between the professional and the damaged party, on the ground of which the surveyor could reasonably foresee the third party would suffer damage by reason of his misrepresentation. In the Hetch V[33] case, the Court of Appeal of Hamburg applied the figure of the "contract in favour of a third party" to a contract concluded by the owner in anticipation of the sale of the vessel.

**22.** In synthesis, "a classification society cannot be held liable toward a third party purchaser of a ship merely because it routinely issued a class certificate in the ordinary course of its business. To create a relationship of confidence it is necessary that the class society's assessment of ships must be made for a specific contract that involves the third party"[34], such as, for instance, a confirmation of class[35] which states that the ship is still in class.

**23.** In addition, the French Courts would appear to be inspired by the principle of justice and environmental responsibility. Although not directly applicable to the subject, it leads the judge to question the traditional defence of classification societies, that is, the exclusive obligation of the owner to ensure the seaworthiness of the ship; more than ever, others are being required to pay damages that they have contributed to create.[36]

28 Perret v. Collins and others, (1998), 2, *Lloyd's Rep.*, 255.

29 Lagoni N., cit., 136.

30 The requirement of near privity operates as a limiting factor in actions for negligent misrepresentation in several jurisdictions, notably New York, to avoid the threat of indeterminate liability; according to this requirement, liability is limited to those in privity with the defendant, or those for whose information is provided: see Freinman J., *Professional Liability to third Parties*, II edn, ABA, Chicago, 2007, 33 ff.

31 Lagoni N., cit., 137.

32 Karaman T.A., cit., 145 ff., spec. 156. Under art. 311 of BGB "such an obligation arises in particular if a third party, by enlisting a particularly high degree of reliance, materially influences the contractual negotiations or the conclusion of the contract".

33 Judgment of 14 June 1990, *Droit Maritime Français*, 1998, 496 ff.

34 Karaman T.A., cit., 141.

35 According to Norwegian Saleform, under which most vessels are bought and sold, the seller is requested to present a confirmation class which states that the ship is still in class: see Lagoni N., cit., 45.

36 In this argument see Jacobsson M., "The French Court of Cassation and the Erika case; some issues relating to civil liability", (2014) 20 *JMIL*, 19 ff.

## III. Contribution of the Reference Principles and Model Rules of European Private Law to the Debate on Non-Contractual Liability of Classification Societies

**24.** The aforementioned judgments demonstrate that in a high number of cases different legal systems produce substantially common answers to common problems. Therefore, we can conclude that there is a common framework of principles and general rules of law according to which it is possible to define a wide area of non-contractual liability of classification societies.

**25.** More than one argument to support this conclusion comes from the model rules and principles of European Private Law, fixed by the Draft Common Frame of Reference (DCFR): we refer especially to the rules regarding non-contractual liability arising out of damage caused to another (Book VI)[37], regarding principles of security and justice on the one hand, and of efficiency on the other.

**26.** Under the so-called Book VI, the basic rule on non-contractual liability confers on a person who suffers legally relevant damage, a "right to reparation from a person who caused the damage intentionally or negligently or is otherwise accountable for the causation of the damage (VI.-1:101).[38] As mentioned in the DCFR, the "substance of this rule is common property in Europe".

**27.** According to this rule, the central elements of non-contractual liability are: a) accountability; b) legally relevant damage[39]; c) causation.

**28.** Sub a), when can classification societies be considered accountable under this rule (source of liability)?

The concept of accountability embraces all the potential grounds of non-contractual liability: fault or position.[40] In short, accountability involves all matters that national jurisprudence has tried to solve under the concept of "duty of care". According to the examined case law, liability of classification societies can arise from a fault in carrying

[37] Under rules VI.–7:103 (Public law functions and court proceedings) of the DCFR, this Book does not govern the liability of a person or body arising from the exercise or omission to exercise public law functions or from performing duties during court proceedings. Thus, our considerations cannot be extended to liability under public law.

[38] The difference between negligent and intentional tort is not central in recognizing civil liability. The concept of malicious tort (*dolus*) is more common.

[39] In the context of non-contractual liability, the term damage has a wide meaning, including loss and injury. Economic loss includes loss of income or profit, burdens incurred and a reduction in the value of property. Non-economic loss includes pain and suffering and impairment of the quality of life (VI.-2:101, §4).

[40] *Ie* liability without intention or negligence, deriving from a source of danger under responsibility of the defendant.

out surveys or in providing truthful certificates (misrepresentation).[41] The concept of fault includes negligence, intention and malicious tort; as we will see better onward (examining the concept of "legally relevant damage") negligence, according to Article VI. 3:102 of DFCR, refers to failure in complying with standards of care requested by a statutory provision[42] (whose purpose is the protection of the damaged interest) or by the general duty of skill and care. This rule does not require wrongfulness or unlawfulness of the conduct, which is requested in several European legal systems for liability in tort[43]: according to common interpretation of this rule[44], it is sufficient for the conduct to be contrary to the spirit of the legal order, or that it violates obligation of good faith, or fails to correspond to legitimate expectations, in infringing a duty of care. The rules of a classification society, engaged to carry out surveys, are incorporated in the contract: thus, negligence in verifying compliance with requirements for maintaining a ship in class represents, first of all, a breach of contractual duties on the part of a classification society and, as a consequence, a private wrong. Overall, we can conclude that, in classification services the concept of wrongfulness is included in the notion of negligence, which involves any infringement of a specific safety standard and requirement, or general rule aimed at protecting the injured interest.[45]

**29.** Sub b), when can damages suffered by a third party be considered legally relevant?

Under Book VI, Rule 2:101, damage includes loss, both of an economic and non-economic type, and injury as such. This loss is legally relevant if, inter alia:

(a) [...]
(b) The loss or injury results from a violation of a right otherwise conferred by the law (for instance, rights and interests which enjoy protection against all comers, such as absolute rights, formally included under VI.–2:201). Purely contractual rights are, as a rule, excluded.
(c) *or* the loss or injury results from a violation of an interest worthy of legal protection.

41 According to VI.–2:210 "loss caused to a person as a result of another's fraudulent misrepresentation [...] is legally relevant damage". A misrepresentation is fraudulent if it is made with knowledge that the representation is false and is intended to induce the recipient to make a mistake. The difference between this article and the VI.–2:207 model rule, on reliance on incorrect advice and information, is that the former relates to losses caused by misinformation outside professional or trade activities.

42 The term "statute" covers primary legislation, regulations and rules from local authorities, but not guidelines or anything similar: see VI.–3.102.

43 Wrongfulness of conduct is requested by German Civil Code, Article 831 and Italian Civil Code, Article 2043, where we find the notion of "danno ingiusto", meaning breach of a legally protected interest. The concept of "wrongfulness" is completely foreign to Common Law.

44 DCFR, Book VI.–3.102, sub-paragraph b.

45 According to the "result orientated" notion of wrongfulness, which has flourished in Germany, every infringement of a right or a protected legal interest enumerated in the German Civil Code by a positive act automatically entails wrongfulness. According to the opposing "conduct oriented" theory, an unintentional violation of a right or legally protected interest is only regarded as wrongful if the actor infringes a specific norm of conduct set out in the relevant legal provision, or if the actor has failed to heed the due care required to avoid the onset of damage: Karaman T.A., *loc. cit.*

In the case of negligent misrepresentation, we can refer to model rule VI.–2:207 concerning "loss upon reliance on incorrect advice or information". It provides that "loss caused to a person, as a result of making a decision in reasonable reliance on incorrect advice or information, is legally relevant damage if: (a) the advice or information is provided in pursuit of a profession or in the course of trade; (b) the provider knew, or could reasonably be expected to have known, that the recipient would rely on the advice or information in making a decision of the kind made". The professional status of classification societies is, of course, not questioned. The above mentioned second condition requires an adequate level of proximity between the contractor and the third party: it is requested that the injured party belongs to a restricted circle of people to whom the information is directed by a professional who is aware (or should be aware) that those recipients will rely on information to come to a decision of substantive significance. From this point of view, it is important to underline that, under VI.–2:207, liability arises in giving, together, incorrect information and advice: both these elements are requested as part of a single unlawful conduct in which a misrepresentation of fact is present with a recommendation (that is usually implicit or deducible by circumstances, such as during an audit or a special visit before a purchase) to make a decision based thereon.[46] With this in mind, we can conclude that reasonable reliance on the trustworthiness of the class is missing if the ship is working and the last inspection is far off in time. In such case, a diligent recipient must verify the accountability of existing information. On the contrary, if the certificate is up-to-date on the current status of the vessel, reasonable reliance of the third party is worthy of protection (according to VI. – 2:101, c), and requires compensation for losses resulting from a decision made in reasonable reliance on incorrect information (pure economic loss). In this case, a classification society assumes a qualified position toward third parties, a type of "qualified contact/ near privity" position, between contract and tort.[47] In conclusion, according to the principles of good faith and loyalty, loss or injury constitute legally relevant damage only if it would be fair and reasonable for there to be a right to reparation or prevention, on the grounds of accountability, the nature of the damage (or impending damage), reasonable expectations of the person who suffers (or would suffer) the damage, and considerations of public policy.[48]

**30.** Sub c), when can the damage be considered caused by classification providers?

[46] De Bruyne J., Vanleenhove C., "An EU perspective on the liability of classification societies: selected current issues and private international law aspects", (2014) 20, *JIML*, 103 ff.

[47] Karaman T.A., p. 136, argues that the liability of information provider is neither contractual nor tort liability, but stems from a breach of the principle of good faith, determining a breach of confidence. The source of liability is the implied contract between the person who materially influenced the contract and the person who incurred damage from this reliance. If a classification society could be considered accountable toward any third parties for any certificate, of course, it assumes an unbearable risk of liability.

[48] Trivial damages are excluded, and also interests which are assigned to the commonalty as a whole, such as pure ecological damage (see VI.–2:209, Burdens incurred by the State upon environmental impairment). If the environmental impairments also infringe property or personal rights, the injured party can claim reparation for it.

In the case of negligence in conducting surveys, liability of classification societies could be regarded as a consequence of the principle of proper allocation of responsibility for creation of risks: according to this principle, Courts can condemn the controlling entity to compensation for damages resulting from an accident of navigation, due to structural defects, that would not have occurred if surveys had been conducted with due diligence.[49] Under model rules, there is no difference between "cause in fact" and "in law", nor is fulfilment to a "*conditio sine qua non* formula" required (VI.- 4:101): when legally relevant damages may have been caused by any number of occurrences, for which different persons are accountable, and it is established that the damage was caused by one of these occurrences, but not which one, there is a rebuttable presumption that each person who is accountable for any of the occurrences has caused that damage (VI.-4:103). In detail, according to the rule on alternative causes (VI.-4:101), a person who breaches a right owed to the injured person, or exposes that person to a greater risk, should not be exonerated from liability solely because another person also breaches a duty owed to the injured person, and it is no possible to say which of the breaches of duty has caused the damage. This rule appears to be a codification of the criterion that was formulated by civil law Courts, especially in the *Wellborn* case[50], according to which liability of the ship-owner for seaworthiness does not exclude liability of the classification society. With regard to clauses on limitation of liability, according to the DCFR, liability for causing legally relevant damage intentionally, or as a result of a profound failure to take such care as is manifestly required in the circumstances, cannot be excluded or restricted (VI.–5:401).[51] Pre-emptive exclusion or restriction of liability is admitted just in cases of ordinary liability in negligence.

## IV. Conclusion: Classification Services Market Efficienies and Purposes of General Interest

**31.** According to classification contracts, classification societies are not obliged to guarantee the seaworthiness of a vessel[52]; they have only to verify the structural and mechanical properties of the ship, with the professional diligence required by their role, and declare them faithfully: inspection, assessment and declaration are integrated into the class certificate, a document that declares the "class" of the vessel by virtue of the conditions of the inspected parties at a definite date. The issuance (or renewal) of the

49 See Erika case, note 25.

50 See note 24.

51 DCFR, VI.-5:401. In any case, restrictions are excluded: (a) in respect of personal injury (including fatal injury); or (b) if the exclusion or restriction is otherwise illegal or contrary to good faith and fair dealing. Where damage of another type is at issue (for example damage to property), an exclusion of liability for causing such damage through gross negligence is invalid where it is illegal or offends the precepts of good faith. Hence, paragraph (2)(b) is linked to the rules in II.–7:301 and in II.–7:302 (Infringement of fundamental principles or mandatory rules) and refers to the rules of the applicable contract law.

52 See Antapassis A., *Liability of Classification Societies*, cit., 3; BerLev O., "Liability of a Vessel Classification Society cannot be based on warranty of seaworthiness", (1973) *JMLC*, 4, 334; Miller M., "Liability of Classification Societies from the perspective of United State Law", (1997) *Tulane Mar. L. J.*, 21, 75.

certificate realizes the interest of the contractor, allowing the ship to sail and to be involved in numerous business transactions.

**32.** In the event of damage due to structural failure of the vessel, classification societies may be sued to the extent to which the contracting party can prove poor or non-performance of classification contractual obligations. Liability toward third parties is recognized under strict limits, in the case of personal injuries, property damage and, in certain circumstances, also for pure economic loss.

**33.** Rules of national legislation are different in this respect: tort of negligence under English law only protects life and health. In the case of property damages, limits such as proximity and foresee-ability are related to the need of the classification society to assess the liability risk, mainly for insurance issues. A tort of deceit only could grant an actionable claim in the case of pure economic loss.[53] Under German law, application of the figure of "contract with protective effects toward third parties" is possible if a qualified relationship of proximity between the damaged party and contractual performance, is proven. According to the French case law, in the event of loss suffered by third parties, due to structural failure of the vessel, classification societies may be sued to the extent to which the injured party can prove that the defects, that have caused the damage, should have been detected during inspections and, therefore, should have led to non-renewal (or withdrawal) of the class.

**34.** In Italian case law, there is a precedent of wide protection of the reliance of third parties on the attested class. There is no doubt, in fact, that classification accomplishes a function which is outside the contract, which is neither incidental nor secondary, since the class certificate contains information on compliance with class requirements and gives some indication on fulfilment of standard of ships' safety, in the interests of a large part of the shipping industry.[54] The group of consultants of information (who rely on class certificates, or on-line Ship Register of Classification societies), includes insurers, cargo owners, cruise liners, potential purchasers, and so on. The importance of this function is directly related to the growing use of modern technologies in marketing of classification services, and to open access to information on class[55], accredited as a quality measure of world fleets. As was pointed out by the Italian Court of Genoa in the Redwood case, the reputational *status* of classification societies gives a relevance of general interest to the certificates and heightens the need for protection of legitimate expectations of third parties afflicted by incorrect information.

53 Lagoni N., cit., 233.

54 On the informative function of the class, and its relevance in the modern shipping market, see De Bruyne J., Vanleenhove C., cit., 108 ff.; Karaman T.A., cit., 125 ff.; Beurier J.P., "La sécurité maritime et la protection de l'environnement: évolutions et limites", *Droit Maritime Français*, 2004, 99 ss.

55 All members of IACS enter their vessels in a ships register that is openly accessible to the public. This register contains information about class, class notations, installation of the ship, ship-owner, Flag State and so on: Lagoni N., cit., 50.

35. Despite of the different positions of EU domestic Courts, the general principles of non-contractual liability are common to different European legal systems and permit us to identify the source of liability of classification societies towards third parties in violation of the duty to conduct inspections with professional diligence (negligence in conducting the survey)[56], or in violation of the (contractual) obligation to certify, with truth, the observed conditions of the vessel (misrepresentation).

36. For the criterion of unlawfulness of conduct, violation of a specific rule is not necessarily required: rather, an infringement of more the general duty of safety and care is enough, deducible from the international rules on protection of human life at sea and of the marine environment, which refer to the standards of the classification society.[57]

37. In this context, when the national rules, principles and criteria applied by different jurisdictions present some common elements, which find correspondence in the principles and model rules of DCFR, these acquire a special significance: I am referring to a common interpretation of core notions, such as "negligence", "foreseeability" and "legally relevant damage".

38. Under the DCFR, the underlying principles of security and justice, including key elements such as proper allocation of responsibility for the creation of risks (that is social responsibility, holding people responsible for the consequences of their own creation of risks), and protection of reasonable reliance (especially of those in a weak or vulnerable position), could furnish a common frame of reference for the criterion of the duty of care and proximity.

39. In this vein, I wish to add that also the principle of efficiency is of vital importance, and presents a wider scope than protection of the interests of the parties, since it aims at fulfilling public purposes, such as sustainable growth. In this respect, there is a public value in promoting better-informed decision-making in a field, such as shipping, that involves economic aims, but also environmental, competition and social matters.

40. Connecting European jurisprudence to the common rules of European private law, whose essential elements are inferred (*inter alia*) from the "Acquis Principles of the Existing EC contract law"[58], allows us to look at the proposed solutions not only as the product of Courts, but also as the result of legal frameworks that could affect future judgments and push decisions into line by their common application. In conclusion, these principles may provide a strong reference point for a common legal basis in

56 In the "Somarelf v. American Bureau of Shipping case", the United States District Court for the District of New Jersey, 720 F. Supp. 441, 453, 1989, *AMC* 2330, 2349, points out that a professional body, that issues formal certificates essential to commerce, can cause economic loss when it does not carry out inspections carefully.

57 Antapassis A., cit., 30 ff.

58 DCFR, Introduction, 30.

drafting any future EU legislation in the field of non-contractual liability of classification societies.

Pablo Constenla*

# TOWARDS A EURO-MARITIME CONTRACT LAW?

## I. Introduction

1. This paper will seek to give a response as to whether there is a room for an EU maritime law on its own or, on the other hand, the EU should rather stand by the path of the International Maritime Conventions and seek a world-wide uniformity. In other words, it is intended to address the current problem of the EU to find a way to regulate private Maritime law.

2. EU law relating to transport and, specifically to maritime transport, has been widely described in many sources.[1] The main current concern seems to be the continuing decline of EU-flagged vessels. It is important for the industry to find a solution in order to stop this negative trend.[2]

3. It will be argued that, despite the incompleteness of the International Conventions[3] on, for example, multimodal carrier liability, the European Union (and particularly the Commission) should not try to navigate around them with PECL or DCFR but rather accept the ratification of the Convention with the power that was conferred. This would also avoid the question of EU competency and the conflict between Member States with obligations both to an International Convention and to the Union.

* Degree in Law Universidad Pontificia Comillas, LLM Swansea University, Spanish Bar Association.

1 Power, V., *EC Shipping Law*, 1992. See also a presentation by Hannu Honka, "European Union Shipping Policies", included in *United States Shipping Policies and the World Market*, ed. William A. Lovett, 1996.

2 As a clarification, the global share of EC-owned shipping has not declined in the 1990s. Compared with the strong decline of the share related to EC-flagged ships this cannot mean anything else, but operators outflagging their ships for economic reasons.

3 United Nations Convention on International Carriage of Goods Wholly or Partly by Sea (the Rotterdam Rules) (formally adopted by UN General Assembly December 2008, annexed to General Assembly Resolution 63/122).

## II. The Roots for a Complete EU Maritime Law Arose Incidentally

4. In highlighting the emphasis of EU law in the maritime sector there are three areas to be considered.[4] Firstly, the EU has gradually been considering and regulating maritime safety, including the ship safety and the protection of the maritime environment. This is the starting point to create a complete EU Public Shipping Law. For example, Sulphur contents of certain liquid fuels were originally regulated by Directive 93/12/EC. The Directive has been revised by the Commission with the strategy to reduce atmospheric emissions from seagoing ships and was reflected in Directive 2005/33/EC, which introduced, inter alia, the IMO concept of Sulphur Emissions Control Areas (SECAs).

(A) Current EU Commission Proposal to introduce measures towards reducing greenhouse emissions from ships.
(B) Prevention of pollution after the ERIKA ad PRESTIGE disasters: ratification of the Hazardous and Noxious Substances by Sea Convention 1996, Directives 2004/35/CE and 2005/35/CE and Decision 2005/667/JHA.

5. Secondly, competition matters as a natural consequence of the TFEU, whose articles 101 and 102 prohibit cartels and suchlike arrangements and misuse of a dominant position respectively:

(A) The EU legislated more comprehensively on maritime transport and competition in 1986 in the Council Regulation (EEC) No 4056/86 of 22 December 1986 laying down detailed rules for the application of the old articles 85 and 86.
(B) The Council Regulation (EC) No 1419/2006 of 25 September 2006 repealing Regulation (EEC) No 4056/86 lays down detailed rules for the application of Articles 85 and 86 of the Treaty to maritime transport, and amending Regulation (EC) No 1/2003 regarding the extension of its scope to include cabotage and international tramp services Official Journal L 269, 28.9.2006, p. 1–3.

6. This is strengthened by decisions of the EU institutions, such as the ECJ and its recent Judgment dated 8 July 2014.[5] This has very recently laid down that a company national in an EEE country can benefit from the free provision of services – with the consequence that "restrictive measures" such as strikes will be prohibited – even if the vessel is flagged in a third State.

7. Therefore, the roots for a EU Public Maritime Law have been developed, including the aspects of competition. The EU institutions and even the ECJ seem willing to protect the shipping industry but it is not clear whether the intention will stop the decline of EU-flagged vessels. However, the main question remaining is the position that the EU

[4] Obviously, there is a much wider perspective to EC shipping. A clarifying position could be found in "Towards a new maritime strategy", COM (96) 81, adopted 14 March 1996.
[5] ECJ Judgment C-83/13, 8 July 2014.

must adopt regarding EU private law and whether it would be possible and convenient to legislate on private law.

## III. EU is Supported by the Law and the Industry to Achieve Its Foundational Aim

**8.** To "Europeanise" means to unify or harmonise European Law and many of the reasons to unify private shipping law is valid both for Europe and for the world. The debate cannot be initiated without considering:

- The aim that led to the establishment of the EU, namely the free flow of goods, persons, services and capital as well as the development of a Common European Transport Policy ("CTP"), which started 20 years ago with a White Paper.[6]
- The importance of transport to achieve these aims. Particularly, a transport that is "*sustainable, energy-efficient and respectful of the environment. The aim is to disconnect mobility from its adverse effects. This means, above all, promoting co-modality, i.e. optimally combining various modes of transport within the same transport chain, which is the solution for the future in the case of freight.*"[7]
- The relevance of the law to comply with the CTP. The transport industry itself was incapable of reforming the transport system mainly because any change of mode in the current modally-oriented transport system involves a change of system – legal system – rather than a mere technical transhipment. This change creates "friction costs"[8] that prevent the formation of a competitive intermodal transport chain.

## IV. The Complexity of Shipping Business

**9.** Shipping is a difficult and complex business. It is not easy for everyone to understand the mechanisms of the market, the number of parties involved, the "forum shopping" strategies, the out-flagging of vessels and the pressures that the players can exercise to circumvent the law.

**10.** Most parties to a contract can understand contract law including (a) formation, validity, interpretation and content of contracts; (b) performance of obligations and remedies of non-performance;[9] (c) content of specific contracts and the rights and

[6] White Paper "The Future Development of the Common Transport Policy – A Global Approach to the Construction of a Community Framework for Sustainable Mobility" COM (92) 494 final, Bulleting of the European Communities Supplement 3/93.

[7] The European Commission, http://ec.europa.eu/transport/sustainable/index_en.htm.

[8] Friction costs are defined a measurement of the inefficiency of a transport operation. They are expressed in the form of higher prices, longer journeys, less punctuality, lower availability of quality services, limitations on the types of goods available, higher risk of damage and more complex administrative procedures.

[9] This is the coverage of the PECL.

obligations arising from them; (d) private law rights and obligations that do not arise from a contract (i.e. unjustified enrichment and damage caused to another); and (e) matters of moveable property: acquisition and loss of ownership trust law.[10]

**11.** In other words, if you cause damage to an injured party, you know that you will have to pay damages. If you prepare a contract to buy a house, you know that if it is destroyed, the contract is then frustrated. However, it is not so easy to understand that if a vessel is carrying cargo and it encounters a maritime adventure but it is saved, the cargo owners will have to contribute in general average; or, that if a hurricane happens, the shipowner might raise the "Act of God" defence and escape liability.

## V. Suitable Method to Regulate Private Maritime Law

**12.** Once it is clear that the industry needs the support of the EU, it should be clarified the method by which the law could contribute to improve the free movement of goods by a sustainable transport.

### *5.1. PECL and DCFR as voluntary private rules*

**13.** The areas of contract law that have been previously mentioned – part D – are the areas covered by the PECL and the DCFR respectively. It is important to explain that the coverage of the DCFR is broader than what the EU Commission seemed to have in mind for the coverage of the CFR. The "academic" frame of reference is not subject to the constraints of the "political" frame of reference. While the DCFR is linked to the CFR, it was conceived as an independent text.[11]

**14.** When the DCFR started there were no political discussions underway, neither of contract law nor for any other part of the law. Then, a comprehensive DCFR created a concrete basis for the coverage of the political CFR. The question that remains is whether adequate PECL for the shipping business would encourage the Institutions to regulate private maritime law.

**15.** However, this solution seems not to be adequate in shipping. Shipping is too complex and involves too many parties to be regulated in voluntary rules. The contracts are usually concluded in an urgent manner and the parties do not spend much time drafting them, so they would be reluctant to incorporate new voluntary rules that escape their day-to-day negotiations.

10 This is the coverage of the DCFR, which is wider in scope than the PECL.

11 Von Bar, C., Clive, E., Schulte-Nölke, H., *Principles, Definitions and Model Rules of European Private Law*, Germany, 2009.

16. Moreover, the past experience with similar instruments – FIATA Model Rules 1996 and UNCTAD/ICC Rules 1992[12] – was not successful due to the pressure of the operators. "*None of the sets of Multimodal Rules, including the latest UNCTAD/ICC Rules 1992, provides those operating the supply chain with a truly multimodal solution.*"[13] Having said this, redacting maritime principles could help to receive a political call to regulate the EU private maritime law, as the DCFR aimed to do with the CFR.

## 5.2. *Choice of law as an option*

17. There have been suggestions in the line that the players-traders-parties to a contract must afford the so protected autonomy of the parties or freedom of contract. This is supported by the choice-of-law rules of the Rome Convention on the Law Applicable to Contractual Obligations of 19 June 1980 (and, now, the Regulation).[14]

### 5.2.1. Uncertainty remains

18. However, a choice of law will not always give them certainty, and if the parties to the contract have not chosen the applicable law, the rules of the Regulation also leave uncertainty as to which law the particular court will apply. Not only problems related to the choice of law arise, but also to choice of forum can lead to many problems in shipping, as the Tilly Russ case showed.[15]

19. In addition, the contracts which are governed by an unknown foreign law will cause the businessmen the following problems:

- First, when foreign law is applicable it must be ascertained. This ascertainment is manageable when the parties or the court have good access to reliable sources of information on foreign law. In general, the law of a country that belongs to the same family of laws and which is expressed in the same or in a related language can be ascertained. An English court will not have great trouble with Irish law, nor will a German court with Austrian or Swiss law.

12 The 1980 UN Convention on Multimodal Transportation of Goods failed to attract sufficient support and did not enter into force. Then, the UNCTAD/ICC drafted the Model Rules as a compromise. Although they do not have the status of mandatory law, they may be incorporated by contract. However, they give preference to mandatory law (Rule 13). As the Rules are based on the "network principle" (Rule 6.4) so the liability limit that applies (providing that the unimodal stage of the transport where the loss occurred can be identified) is that which corresponds to the national or international law that would have applied for that stage under a unimodal contract.

13 Kindred and Brooks, *Multimodal Transport Rules*, the Hague, 1997.

14 Regulation (EC) No 593/2008 of the European Parliament and the Council of 17 June 2008 on the law applicable to contractual obligations (Rome I).

15 ECJ Judgment C-71/83, 19 June 1984. A choice-of-forum clause in a Bill of Lading will be valid if: the consent of both parties was given in writing, consent relating to the clause was given orally and confirmation is in writing, the Bill of Lading is the form of the usual dealings between the parties.

- Further, the party who pleads foreign law will most often have to prove that the foreign law provides his submissions. Therefore, foreign law will only be pleaded and proven when a party believes that he can provide the information that is necessary to convince the court that the foreign law should be applied to his advantage.

**20.** Therefore, the choice-of-law rules do not consider whether the applicable foreign rule leads to a result that the court will accept. As the American author *Cardozo* expressed the choice of law rules are "*more remorseless, blinder to the final cause than in other fields*".[16] Many courts resent this blind neutrality and apply the rules they like best, and very often they prefer the rules of the forum to the foreign rules.[17]

**21.** Most writers on the conflict of laws believe that the courts are wrong in preferring what they believe to be the "better law". The choice-of-law rules provide a special kind of justice to distribute in a fair and equitable manner the power of the legal systems to govern legal situations.[18]

**22.** Even if the writers tell a party who appears in a foreign court that his national law is the one applicable to the particular case, he still cannot be assured that it will be applied. As the average lawyer is afraid of private international law, the party will often find that his counsel in the foreign country and the judge try to avoid the refined mechanisms of private international law and an unknown foreign law with the result that his law is not applied.[19]

### 5.2.2. Rome I Regulation and the Rotterdam Rules

**23.** In the carriage of goods by sea, the Rome I Regulation (Article 5)[20] might conflict with the Rotterdam Rules (Article 5).[21] Rome I provides a set of conflict rules that differ from those in the Rotterdam Rules. Therefore, in case the applicable law to the carriage is not agreed, the law applicable shall be the law of the country of habitual residence of the carrier, provided that the place of receipt or the place of delivery or the habitual

16 Cardozo, *Paradoxes of Legal Science*, Lawbook Exchange, 2000.

17 See European University Institute, *Integration through Law*, (eds. Cappelletti, Seccombe and Weiler) Volume 1, Book 2, Part II, p 161ff, *Conflict of Laws as a Technique for Legal Integration*, by Hay, Lando and Rotunda, at pp 168ff.

18 See Kegel *The Crisis of Conflict of Laws*, Recueil des Cours de l'Académie de Droit International 1964 II, 94, 185. Bernard Audit, *Droit international privé*, 1991 no 96 ff, and Jan Kropholler, *Internationales Privatrecht*, 2nd. ed. 1994 §4 seem to agree with *Kegel*.

19 Op.cit. no.18.

20 To the extent that the law applicable to a contract for the carriage of goods has not been chosen in accordance with Article 3, the law applicable shall be the law of the country of habitual residence of the carrier, provided that the place of receipt or the place of delivery or the habitual residence of the consignor is also situated in that country. If those requirements are not met, the law of the country where the place of delivery as agreed by the parties is situated shall apply.

21 General scope of application.

residence of the consignor is also situated in that country. If these common elements with the country of habitual residence of the carrier do not exist, the law of the place of delivery will be applicable.

**24.** However, the aim of Article 5 of the Rotterdam Rules should be read as a provision of the scope of application and not as a conflict rule. Rome I aims to be applied as a conflict rule. This means that when the applicable law is not agreed and the conditions in Article 5 of Rome I are met, the Rotterdam Rules will apply with mandatory effect.

## 5.3. *Mandatory and uniform system*

### 5.3.1. International agreements concluded by the EU have preference over EU secondary law and Member States national law

**25.** Agreements concluded by the Union are binding upon both the Union institutions and the Member States.[22] The agreements, when concluded and entered into force, become integral parts of Union law and are directly applicable also in the Member States. Whether they also have direct effect – i.e. they may be invoked directly by private parties before courts and authorities – will depend on the nature of the agreement and the individual provisions invoked.

**26.** In the EU hierarchy of norms, agreements concluded by the Union are situated between primary law – such as the TEU and the TFEU – and legislative acts – such as regulations and directives.[23] Similarly to all norms of EU law, they have primacy over national laws of Member States.[24]

**27.** On the other hand, agreements concluded by EU Member States but not by the Union are even more clearly extraneous to Union law. They form part of the national law of the Member States that have concluded them.

**28.** The ECJ ruled in the "Tatry" case[25] that the priority of the specific maritime Conventions shall be applicable only to matters of jurisdiction and recognition of foreign judgments.

[22] TFEU Consolidated Version of the Treaty of Functioning of the European Union, Article 216.2, 2010 OJ C 83, at 144.

[23] See Int'l Air Transp. Ass'n v. Dep't for Transp., Case C-344/04, [2006] E.C.R. I-403.

[24] On the principle of primacy, see, e.g., Costa v. ENEL, Case 6/64, [1964] E.C.R. 585; Internationale Handelsgesellschaft mbH v. Einfuhr- und Vorratsstelle fdr Getreide und Futtermittel, Case 11/70, [1970] E.C.R. 1125.

[25] ECJ Judgment C-406–92, 6 December 1994.

### 5.3.2. EU institutions are competent in regulating EU transport

**29.** According to Article 90 TFEU, "*the objectives of the Treaties shall, in matters governed by this Title, be pursued within the framework of a common transport policy.*" Considering that one of the aims of the EU was the free movement of goods, that transport policies are within the EU competence and that International Agreements concluded by the EU have primacy over EU secondary law and Member States national law, it is no longer reasonable that the EU does not ratify the Private Maritime Law International Conventions. There might be three reasons justifying the non-ratification of the Conventions by the EU as a party:

(A) The agreements may have been concluded by Member States before the EU had competence in a particular area;
(B) The agreement may concern a matter that is still outside an EU competence; and
(C) The EU Commission or the Council may prefer not to conclude agreements despite of an EU competence. However, if the EU does not become party to the Private Maritime Law International Conventions problems will arise such as:

- *Increase of "forum shopping"*

**30.** For example, if one State is party to the 1952 Arrest Convention – i.e. Belgium, Germany – with 17 categories that give rise to a maritime claim and another State to the 1999 Arrest Convention – i.e. Spain – with 22 categories, the interested person will wait the vessel to be in the jurisdiction that better protects his right (probably a 1999 Convention State) with the prejudice that it brings for the person suffering the arrest – although well-founded.

- *Conflicts between Member States' obligations both to an International Convention and to the Community.*

**31.** For example, if the EU finally decides to regulate multimodal transport in a regional level and the Rotterdam Rules enter into force – or the Member State still applies unimodal Conventions – at the same time in one or various Member States the debate about priority will be in place.

**32.** On another matter, the controls over class societies in the "Erika I package"[26] and the Regulation 391/2009/EC[27] might be in breach of the International Convention that is being debated in the CMI.

[26] Http://ec.europa.eu/transport/library/erika-en.pdf.

[27] Regulation (EC) No 391/2009 of the European Parliament and of the Council of 23 April 2009 on common rules and standards for ship inspection and survey organizations.

**33.** It must be pointed out that in some Member States the primacy of EU law over treaty law may not be accepted. The example of France is relevant, as the French Administrative Court has never accepted to rule that EU law would supersede another treaty because Article 55 of the French Constitution does not establish any hierarchy between international treaties.

- *Legal conflict between International Agreements concluded by the EU and the EU secondary law.*

**34.** By way of example, if the EU decides to be party to the Nairobi Convention of Wreck Removal 2007 and, at the same time, the EU legislates – by way of Directive – the procedure or the obligations to remove wrecks or the liability in doing so, the conflict will arise again due to the direct effect of Directives. The same would happen with the Limitation of Liability for Maritime Claims Convention 1976 or even Conventions that are likely to enjoy their validity soon.[28]

### 5.3.3. The transport of goods as the "mirror image"

**35.** In multimodal transport there is more than one mode of transport involved in a multimodal carriage and thus different unimodal legal regimes may apply. The problem has been solved by identifying under which method of transport the damage, loss or incident causing delay occurred and by applying the particular unimodal regime.

**36.** A number of obstacles which prevent the extensive use of intermodal transport have been identified. These include the lack of a coherent network of modes and interconnections, the lack of technical interoperability between the modes, a variety of regulations and standards for transport means, data interchange and procedures.[29]

**37.** The law cannot increase the problem and practitioners should collaborate to facilitate life to the operators. The intermodal operators should be able to offer their customers a clear set of transparent liability conditions and procedures for any cargo

28 Three major organizations move forward in 2013 promoting Maritime Treaty ratification and claim to promote the ratification of a package of up to 11 Maritime Conventions, including seven from IMO, namely, Protocol 1977 to MARPOL; Recycling of Ships, Hong Kong Convention 2009; Facilitation of International Maritime Traffic Convention 1965; Protocol 1996 to "LLMC1976"; Protocol 2002 to the Athens Convention relating to the Carriage of Passengers and their Luggage by Sea 1974; "HNS1996" and Protocol 2010; Nairobi Convention on the Removal of Wrecks 2007. Other two promoted ILO, namely, the Maritime Labour Convention 2006 and the Seafarers' Identity Documents Convention, revised, 2003. Lastly, one UNCITRAL instrument (the so-called "Rotterdam Rules 2009"). Also, the BWM (Ballast Water Management Convention 2004) would be later added up to the bouquet.

29 Communications from the Commission to the European Parliament and the Council "Intermodality and Intermodal Freight Transport in the European Union."

that is damaged or lost in journey. From the end-user's point of view, the liability rules should not be mode-specific and should not distinguish between national and international transport.

**38.** Efforts to draft a European regional liability regime on multimodal transport have been based on an understanding of the multimodal contract as *sui generis,* a contract with its own characteristics. This view was taken by the legal experts assisting the EU Commission in drafting the 2005 proposal for an EU regional multimodal regime,[30] which did not attempt to provide a mandatory new regional legal instrument, but as an "opt out" system. However, the *sui generis* approach would not solve the problem of a "collision of conventions" if the EU decides on a regional solution for international European transport. On the contrary, there would have been two competing international legal regimes.[31]

**39.** The experts expressed that a European regime on multimodal transport might conflict with the existing applicable unimodal conventions, such as the Convention on the Contract for the International Carriage of Goods by Road (CMR),[32] although it is stated in the proposal that "*the intention behind the Regime, however, is that in all such cases it is the Regime and not CMR that should prevail*".[33]

**40.** The latest report was published in June 2009,[34] where the stakeholders agreed on the need for a uniform system with the exception that they could not accept any increase in liability.[35] Most stakeholders believed that any attempt at regulating multimodal transport should take place at a global level.

**41.** A new European regime would add a new player of complexity to the rather complex cargo liability regimes.[36] This is another debate but the problems might to be solved by the Rotterdam Rules although other issues will arise – mainly due to volume contracts, the carriage preceding or subsequent carriage;[37] collision with unimodal conventions in

30 Integrated Services in the Intermodal Chain (ISIC) Final Report Task B: Intermodal Liability and Documentation (Southampton 28 October 2005) (ISIC 2005) p 13.

31 Eftestol-Wilhelmsson, E., "The Rotterdam Rules in a European multimodal context" (2010) 16 *JIML.*

32 Convention on the Contract for the International Carriage of Goods by Road (CMR) (Geneva 19 May 1956).

33 ISIC 2005 (n 12) p 13.

34 Http://ec.europa.eu/transport/strategies/studies/strategies_en.thm.

35 This was also the conclusion of the UNCTAD report "Multimodal Transport: The Feasibility of an International Legal Instrument" UNCTAD/SDTE/TLB/2003/1.

36 The 2009 expert report (n 36) p 8.

37 Rotterdam Rules Article 26 regulates the situation where the liability regime of the Rotterdam Rules has extended its scope of application to multimodal carriage outside the vessel.

multimodal transport;[38] jurisdiction,[39] arbitration[40] and their relation with the Brussels I Regulation).

**42.** The Rotterdam Rules, which are in line with the alternatives presented in the 2007 Freight Logistic Action Plan, offer a "modified network liability system"[41] (Article 26) combined with an extension in the applicability of existing unimodal regimes in multimodal transport (Article 82). They also offer a global solution as required by the European stakeholders in the 2009 survey.

**43.** However, as we a have previously stated, it is not a truly multimodal legal regime. The "modified network liability system" is based on an interaction between the different unimodal liability systems on carriage by road,[42] rail, air[43] and inland waterway[44] and the liability system of the Rotterdam Rules. Being the period of responsibility of the carrier under the Rotterdam Rules extended to include the place of receipt to the place of delivery,[45] both the Rotterdam Rules and different unimodal liability regimes may be applicable simultaneously and lead to conflicts of conventions. Also, the unimodal conventions have an extended scope of application and are applicable to what might be seen as traditional maritime carriage.[46]

**44.** Nevertheless, while the European Parliament has gone some way encouraging the Member States to sing up to the Rotterdam Rules, the Council of the EU has still not reached an official conclusion.[47] The revision of the maritime transport policy in the period 2018–2020, held on 3 June 2014 would have been a great opportunity.

38 Rotterdam Rules Article 82 regulates situations where the unimodal regimes have extended their scope of application to what might be characterised as traditional maritime carriage, such as when the cargo is on board a ship or if the sea leg is supplementary to the land transport.

39 Chapter 14.

40 Chapter 15.

41 Nikaki, T., "Conflicting Laws in "Wet" Multimodal Carriage of Goods: The UNCITRAL Draft Convention on the Carriage of Goods Wholly or Partly by Sea" (2006) 37 *Journal of Maritime Law & Commerce* 521–44 at p 528.

42 Convention on the Contract for the International Carriage of Goods by Road (CMR) (Geneva 19 May 1956).

43 See Convention for the Unification of Certain Rules for International Carriage by Air (Montreal 28 May 1999) (the Montreal Convention) Article 23 and Convention Concerning the Contract for International Carriage by Rail (COTIF) – Annex B Uniform Rules Concerning the Contract of International Carriage of Goods by Rail 1999 (CIM) (COTIF-CIM) art 30.

44 Budapest Convention on the Contract for the Carriage of Goods by Inland Waterways (CMNI) (Budapest 22 June 2001).

45 Rotterdam Rules, Article 12.

46 (2010) 16 JIML.

47 In an informal meeting in Antwerp, 15–16 September 2010, the Council of Ministers of Transport of the EU concluded that "the Rotterdam Rules seem to have great potential."

## VI. Conclusion

**45.** It might be the time for scholars to address the matter to the EU and suggest the ratification of the Private Maritime International Conventions being the power conferred in Article 216 TFEU[48] in order to achieve one of the objectives in the Treaties, being the regulation of transport with the procedure established in Article 218 TFEU.

**46.** In other words, the EU private maritime law should pass through the connection with the world and both the unification and uniformity of the law. Quoting prof. Thibaut, *"if there is no unity of laws then the terrible and odious practice of the conflict of laws will arise ... so that in their intercourse the poor subjects will be stuck and suffocated in such a constant maze of uncertainty and shock that their worst enemies could not advise them worse. Unity of law would, however, make smooth and safe the road of the citizen from one state to the other, and wicked lawyers would no longer have the opportunity to sell their legal secrets and thereby extort and maltreat the poor foreigners."*

48 The Union may conclude an agreement with one or more third countries or international organizations where the Treaties so provide or where the conclusion of an agreement is necessary in order to achieve, within the framework of the Union's policies, one of the objectives referred to in the Treaties, or is provided for in a legally binding Union act or is likely to affect common rules or alter their scope.

José Manuel
Martín Osante*

# PRINCIPLES OF EUROPEAN INSURANCE CONTRACT LAW AND MARINE INSURANCE**

## I. Introduction

1. The present paper seeks to examine the outlines of the European Insurance Contract Law, which aims at setting a model of insurance contract that can be used as an alternative approach to the various national legal frames, as well as the impact they will probably have on marine insurance. In this regard, it should be borne in mind that there are many national marine insurance contract regulations that are non-mandatory (for example, the Spanish Law 14/2014, of 24 July 2014, of Maritime Navigation[1] – hereinafter LMN), so that the policy models for insurance contracts (or what is the same, what is agreed by the parties) are the first regulatory source of the marine insurance contract. And, in the practice, the parties use, among others, the English policy models for marine insurance contracts: the Institute Time Clauses Hulls 01/10/83 and the Institute Cargo Clauses 01/01/82, in modes A, B and C, drawn up in accordance with the British 1906 Marine Insurance Act. There do thus exist different – optional – models of reference for the contracting of marine insurance on an international level that serve as an alternative to national rules. It is therefore necessary to establish the advantages and drawbacks the European model of insurance contract may imply for the contracting parties of marine insurance with respect to the existing insurance policies, a work that shall be done in the present study.

## II. Principles of European Insurance Contract Law

### 2.1. *Scope of application*

2. The Principles of European Insurance Contract Law (PEICL) apply to private insurance in general, including mutual insurance (Article 1:101.1), and also to marine

* Assistant Professor of Commercial Law, University of the Basque Country (UPV/EHU), Bilbao, Spain.
** This article has been produced in the course of research project Ref. DER2012-37543-C03-02: "New Legal Solutions regarding Documentation and Liability in view of the Restructuring of the Transport Market", subsidised by the Spanish Ministry of Economy and Competitiveness.
1 Published in the Spanish Official Gazette, n. 180, of 25 July 2014.

insurance.[2] This is because of the substantive scope of application: "private insurance in general", and marine insurance is part of private insurance contract law. In any case, parties to a marine insurance contract may opt into the Principles (optional application, *opt-in*), but are not obliged to apply them to their contracts (Article 1:102).

**3.** The Principles do not follow the traditional distinction between general insurance contract law and marine insurance contract law.[3] The Principles apply to both of them. Moreover, the PEICL does not apply to reinsurance (Article 1:101.2).

**4.** So it refers to the territorial scope of application, raises the question of whether the principles apply only to international contracts or apply also to the national contracts. The answer that best suits the interests of the contracting parties seems to be that the Principles must also be applied to contracts which are developed exclusively in a Member State, in such a way that the parties can choose the application of such Principles to the national contracts.[4] This response is obtained, also, applying Article 1:104, which sets that the Principles "must be interpreted in the light of their text, context, purpose and comparative background. In particular, regard must be had to the need to promote (...) uniformity of application and the adequate protection of policyholders". And it seems to be that the "uniformity" and the "adequate protection of policyholders" require the application of the PEICL to the national contracts.

**5.** The Principles constitute an alternative to national law, not a complement to it. Then, "no recourse to national law, whether to restrict or to supplement the PEICL, is permitted. This does not apply to mandatory national laws specifically enacted for branches of insurance which are not covered by special rules contained in the PEICL" (Article 1:105.1).[5]

**6.** Not resolved aspects of the insurance contract in the PEICL, shall be resolved as they point out the Principles of European Contract Law (PECL)[6] and, in their absence, in accordance with the general principles common to the laws of the Member States.

2 In this sense, Reichert Facilides, F., "Substantive Scope of Application", in Basedow, J., Birds, J., Clarke, M., Cousy. H. and Heiss, H., *Principles of European Insurance Contract Law (PEICL)*, Munich, 2009, p. 31; and Quintans Eiras, M.R., "El contrato de seguro en el proyecto de armonización del Derecho contractual europeo", *Revista de Derecho Mercantil*, n. 290, 2013, p. 305.

3 See Reichert Facilides, F., "Comparative Insurance Contract Law: General Aspects", in Heiss, H. and Lakhan, M., *Principles of European Insurance Contract Law (PEICL): A Model Optional Instrument*, Munich, 2011, p. 119.

4 Likewise, Bataller, J., "Los principios de Derecho europeo del contrato de seguro: la técnica del instrumento opcional", in Bosch, E. (Dir.), *Derecho contractual europeo: problemática, propuestas y perspectivas*, Barcelona, 2009, pp. 439 and 440; and Bataller, J., "¿Hacia la unificación de la normativa del contrato de seguro en Europa? Tópicos para un debate", in Prats, L., Palao, G. and Reyes, M.J. (Coords.), *Derecho patrimonial europeo*, Navarra, 2003, p. 63.

5 Cf. Basedow, J., "National Law and General Principles", in Basedow, J., Birds, J., Clarke, M., Cousy. H. and Heiss, H., *Principles of European Insurance Contract Law...*, cit., p. 46.

6 Cf. Lando, O. and Beale, H., (eds.), *Principles of European Contract Law*, Parts I and II, The Hague, 2000; and Lando, O., Clive, E., Prüm, A. and Zimmermann, R., (eds.), *Principles of European Contract Law*, Part III, The Hague, 2003.

### 2.2. *Mandatory application versus freedom of contract*

7. Once they have been selected as applicable law, the Principles are mandatory, in general (Article 1:103.1). Then, the parties to a marine insurance contract can opt to use (opt-in) the Principles, they have freedom of contract (Article 1: 103.2.a). On the other hand, the Principles are not mandatory in the following cases connected with the marine insurance:

- Liability for ships (sea, lake, river and canal vessels). All liability arising out of the use of ships, vessels or boats on the sea, lakes, rivers or canals (including carrier's liability).
- All damage to or loss of river and canal vessels, lake vessels, sea vessels.
- Goods in transit (including merchandise, baggage, and all other goods). All damage to or loss of goods in transit, irrespective of the form of transport.

**8.** Also, it must be taken into consideration that "The contract may derogate from all other provisions of the PEICL as long as such derogation is not to the detriment of the policyholder, the insured or beneficiary" (Article 1:103.2).

### 2.3. *Form of the contract*

**9.** The Principles do not require a specific form for the conclusion of the contract.[7] An insurance contract is not required to be concluded or evidenced in writing nor subject to any other requirement as to form. The contract may be proved by any means, including oral testimony (Article 2:301). So, the insurance contract is a consensual contract. When concluding the insurance contract, the insurer shall issue an insurance policy, together with the general contract terms as far as they are not included in the policy (Article 2:501).

### 2.4. *Obligations of the parties*

#### 2.4.1. **Duty of disclosure**

**10.** A duty to declare risks is imposed on the applicant. This declaration is the mechanism that the insurance company has for obtaining direct information from the future policyholder about the risk to be assumed (or not), for the purposes of delimiting and valuing it.[8] In particular, Article 2:201 PEICL reads as follows: "When concluding the contract, the applicant must inform the insurer of any circumstances of which he is or ought to be aware, and which are the subject of clear and precise questions put to him by the insurer".

7 Cf. Dufwa, B.W., "Manner of Conclusion", in Basedow, J., Birds, J., Clarke, M., Cousy. H. and Heiss, H., *Principles of European Insurance Contract Law...*, cit., pp. 103 and following.

8 See, Clarke, M. and Rudish, B., "Duty of disclosure", in Basedow, J., Birds, J., Clarke, M., Cousy. H. and Heiss, H., *Principles of European Insurance Contract Law...*, cit., p. 77.

11. The duty of the applicant is a duty to answer the questionnaire ("clear and precise questions"). Then it is a passive obligation: the obligation to answer the questionnaire. It is not an active obligation: active or spontaneous obligation of the holder to make a pre-contractual declaration of risk, with the obligation to send all the data involved in the assessment of the risk to the insurance company.

12. When the policyholder is in breach of the duty of disclosure (Article 2:102), the insurer is entitled to propose a reasonable variation of the contract or to terminate the contract. To that end the insurer must give written notice of its intention, accompanied by information on the legal consequences of its decision, within one month after the breach becomes known or apparent to it.

### 2.4.2. Payment of the premium

13. Failure to pay the first or single premium, or the subsequent premium, releases the insurer from the obligation to pay compensation for any losses occurring prior to the payment, only when the requirements listed in Article 5:101/102 are fulfilled. In particular, in the case of the first or single premium, when the insurer makes payment of the first or single premium a condition of formation of the contract or of the beginning of cover, that condition shall be without effect unless: (a) the condition is communicated to the applicant in writing using clear language and warning the applicant that he lacks cover until the premium is paid, and (b) a period of two weeks has expired after receipt of an invoice which complies with requirement (a) without payment having been made (Article 5:101).[9] And in the case of the subsequent premium, a clause, providing for the insurer to be relieved of its obligation to cover the risk in the event of non-payment of a subsequent premium, shall be without effect unless: (a) the policyholder receives an invoice stating the precise amount of premium due as well as the date of payment; (b) after the premium falls due, the insurer sends a reminder to the policyholder of the precise amount of premium due, granting an additional period of payment of at least two weeks, and warning the policyholder of the imminent suspension of cover if payment is not made; and (c) the additional period in requirement (b) has expired without payment having been made (Article 5:102).[10]

### 2.4.3. Notice of insured event

14. Any insured event must be notified to the insurer without undue delay (i.e. as quickly as possible). If the contract requires notice to be given within a stated period of time, that time must be reasonable and in any event no shorter than five days (Article 6:101).

9 For details see, Heiss, H., "First or Single Premium" in Basedow, J., Birds, J., Clarke, M., Cousy. H. and Heiss, H., *Principles of European Insurance Contract Law...*, cit., pp. 192 and following.

10 Cf. Heiss, H., "Subsequent Premium" in Basedow, J., Birds, J., Clarke, M., Cousy. H. and Heiss, H., *Principles of European Insurance Contract Law...*, cit., pp. 196 and following.

### 2.4.4. Payment of the indemnity

15. When a claim has been accepted, the insurer shall pay or provide the services promised, as the case may be, without undue delay (Article 6:104.1). In this line, the Principles establish that the payment of insurance money shall be made no later than one week after the acceptance and quantification of the claim or part of it, as the case may be (Article 6:104.3). In relation to the late performance, the PEICL provide that if insurance money is not paid in accordance with Article 6:104, the claimant shall be entitled to interest on that sum from the time when payment was due to the time of payment and at the rate applied by the European Central Bank to its most recent main refinancing operation carried out before the first calendar day of the half-year in question, plus seven percentage points.

## III. The Spanish Law 14/2014 of Maritime Navigation

### *3.1. Introduction*

16. Marine insurance contracts are currently regulated in Spain by the Law of Maritime Navigation – Law 14/2014, of 24 July 2014 (LMN) –, specifically Title VIII: Articles 406–467. The provisions about marine insurance contract of the Law 14/2014 are the culmination of the work undertaken by the Commercial Law Section of the Spanish General Commission of Codification. The aim was to adapt the articles regarding marine insurance in the Commercial Code to the current situation. In 1978 the Spanish Maritime Law Association entrusted the task of drafting the provisions governing marine insurance contracts. The proposed text was then discussed and relevant observations were made by the insurance companies and shipping associations. An initial version was drafted in 1980, which was succeeded by others, such as the 1991 draft Bill, the 2004 proposal, the 2006 Bill and the 2008 Bill.

17. The Spanish regulation of marine insurance – in the LNM – is inspired by the English policy models. The reason it is that the Spanish operators in the sector of marine insurance have used, long time ago, the English policy models of the Institute of London. Then, the LNM 14/2014 provides the necessary framework for this insurance practice.

18. The LNM 14/2014 regulates marine insurance in the VIII Title, in three chapters. The first chapter contains the general provisions. The second chapter considers the common provisions for the different types of marine insurance. And the third chapter looks at the special provisions of any type of insurance: ship insurance, cargo insurance and civil liability insurance.

19. The new maritime Law reflects the specific nature of the marine insurance, which intended to indemnify the damages produced by the special risks inherent to maritime shipping (Article 406.1 LNM). In any case, the mandatory insurance for pleasure and

sporting vessels is excluded of the LNM (Article 406.2 LNM) and is regulated under the General Insurance Contract Act, Ley de Contrato de Seguro (Act 50/1980, of 8 October 1980 – hereinafter LCS).[11]

### *3.2. Legal sources*

**20.** The provisions of the Law of Maritime Navigation are non-mandatory (Article 407.1 LMN). Then, contracting parties are not required to follow the LNM and can agree clauses that best meet their needs. Consequently, the Law 14/2014 will only apply when there is no agreement between the parties, or when the parties specifically agree that the Law 14/2014 will govern their marine insurance contract.

**21.** In this sense, Article 407.1 prioritises the freedom of choice regarding the legal system envisaged in the LNM, except in those cases where the legislation expressly excludes the possibility of a contract agreed under a different system. These exceptions occur: in the direct action against the insurer (Article 465); in the case of negligence or wilful delay in the notification of a loss (Article 426); when the insurer is unable to dispute the defaulting on premium with the purchaser of the cargo in good faith where the insurer has issued and handed over an insurance certificate to that purchaser (Article 425.3); in consideration of the limit of compensation in the case of multiple insurance (real amount of the damage in Article 415.1). It is appropriate to maintain the principle of freedom of contract. The parties can provide their own norms by preparing the relevant general clauses where their interests are laid down in a balanced manner, although this does not prevent some insurance contracts reflecting an imbalance between the parties and creating a weak party in the contract.

**22.** Then, the policy is the first regulatory source of the marine insurance contract.[12] If the policy is incomplete, the LNM 14/2014 is applicable (in second place), and in matters not specifically regulated in the LNM will apply the General Insurance Contract Act 50/1980, of 8 October 1980 (in third place).

**23.** Spanish insurance companies and policyholders use English policy models for marine insurance contracts. These are the English marine insurance policies: the *Institute Time Clauses Hulls 01/10/83* and the *Institute Cargo Clauses 01/01/82*, in modes A, B and C, drawn up in accordance with the 1906 Marine Insurance Act. The English insurance policies are used even though the Spanish authorities approved two marine insurance policy models in 1934: the *Spanish Ships Insurance Policy* and the *Spanish Insurance Policy for Cargo and Other Goods*. Both policy models make up the general

11 See, Díez Ramos, D. and García Villar, L.A., "The new Spanish Law of Maritime Navigation 14/2014. The Contract of Marine Insurance – An Overview", *TranspR*, 11–12/2014, p. 417.

12 In this sense, Martín Osante, J.M., "Aplicación supletoria del artículo 20 de la Ley de Contrato de Seguro al Seguro Marítimo", in Yzquierdo Tolsada, M., (Dir.), *Comentarios a las sentencias de unificación de doctrina (civil y mercantil)*, Vol. 3, Madrid, Dykinson S.L., 2010, pp. 49 to 78.

conditions for ship insurance and cargo insurance, respectively, as expressly stated in those policies. The reasons why the English clauses are used have been highlighted elsewhere[13] and can be summarised as follows:

1. The requirement that cargo insurance conditions be internationally known, given the use of standard models for international trade (CIF conditions).
2. The lack of initiative shown by Spanish insurers to work on new standard general conditions.
3. English reinsurance, to which Spanish insurance necessarily resorts, requires the marine insurance contract to be entered into under English conditions, so that its contents can be assessed and interpreted easily.
4. The Spanish Public Authorities require the English conditions to be used for ships under the 'Crédito Naval' shipbuilding loans.
5. The successive updating of the English general conditions to the requirements of the shipping industry and the relevant extensive existing jurisprudence make them a more precise and up-to-date than the Spanish general conditions.

**24.** It is inevitable that there is overlap of the general conditions within marine insurance contracts which generates problems of interpretation and application, since the English and Spanish standard policies were drafted from different legal sources. As mentioned above, the English standard policies were drafted in accordance with the 1906 Marine Insurance Act, while the Spanish standard policies are based on the 1885 Commercial Code. There are significant differences between them and they are based on very different legal systems.

**25.** The power of the parties to select the applicable law for the insurance contract is restricted to international cases, as laid down in Article 10.5 of the Spanish Civil Code, Articles 1, 3 and 15 of the 1980 Rome Convention on the law applicable to contractual obligations, and Article 107 of the Spanish Insurance Contract Act (LCS), then, the applicable law will be Spanish in national cases.[14]

### *3.3. Form of the contract*

**16.** The contract of marine insurance does not require a specific form for its valid conclusion (Article 407.2 LMN). However, the insurer is obliged to deliver to the

13 Cf. Sánchez Calero, F., "Sobre la regulación del contrato de seguro marítimo", *Revista Española de Seguros*, n. 73 y 74, 1993, p. 76; and Ruiz Soroa, J.M., "Un nuevo modelo de póliza de seguro marítimo", in Eizaguirre, J.M. (Coord.), *IV Jornadas de Derecho marítimo de San Sebastián*, Donostia, 1997, pp. 127 and 128.

14 See Arroyo, I., "La reforma del seguro marítimo español", in Arroyo, I. and Beltrán, E. (Dirs.), *La reforma de la legislación marítima*, Navarra, 1999, pp. 172–174; and Rodríguez Carrión, J.L., *Los seguros marítimos y aéreos*, in Olivencia, M., Fernández Novoa, C. and Jiménez De Parga, R. (Dirs.); Jiménez Sánchez, G. (Coord.), *Tratado de Derecho Mercantil*, XLVIII, *Derecho de la navegación*, Vol. 5, Madrid, Barcelona, 2003, p. 426.

policyholder an insurance policy or the provisional document or certificate of cover. Until these documents are delivered, the contract can be proven by any means which demonstrate the acceptance of coverage by the insurer (Article 421 LMN).

### 3.4. *Obligations of the parties*

#### 3.4.1. Duty of disclosure

**17.** The LNM 2014 sets the duty of the policyholder to declare to the insurer, prior to contracting the marine insurance, all the circumstances that are known and can influence in the appreciation of the risk by a prudent insurance company (Article 423.1 LNM).[15]

**18.** In maritime insurance agreed between enterprises, an obligation on the policyholder to make a pre-contractual declaration of the risk, sending all the data involved in the assessment of the risk to the insurance company (active obligation), is a more practical obligation, than the obligation to answer the questionnaire (passive obligation). This is due to the fact that it is difficult, in the sphere of maritime insurance, for any general form to contain all the questions required adequately to assess the risk. It is the insured who are in a position to distinguish what should be taken into account when assessing the insurable interest and what should be provided to the insurer. Therefore, Article 423.1 LNM includes the active obligation to declare the risk.

**19.** The passive obligation to answer the questionnaire applies to the mandatory insurance for pleasure and sporting vessels. This type of insurance is excluded of the LNM (Article 406.2 LNM) and is regulated under the General Insurance Contract Act (LCS), and the LCS (Article 10) imposes the obligation to answer the questionnaire.

**20.** During the course of the contract, the policyholder or the assured must communicate to the insurer, and as soon as possible, all the circumstances that aggravate the risk and are of a nature that had the insurer been aware of such circumstances at the time of agreeing the marine insurance contract, would not have provided cover or would have provided cover on very different terms (Article 423.2 LMN).

**21.** If an insured event is caused by an element of the risk which is the subject of negligent non-disclosure or misrepresentation by the policyholder, and occurs before the insurer had appreciated the real risk, no insurance money is payable, in those cases where there has been wilful misconduct or gross negligence of the policyholder or the assured. If, however, the insurer would have entered into the contract at a higher premium or on different terms, insurance money is payable proportionately or in accordance with such terms (Article 424.2 LMN).[16]

[15] Cf. Díez Ramos, D. and García Villar, L.A., "The new Spanish Law of Maritime Navigation 14/2014…", cit., p. 420.

[16] Arroyo, I., *Compendio de Derecho Marítimo,* 5th ed., Madrid, 2014, p. 367.

### 3.4.2. Payment of the premium

22. When the policyholder fails to pay the premium or instalments, the insurer can terminate the marine insurance contract or suspend cover until payment is made. In this line, the LMN 2014 establishes that failure to pay the single premium or the first instalment of the premium, releases the insurer from the obligation to pay compensation for any losses occurring post agreement but prior to the payment, even if the insurer has not sent a demand for payment to the insurance holder (Article 425.2 LMN).[17]

23. The regulation of the LMN relating to the payment of the premium is similar to that provided for in the General Insurance Contract Act (LCS).[18] However, as far as marine insurance for cargo is concerned, contracts are effective immediately from agreement so as to perform a specific type of operation, namely transporting goods, which means that the exposure to the risk may start prior to the payment of the premium. Thus, the automatic release of the insurer from any obligation to pay compensation prior to payment of the premium is not appropriate for the insurance of cargo and the LMN 2014 establishes in consequence that upon issue of a cover note for the insurance of cargo, the insurer cannot then claim the failure to pay the premium against the party who has purchased the cargo in good faith and who has received the certificate (Article 425.3 LMN).

### 3.4.3. Notice of insured event

24. The insured or the policyholder should notified to the insurer or to the average adjuster named in the policy, the accident whereby loss or damage may result in a claim under the insurance, within the period of seven days running from the date of knowledge of the accident (Article 426 LMN). The seven-day period is also foreseen in the Spanish General Insurance Contract Act (Article 16 LCS).[19] However, the Spanish Ships Insurance Policy (Article 26) and the Spanish Insurance Policy for Cargo and Other Goods (Article 26) establish that the insured event should be notified "by next mail" and "by telegraph, where applicable", which should be interpreted currently that the loss should be notified as quickly as possible, by any means of communication. The failure or delay of this notification will cause the loss of the right to compensation only if there had been wilful misconduct or gross negligence of the insured or the policyholder.

17 See Judgment Spanish Supreme Court, 01.4.1987 (Repertorio de Jurisprudencia Aranzadi, number 2482).

18 Cf. Díez Ramos, D. and García Villar, L.A., "The new Spanish Law of Maritime Navigation 14/2014...", cit., p. 420.

19 Cf. Gabaldón García, J.L. and Ruiz Soroa, J.M., *Manual de Derecho de la navegación marítima*, 3rd. ed., Madrid-Barcelona, Marcial Pons, 2006, p. 892.

#### 3.4.4. Avoidance or mitigation of the damage

**25.** Article 427.1 LMN 2014 establishes that the policy holder or the insured and its dependents shall use all reasonable measures in their power to salvage or recover the insured effects and, in general, to avoid or reduce the damage arising from an insured risk. The obligation to adopt measures aimed at reducing the damage after the loss is an obligation that can be included in any maritime insurance contract.[20]

#### 3.4.5. Payment of the indemnity

**26.** The Spanish Law of Maritime Navigation retains the two different liquidation procedures for a maritime accident covered for the marine insurance: average and abandonment (Article 433.1 LMN).[21] Liquidation due to abandonment is reserved for cases, mainly, of total loss of the vessel or the cargo. Should the insured exercise abandonment, the ownership of the abandoned effects is transferred to the insurer and the latter is required to pay the whole of the insured sum. Liquidation by average is envisaged for the cases of partial loss, where the insured receives compensation pursuant to the damage caused to the insurable interest. In the cases of total loss, the insured is empowered to choose whether it opts for liquidation or abandonment (Article 433.2 LMN).

### 3.5. *Special provisions for certain types of marine insurance*

#### 3.5.1. Ship insurance

##### 3.5.1.1. Voyage or time insurance

**27.** After stating that ship insurance may be taken out for either one voyage or several successive ones or for a specific term (Article 439), the Spanish Law of Maritime Navigation 14/2014 establishes a series of guidelines regarding the time limits of the cover, in accordance with common practice in this field. In specific terms, if insurance is contracted for one or several voyages, cover commences the moment the cargo is received on board and ends when unloading has concluded, and in all cases "fifteen days after arrival at the destination port" (Article 440.1 LMN). If the voyage is performed under ballast, cover begins upon raising anchor or casting off at the port of departure and ends when the ship anchors or moors at the destination port (Article 440.2 LMN).

20 See, Uría, R., *El seguro marítimo*, Barcelona, 1940, pUría, R., *El seguro marítimo*, Barcelona, 1940, p. 152.

21 In this sense, Arroyo, I., *Compendio...*, cit., p. 371.

**28.** Should the insurance be contracted by time, the LMN states that cover commences "at zero hours on the day following entering into the contract" and ends "at twenty-four hours on the last day" (Article 441 LMN).

3.5.1.2. Collision

**29.** One of the typical navigation risks to which ships are exposed is collision, or in other words, ships, vessels or naval artefacts running into one another and causing damage.[22] For the purposes of ship insurance, collision is considered in two different ways. Firstly, it may be the cause of the damage suffered by the insured ship; and secondly, it may generate civil liability for the insured shipping company as a result of the damage caused by the collision. The Spanish Law of Maritime Navigation 14/2014 expressly anticipates both aspects of collision by extending the cover of the ship insurance to both the damage caused to the insured ship and the civil liability of the shipping company in the event of collision (Article 443.1 LMN).

**30.** The limits of the cover established in the LMN are in accordance with the English Hull Clauses (clause 8 "3/4ths collision liability" ITCH/83), in that they structure the cover for the shipping company's liability in the event of collision as a complement or addition to the damage to the insured ship itself.[23] In short, compensation is determined by establishing two limits (one for damages and the other for liability), each for the amount of the sum insured. This stands in opposition to Article 34 of the Spanish Ships Insurance Policy, which prohibits the adoption of two different limits and states that only one limit to the cover may be established (i.e. the sum insured) for both types of collision, considered jointly. Therefore, under the Spanish policy, the insurer will never pay out a sum that is higher than the insured value.

3.5.1.3. Seaworthiness

**31.** Article 444 LMN states that "the assured shall maintain the seaworthiness of the ship, vessel or naval artefact insured during the whole term of the cover".[24] However, this obligation is linked to no sanction, which means that no consequences are specified for failure to comply. What we have here is not an English *warranty*, in the sense that any violation of the guarantee or failure to comply with the condition (in this case maintaining the seaworthiness of the vessel) automatically renders the cover null and void. These guarantees or conditions are not contemplated in the Spanish legal system. According to Spanish Law, this infraction or non-compliance must be the cause of the accident in

22 See, Martín Osante, J.M., *La responsabilidad civil del naviero por abordaje*, Vitoria, 2001, pp. 23 to 61.

23 Cf., Sánchez Calero, "Seguro marítimo", cit., p. 85; and Rodríguez Carrión, *Los seguros...*, cit., p. 226.

24 For a practical application of the obligation to maintain the seaworthiness of the ship in the field of maritime insurance, see Spanish High Court Ruling 27.2.04 (Repertorio de Jurisprudencia Aranzadi, number 1.440).

order for exclusion of cover to come into effect. Thus, in our opinion, the unsanctioned obligation outlined in Article 444 LMN has no specific, practical, legal form.

**32.** It is a completely different matter when, as the result of a negligent action or wilful misconduct, the ship stops being seaworthy and causes an accident. In this case, the negligence or wilful misconduct is considered the cause of the accident, and is regulated in Article 419 LMN, which outlines the specific consequences of such conduct.

3.5.1.4. Maximum limit per claim

**33.** In Article 447, the LMN states that the maximum limit for compensation to be paid by the insurer (the sum insured) will be applied to each claim arising during the term of the insurance contract. The insured sum is automatically reinstated after every claim.

3.5.1.5. New for old deductions

**34.** New for old deductions are reductions in the compensation to be paid to the assured. They are traditionally based on the theoretical increase in value undergone by the ship as a result of the repairs carried out at the expense of the insurer when old parts are replaced by new ones, etc. When this increase occurs, it is deemed to go against the compensatory principle that governs the insurance contract, and the compensation due is therefore be reduced. In this sense, the Spanish Ships Insurance Policy (Article 15) establishes the application of these old for new deductions.

**35.** However, said reductions in the compensation owed were excluded from the English Hull Clauses (clause 14, ITCH/83) in response to protests from insured parties. Given that international insurance practice no longer applies these deductions[25], Article 448 LMN establishes that claims shall be payable without new for old deductions. We believe that this provision is correct, since in our opinion, the increase in a ship's value due to the repairs carried out by the insurer are either non-existent or insignificant for the assured, who generally simply wishes to continue using the ship in the same conditions as they did prior to the accident; thus, the theoretical greater value of the ship should not be taken into consideration when establishing the compensation due.[26]

3.5.1.6. Subrogation and crew

**36.** Since it regulates ship insurance, the Spanish Law of Maritime Navigation 14/2014 contains a specific provision on subrogation (Article 446 LMN) which, in the event of a claim, prevents the insurer from exercising the rights in which it has subrogated itself

25 In this sense, González Hevia, R., *Manual de seguro marítimo*, 2nd. ed., Madrid, 1980, p. 52.

26 See, Ruiz Soroa, J.M., en Ruiz Soroa, J.M., Zabaleta Sarasua, S. and Arranz de Diego, A., *Manual de Derecho del seguro marítimo*, Vitoria, 1993, p. 165.

against the crew members of the insured ship, unless said crew members caused the claim by wilful misconduct.

3.5.1.7. Indivisibility of the premium

**37.** The principle of the indivisibility of the premium is established in Article 451 of the LMN, which states that said premium is owed in full by the assured from the moment in which the cover period commences.[27] In other words, in voyage insurance it is due from the beginning of the voyage and in time insurance it is due from zero hours on the day after the contract is entered into. In this sense, the LMN foresees certain conditions (Article 460) under which, due to increased risk (transfers, changes in the voyage or route, etc.), a premium surcharge may be applied.

3.5.1.8. Subsidiarity

**38.** The types of maritime insurance regulated by the LMN are, as indicated above, ship insurance, goods insurance and civil liability. There are, however, other types of insurance that are not legislatively developed in this legal text. These include, for example, freight insurance (*Institute Time Clauses, Freight 1/10/83, 1/8/89 and 1/11/95, Institute Voyage Clauses, Freight 1/10/83, 1/8/89 and 1/11/95*) and anticipated profit insurance or disbursement insurance (*Institute Time Clauses – Hulls, Disbursements and Increased Value 1/10/83,* clause 21 ITCH/83 and clause 24 IHC/03).

**39.** In relation to this issue, the special section on ship insurance ends (Article 452 LMN) by establishing the principle of the subsidiary application of said section to freight insurance or other interests of the shipping company (such as pay outs, for example), providing this is so established by the parties and that the provisions relative to ship insurance are compatible with the nature of these other types of maritime insurance.

### 3.5.2. Cargo insurance

**40.** The second block of special provisions focus on cargo insurance. These provisions are outlined in section 2 of Chapter III of the LMN.

3.5.2.1. Time limit of the cover

**41.** The LMN is particularly thorough when outlining the time limits of cargo insurance cover. The regulation proposed establishes as a general norm that the cover begins at the moment when the goods leave the ground for loading on board, and ends when they are placed on land at the destination port (Article 455 LMN). Despite this, however, the

27 Sánchez Calero, "Seguro marítimo", cit., p. 85.

parties may include a "warehouse to warehouse" or other similar clause in the contract, thus extending the cover to run from the moment "the goods leave the warehouse of origin at the place stated in the policy until they reach that of destination at the place stated in the policy" (Article 456 LMN). It may also occur that goods are already in transit when the insurance is contracted. In such cases, the cover commences at zero hours on the day on which the contract is entered into (Article 457 LMN).

**42.** The Law of Maritime Navigation also extends the cover of goods insurance to the non-maritime phases of transport "as long as these are accessory to the maritime voyage" (Article 453 LMN).

**43.** Later on, the LMN specifies that cargo insurance covers the "whole voyage" (Article 460 LMN). This includes periods in which the goods are not actually travelling by sea, due to transfers, loading and unloading operations at ports of transit or arrival or when they remain, for whatever reason or circumstance, on the dock or in the warehouse in ports of transit or arrival.

3.5.2.2. Floating policies

**44.** The section of cargo insurance regulates the way in which floating policies work (Articles 458 and 459, LMN). Of the aforementioned regulation, the following points are particularly worth noting:

1. The presumption of the obligatory nature of the policy for both parties. Thus, during the period for which the cover is in force, the assured is obliged to apply it to all shipments defined in the policy; for its part, the insurer must provide automatic cover of all such shipments or consignments.
2. The floating policy must specify the "maximum sum that the insurer agrees to guarantee for each consignment".
3. It is the insured party's duty to notify the insurer of a consignment in progress within forty-eight hours from the moment "of the assured obtaining news of the consignment" (Article 459.1 LMN).
4. In the event of failure to notify, the insurer is released from its obligation to cover the specific consignment in question and may request payment of the premium corresponding to said consignment. The insurer may also exercise its right to terminate the contract, without said termination affecting the validity of previously notified consignments.

3.5.2.3. Civil liability insurance

i) Scope of application

**45.** In addition to applying to this specific type of insurance, the articles of the LMN which regulate civil liability insurance also apply to any civil liability cover included in other types of maritime insurance (Article 463 LMN). As indicated above, ship and cargo insurance covers the assured not only for any damage to the insured goods themselves, but also for any hypothetical obligations to compensate third parties as the result of maritime navigation activities (mainly collision, salvage or general average). Over and above that specifically established in the LMN for said events, this type of cover is subject to that laid down in general terms in the LMN in relation to civil liability insurance (Article 463 to 467). Also, the rules established in the LMN regarding civil liability insurance apply secondarily to the compulsory liability insurance required by the LMN itself (Article 464 LMN).

ii) Direct action

**46.** Article 465 of the LMN *imperatively* (binding on both parties) establishes the right of the injured third party to take direct action against the insurer.[28] Therefore, the injured third party may take direct action against the insurer, claiming compensation for the damage suffered as the result of the covered incident. Given its imperative nature, there can be no doubt that this will be the solution when the contract is governed by internal rules (i.e. Spanish Law). However, more doubts have been raised regarding the question of whether direct action should also be admitted when, by agreement between the parties, the contract is governed by English Law, since English Law excludes direct action, as shown below. To our way of thinking, direct action should also be admitted in this case, bearing in mind that, given the public order nature of direct action, the parties to the maritime insurance contract may not exclude or limit the rights and legitimate actions of injured third parties. This affirmation is supported by Article 12.3 of the Spanish Civil Code, Article 107.6 of the Spanish Law on Insurance Contracts and Article 16 of the Rome Convention on the Law applicable to contractual obligations.[29]

## IV. Conclusions

**47.** The Principles of European Insurance Contract Law (PEICL) as a model of insurance contract that can be used in the maritime sector as an alternative approach to the various national regulations of the marine insurance contract, and to the existing marine insurance policies, among others, the English policy models, provide several advantages. The advantages of the PEICL for companies would be that they would only have to adapt their operations to a single legal system (the European system), then they would save on costs and their competitiveness would be reinforced.[30]

[28] Cf. Díez Ramos, D. and García Villar, L.A., "The new Spanish Law of Maritime Navigation 14/2014...", cit., p. 425.

[29] In this sense, Gabaldón García, J.L. and Ruiz Soroa, J.M., *Manual...*, cit., pp. 811 and 812. Against, Hill Prados, M.C., *Los Clubs de Protección e Indemnización en el campo del seguro marítimo*, Barcelona, 1992, p. 116; and Zurimendi, A., "El orden público en el Derecho marítimo", en Eizaguirre, J.M. (Coord.), *XII Jornadas de Derecho marítimo de San Sebastián*, Vitoria, 2005, p. 154.

[30] See Bataller, J., "Los principios de Derecho europeo del contrato de seguro...", cit., pp. 439 y 440.

**48.** The positive effects of the PEICL for the applicant, insured and consumer would be that they would have a broader choice of insurance contracts and services available, the European offer, the English policy models and the domestic (national) offer, allowing them to get better conditions as regards price and quality.[31] Effects for judges and other legal operators (lawyers, etc.) would be that they wouldn't need to deal with foreign legislation when settling legal disputes, and thus reducing costs for the companies and for the Administration of Justice.[32]

31 Cf. Quintans Eiras, M.R., "El contrato de seguro...", cit., p. 303.

32 See Reding, V., "Por qué necesita Europa un derecho contractual europeo opcional", *InDret* 2/2011, pp. 5 and 6.

Rhidian Thomas*

# THE PERSPECTIVES OF ENGLISH AND EUROPEAN CONTRACT LAW TO AGREED DAMAGES CLAUSES IN VOYAGE CHARTERPARTIES

## I. Introduction

1. It is generally an established right of contracting parties to agree in advance the remedy that is to follow in the event of a breach of contract. Such an agreement will customarily be set out as a term of the contract and its precise field of application will be governed by the scope and proper construction of the adopted words. At one extreme it may apply to all breaches, at the other to a single or small number.

2. The precise nature of the agreed remedy may also vary. In the great preponderance of instances the parties will make provision for the payment of a sum of money, which may be characterised as agreed damages, also identified as liquidated damages in the common law. This mode of description derives from the fact that compensation payable for breach does not have to be assessed by reference to applicable legal criteria, but is based on an agreed sum of money. In the event of default an action to obtain payment of the agreed sum is based on debt and not damages.

3. Although the payment of a sum on money represents the paradigm case, the remedy is not necessarily so restricted. Under the common law the parties may agree upon any lawful response, such as the forfeiture of a legal right or an obligation to transfer property without payment or at an undervaluation. But in this regard differences may exist between different jurisdictions.

4. This right to settle the remedy for breach is very clearly an incident of the doctrine of freedom of contract. If it is open to parties to agree the substantive and procedural terms and conditions of their contracts, it must also be the case that they have the right to prescribe in advance the remedy in the event of breach. This stance is also supported by considerations of public policy, because such agreements avoid the complexities that may be involved in the assessment and quantification of damages, speed up the remedial process and avoid the risk of disputes. They also have the overarching benefit of

* Emeritus Professor of Maritime Law, Founding Director of the Institute of International Shipping and Trade Law – Swansea University.

establishing a certain contractual environment and of indicating to the parties the risk inherent in the bargain they have entered into.

5. On the other side of the coin, there are clearly recognisable dangers. There is always the possibility that the parties may agree a remedy the nature and/or scale of which may be outside the limits of legitimate legal perceptions. It is also possible that the parties may not be in a position of equal bargaining power, or with equal access to informed legal advice, with the consequence that the party in the dominant position may impose an agreement which is abusive, unconscionable and oppressive. It is clear, therefore, that an unqualified commitment to freedom of contract carries dangers and some degree of protection is necessary.

6. Precisely how agreed remedies are made subject to legal review will doubtlessly vary as between legal systems. Under the common law the distinction is drawn between a liquidated damages clause and a clause in the nature of a penalty. The former is valid but the latter is not. A different approach is adopted in European initiatives in the realm of private law, as embodied principally in the Draft Common Frame of Reference (DCFR)[1], with the concept of reasonableness identified as the key concept. The court is vested with a jurisdiction to intervene where the agreement is judged to be grossly excessive and may substitute a reasonable agreement.

7. It is proposed in this contribution to analyse and contrast these two legal sources, and to consider their application to demurrage provisions in voyage charterparties.[2] Although these demurrage provisions are rarely spoken of in the express language of agreed or liquidated damages, nonetheless this is their true nature. It follows that they could become subject to review under the common law and also the DCFR, should this Code eventually become part of European contractual law. To consider first the European contract law initiatives.

## II. Draft Common Frame of Reference

### *2.1. Relevant provisions of the DCFR*

8. The relevant provisions are:

Article III.–3:712: Stipulated payment for non-performance

(1) Where the terms regulating an obligation provide that a debtor who fails to perform the obligation is to pay a specified sum to the creditor for such non-performance, the creditor is entitled to that sum irrespective of the actual loss.

1 Prepared by the Study Group on a European Civil Code and the Research Group on EC Private Law (Acquis Group), and based in part on a revised version of the Principles of European Contract Law (PECL).

2 The discussion is equally relevant to demurrage provisions found in international trading contracts and container hire contracts.

(2) However, despite any provision to the contrary, the sum so specified in a contract or other juridical act may be reduced to a reasonable amount where it is grossly excessive in relation to the loss resulting from the non-performance and the other circumstances.

9. Although there are minor differences in the drafting, this provision follows the corresponding provision in the Principles of European Contract Law (PECL), which arguably is better drafted.[3]

"Non-performance" is defined in Article III.–1:102(3), in the following terms –

> Non-performance of an obligation is any failure to perform the obligation, whether or not excused, and includes delayed performance and any other performance which is not in accordance with the terms regulating the obligation.[4]

Regard must also be had of the general duty of "good faith and fair dealing" as defined in Article III.–1:103(1) –

> A person has a duty to act in accordance with good faith and fair dealing in performing an obligation, in exercising a right to performance, in pursuing or defending a remedy for non-performance, or in exercising a right to terminate an obligation or contractual relationship.[5]

The principle and limitations on party autonomy are stated in Article II.–1:102 –

(1) Parties are free to make a contract or other juridical act and to determine its contents, subject to any applicable mandatory rules.
(2) Parties may exclude the application of any of the following rules relating to contracts or other juridical acts, or the rights and obligations arising under them, or derogate from or vary their effects, except as otherwise provided.[6]

3 PECL Article 9:509 (ex Article 4.508) – AGREED PAYMENT FOR NON-PERFORMANCE
Where the contract provides that a party who fails to perform is to pay a specified sum to the aggrieved party for such non-performance, the aggrieved party shall be awarded that sum irrespective of its actual loss.
However, despite any agreement to the contrary the sum may be reduced to a reasonable amount where it is grossly excessive in relation to the loss resulting from the non-performance and other circumstances.

4 PECL Article 1:310(4) defines 'non-performance' – "denotes any failure to perform an obligation under the contract, whether or not excused, and includes delayed performance, defective performance and failure to cooperate in order to give full effect to the contract."

5 PECL Article 1:102 Freedom of Contract.
Parties are free to enter into a contract and to determine its contents, subject to the requirement of good faith and fair dealing, and the mandatory rules established by these principles.
Parties may exclude the application of any of the Principles or derogate from or vary their effects, except as otherwise provided by these Principles.

6 For the corresponding provisions in the PECL, see n 5.

## 2.2. *Comments on the DCFR*

**10.** Article III.–3: 712 is somewhat oddly drafted, referring to the contractual parties as creditor and debtor. Those who think differently would no doubt point to the fact that the contractual obligation is about the payment of a fixed sum of money and therefore the party obliged to pay may be considered the debtor and the recipient the creditor. Although this argument exists, in the present context it remains clumsy, because the obligation has been agreed by the contracting parties as a term of their contract

**11.** Para 1 is founded on the principle of freedom of contract. It provides unambiguously that when the parties agree that a specific sum of money is payable by the party in breach of contract to the innocent party, the agreement is enforceable irrespective of the measure of actual loss. This raises the question whether the provision applies when no actual loss has been caused: it might be thought odd if it did not.

**12.** The provision is confined to an agreement to pay a sum of money and does not extend to any other kind of agreed consequence following a breach. Although this limitation is not recognised expressly, it appears to follow naturally from the drafting of par 1, but it is also the case that the parties are free to extend their agreements beyond the express terms of para 1.[7]

**13.** It applies to all manner of breaches, given the very wide definition of "non-performance" in the DCFR.[8] Nonetheless, the obligation to pay will not necessarily apply to all the obligations in the contract; it will be for the parties to settle the precise ambit of the obligation to pay the stipulated sum of money for breach. This being the case, the obligation to pay will only be triggered by a breach of an obligation to which the clause applies.

**14.** There is no express indication if account may be taken of any breach of duty on the part of the innocent contractor, such as the duty to mitigate loss where it exists, and the appropriate adjustment made. The drafting would suggest a negative answer.

**15.** Contrariwise, Part 2 represents an inroad to the doctrine of freedom of contract. It vests in the courts (and probably also arbitrators) a jurisdiction to reduce the agreed sum, if judged to be "grossly excessive" compared with "the loss resulting from the non-performance and the other circumstances", and substitute a reasonable sum. The rule is expressed in mandatory terms and therefore cannot be excluded or varied by the agreement of the parties. Thereafter, no express assistance is provided as to the assessment and computation of a reasonable sum.[9]

7 *Infra* n.12.

8 *Supra* n.4.

9 A definition is provided of 'Reasonableness' by DCFR I.-1:104.See also *infra*.

**16.** The jurisdiction exists only when it can be established that the agreed sum is grossly excessive. Simply to show that it is excessive is insufficient, the word "grossly" cannot be ignored. This would appear to raise, at least potentially, a difficult question of degree. It appears that the degree of excess is to be gauged at the time of the breach, comparing the loss actually suffered and the sum payable under the agreement. Except where the actual loss is agreed, this issue may involve a separate adjudication, a trial within a trial, and consume much time and expense. It also unclear whether the loss resulting from the breach refers to actual loss or compensatory loss, taking into account the relevant legal criteria in establishing the quantum of damages.

**17.** The requirement that the excess must be "gross" also serves to make it clear that simply because the parties have agreed a payment higher than legally assessed damages for the loss, will not invoke the jurisdiction to intervene. The excess must be significantly higher, such as to be excessive, exorbitant or unreasonable.

**18.** Para 2 indicates that the agreed sum may be reduced to a reasonable amount where it is grossly excessive in relation to the loss resulting from non-performance *and the other circumstances*. How the italicised words are to be understood is a difficult question, as also is what they may allude to. The use of the conjunction 'and' suggests that the other circumstances may amount to additional makeweights to the disparity in the relative sums. Alternatively, the words could be construed disjunctively so that 'other circumstances' represent an alternative basis for reducing the agreed sum. Under either approach, uncertainty prevails. The words could allude to the conduct and intention of the parties, particularly a dominant party who has insisted on the inclusion of the agreement and dictated its term. Where it can be ascertained that the motivation was associated with profiteering and heavy-handed imposition, these may be criteria capable of being taken into account in determining whether the jurisdiction to intervene has been established.

**19.** Under para 2 the jurisdiction relates to the reduction of the sum agreed to a reasonable amount, with the ostensible consequence that the contract is effectively re-written and the reduced sum becomes a contractual term. No guidelines are provided as to the computation of a reasonable sum.[10] The intervention, otherwise, does nothing to undermine the contract and its enforceability.

It is doubtful if the principle of good faith and fair trading can impose upon the matter further because, it is arguable, that the article is itself a particular rule of good faith which exhausts the remedy.[11]

**20.** By contrast with par 2, par 1 has not been expressly designated a mandatory rule and it is improbable that it is such by implication.[12] If this is a correct analysis, it means

10 See *infra*.
11 Cf DCFR I.-1:102(5).
12 Cf DCFR II.-1:102(1).

that its application and the remedy it provides may be excluded or varied or extended by the agreement of the parties, subject, presumable, to the general duty of good faith and fair dealing.[13]

## III. English Common Law

**21.** Agreed damages clauses, alluding to the fact that the parties have agreed in advance the precise sum payable (either fixed or ascertainable) as damages in the event of breach, are valid and enforceable in English law provided that they amount to a liquidated damages agreement and not a penalty.[14] Liquidated damages clauses are supported on grounds of public policy and favourably viewed by the courts, which are predisposed to their enforcement.[15]

**22.** The vital distinction is between a liquidated damages provision and a penalty. The former is compensatory and based on a genuine attempt to arrive at a pre-estimate of the damages payable on breach. There may be a genuine pre-estimate of future damages even though the consequences of a breach are difficulty or even impossible to assess. This probably represents the kind of situation when the agreement of the parties on the question of damages to be paid is most beneficial.[16] The validity of the pre-estimate does not turn solely on the genuineness or honesty of the party or parties involved. It is primarily one of objective fact relating to the intentions of the parties at the time the contract was entered into.[17] The agreement, objectively viewed, must represent a genuine attempt to arrive at a pre-estimate or approximation of recoverable damages in the event of breach.[18] Therefore, anticipated loss which might not be causal or might be too remote does not come into the calculation, but the duty to mitigate loss is not taken into account.[19]

**23.** By contrast, the clause is penal, historically described *in terrorem* the party in breach, but in more moderate contemporary language explained in terms of deterrence, if the predominant object is to deter a party from breaking the contract obligation and penalising any breach that may occur.[20] This position of the law is, at least in part, a reflection of the broad premise underpinning the common law that it always open to a contracting party to intentionally withdraw from performing a contractual obligation upon pain of paying damages. The law of penalties may apply to any provision which prescribes a response to a breach of contract. It may, therefore, apply more broadly than

13 *Supra.*
14 Dunlop Pneumatic Tyre Co Ltd v New Garage & Motor Co Ltd [1915] AC 79.
15 Cavendish Square Holdings BV and another v Makdessi [2013]EWCA Civ 1839, [2014] 2 All ER (Comm) 125.
16 Dunlop Pneumatic Tyre Co Ltd v New Garage & Motor Co Ltd, *supra*, p. 96.
17 Alfred McAlpine Capital Projects Ltd v Tilebox Ltd [2005]EWHC 281(TCC), 104 ConLR 39.
18 Robophone Facilities Ltd v Blank [1966]1 WLR 1428, 447 per Diplock LJ.
19 Murray v Leisureplay Plc[2005] EWCA Civ 963, [2005] IRLR 946.
20 Dunlop Pneumatic Tyre Co Ltd v New Garage & Motor Co Ltd, *supra*, p. 86.

to clauses which provide for the payment of a stipulated sum on breach of obligation, though this is the paradigm case[21] and it is the category of agreement which will be focused upon in this contribution.

**24.** The burden of proof is on the party alleging the clause to be a penalty[22] and, importantly, the test is applied at the time the contract was entered into, not at the time of breach.[23] If it is a penalty the clause is void and damages are assessed as if the contract had not contained the penalty clause.[24] Where the clause is severable, the penal element alone is struck down as invalid.[25]

**25.** In each case it is a question of construction into which category a clause falls: the objective intention of the parties at the time of contracting is to be determined on a proper construction of the contractual words taking into account the surrounding commercial matrix[26], and some regard may also be had to the thought processes of the parties.[27] The Court, therefore, is not confined to the terms of the agreement and may look at the inherent circumstances of the contract judged at the time of its making.[28] The terms of the agreement, without more, may give rise to an inference that it is not a genuine pre-estimate, but the inference may be rebutted by reference to the wider facts and circumstances.[29] It follows that the characterisation is not a question of form, the labels used by parties – liquidated damages or penalty – are not conclusive and may not even carry much weight, though it is always possible that they may be relevant in particular circumstances.

**26.** The authorities have focused principally on the application of the test and the significance of inferences or presumptions arising from the wider facts and circumstances. The *locus classicus* is *Dunlop Pneumatic Tyre Co Ltd v New Garage & Motor Co Ltd*[30], where the House of Lords[31] recognised a number of inferences/presumptions to assist the question of construction.[32] These may be presented as three propositions-

First, there is a presumption of penalty if the sum stipulated for is extravagant and unconscionable in amount in comparison with the greatest loss that could conceivably be proved to have followed the breach.

21 Cavendish Square Holdings BV and another v Makdessi, *supra*, [46] per Christopher Clarke LJ.

22 Robophone Facilities Ltd v Blank [1966]1 WLR 1428; Jeancharm Ltd v Barnett Football Club Ltd [2003] EWCA Civ 58[9], Murray v Leisureplay Plc[2005] EWCA Civ 963, [2005] IRLR 946.

23 Dunlop Pneumatic Tyre Co Ltd v New Garage & Motor Co Ltd, *supra*,p.87.

24 Jobson v Johnson [1989] 1 WLR 1026, 1038.

25 The Angelic Star [1988]1 Lloyd's Rep 122, 126–7; Dalkia Utilities Services Plc v Celtech International Ltd [2006] EWHC 63, [2006]1 Lloyd's Rep 599 [123].

26 Dunlop Pneumatic Tyre Co Ltd v New Garage & Motor Co Ltd, *supra* p.87.

27 Alfred McAlpine Capital Projects Ltd v Tilebox Ltd, *supra*.

28 Murray v Leisureplay Plc, *supra* [52] per Arden LJ.

29 *Supra* n.20.

30 [1915] AC 79.

31 Predecessor to what is now the Supreme Court.

32 Ibid pp 87–88.

Second, there is a presumption of penalty if the breach consists only in not paying a sum of money, and the sum stipulated is greater than the sum which ought to have been paid.

Third, there is a presumption of penalty when a single lump sum is made payable by way of compensation, on the occurrence of one or more or all of several events, some of which may occasion serious and others but trifling damage.

**27.** The first is considered to be in the nature of an overarching presumption: the second represents a straightforward and obvious proposition: the third is by far the most complicated to apply and about which a considerable body of case-law has developed. This it is unnecessary to pursue because it is not relevant to the situation when demurrage is payable under a voyage charterparty, which relates to a single obligation which is breached by a particular form of conduct, and which results in a uniform kind of loss. Consequently, only the first proposition is applicable to demurrage clauses, and the discussion will be restricted to this proposition.

The first proposition requires a highly factual comparison of the damages stipulated by the clause and the maximum loss likely to be suffered in the event of a breach. If the discrepancy is substantial, as when a wide gulf exits between them, it may lead to the conclusion that the stipulated damages are extravagant and unconscionable, and, therefore, a penalty.[33]

**28.** The test will not always be easy to apply because assessing in advance the maximum loss likely to arise from a breach may be factually difficult and involve many speculations. There will also be problematic questions of degree. The key word is "extravagant" which is clearly beyond a stipulated sum which is marginally high or decidedly on the high side – it must be patently disproportionate. As for the additional word "unconscionable", it is doubtful if it adds anything to "extravagant", because once the stipulated sum is held to be extravagant it would seem to follow that in all conscience the court will not recognise its acceptability. An appeal judge has recently observed, "If the maximum possible loss is £1m and the 'liquidated damages' are £2m it is not difficult to conclude that the provision is not a true estimate of loss and is penal in intent".[34]

**29.** In the early authorities the focus was very much on an examination of the disparity between the stipulated sum and the actual recoverable loss under the common law. Over the years the substance of the test has not changed, but the manner of its application has. The modern approach is broader and represents a shift towards freedom of contract: under it the existence of a substantial discrepancy raises only an inference of a penalty, which is capable of being rebutted by an examination of the wider commercial context of the contract.[35] The factual difference between the stipulated and likely damages does not

33 Alfred McAlpine Capital Projects Ltd v Tilebox Ltd, *supra*.

34 Cavendish Square Holdings BV and another v Makdessi, *supra* [73] per Christopher Clarke LJ.

35 General Trading Co (Holdings) Ltd v Richmond Corp Ltd [2008] EWHC 1479 (Comm),[2008] 2 Lloyd's Rep 475.

dominate; it is necessary to look further to the wider commercial context to ascertain if there is justification for the disparity.[36]

**30.** In *Murray v Leisureplay plc*[37] a majority of the Court of Appeal was of the opinion that although drawing a comparison between the stipulated sum and the likely maximum claim for damages was relevant, it was no more than a guide to the question whether a clause was a penalty.[38] To look only at the discrepancy introduced "a rigid and inflexible element into what should be a broad and general question".[39] It was legitimate to look more widely and take into account market expectations, and in that context determine whether the sum agreed was commercially justifiable or not oppressive.[40] This was particularly the case where the parties were in positions of comparable bargaining power and access to informed legal advice. The new approach has inevitably increased the judicial reluctance to intervene and strengthened the predisposition to uphold liquidate damages clauses.[41]

**31.** The guidelines set out in *Dunlop Pneumatic Tyre Co Ltd v New Garage & Motor Co Ltd* are therefore to be approached cautiously. Only when the commercial context fails to provide any justification will a clause which is extravagant and unconscionable in relation to the greatest conceivable loss be struck down as a penalty.[42] In *General Trading Co (Holdings Ltd v Richmond Corp Ltd*[43] the commercial judge, obiter dictum, confessed that his first inclination was to consider the provision before him, namely an undertaking to procure a loan guarantee, breach of which would result in the loan notes being cancelled, a penalty. But applying the broader approach he arrived at a contrary conclusion, as the clause was commercially justifiable, did not amount to oppression and was negotiated and freely entered into by parties of comparable bargaining power.

**32.** More recently, in *Cavendish Square Holdings BV and another v Makdessi*[44] the Court of Appeal affirmed the broader test when considering whether a clause was extravagant and unconscionable with the predominant purpose of deterrence. The development in the modern law was considered to be a reversion to the foundation of the law as expressed in the observations of the Earl of Halsbury LC in relation to the appropriate test to be applied to the agreement of the parties – "whether it is ...

36 Lordsvale Finance plc v Bank of Zambia [1996] QB 752; Cine Bes Filmcilik ve Yapimclik v United International Pictures [2003] EWCA Civ 1669, [2004] 1 CLC 401.

37 [2005] EWCA Civ 963, [2005] IRLR 946.

38 Ibid per Clarke LJ.

39 Ibid per Buxton LJ[115].

40 For a recent review of the law, see Cavendish Square Holdings BV and another, *supra*.

41 Alfred Mc Alpine Capital Projects Ltd v Tilebox Ltd, *supra*.

42 General Trading Co (Holdings)Ltd v Richmond Corp Ltd [2008] EWHC 1479(Comm), [2008] 2 Lloyd's Rep 475; Tullet Prebon Group Ltd v El- Hjjali [2008] EWHC 1924(QB).

43 [2008] EWHC 1479(Comm),[2008] 2 Lloyd's Rep 475.

44 [2013]EWCA Civ 1539, [2014] 2 All ER(Comm)125.

unconscionable and extravagant, and one which no court ought to allow to be enforced".[45] The latter phrase foreshadowing the modern appeal to considerations of commercial justification.

**33.** It has previously been observed that the test relating to the characterisation of the clause is to be applied at the time the contract was entered into and not the time of breach.[46] This is an important feature of the law and leads to a number of conclusions, some of which are surprising. It explains why the sum payable need not be precisely equivalent to the injured party's actual loss[47], and why it may be payable even though the claimant has not suffered any loss. It also explains why a clause may be struck down as a penalty even though the loss actually suffered is greater than the sum stipulated. This is a paradoxical situation but it may be produced by changed circumstances.[48]

**34.** Throughout this discussion the presumption has been that the agreed damages clause specifies a higher sum than the actual loss. Although rare in practice, it is equally open to the parties to agree a sum payable which is known and even intended to be less than the estimated loss arising from a breach. Such a clause was considered in *Cellulose Acetate Silk Co Ltd v Widnes Foundry (1925) Ltd*[49] and held to be binding, as it was not a penalty. It was also held not to be an exclusion clause.

## IV. Comparative Summary of DFCR and the English Common Law

### *4.1. General*

**35.** Both regimes recognise that agreed damages clauses are beneficial and supportable, and also that their validity does not depend on a precise equivalence between the agreed sum and actual loss. They also foresee that the right may be used abusively and that a remedy must be provided to protect against this mischief. It is in the provision of a remedy that they differ radically.

**36.** The DCFR applies only to the mischief of an agreement which provides for the payment of a grossly excessive sum. This fact does not impinge on the validity of the contractual agreement, rather a jurisdiction is established to intervene and reduce the agreed sum, if grossly excessive, to a reasonable amount, taking into account the actual loss resulting from the breach and other circumstances. This judgment is made at the time of the loss and when the jurisdiction is activated it results in the contract being

45 Clydebank Engineering and Shipbuilding Co Ltd v Don Jose Ramos Yzquierdo y Castaneda [1905] AC 6, 10.

46 Dunlop Pneumatic Tyre Co Ltd v New Garage & Motor Co Ltd, *supra*, p.87.

47 Murray v Leisureplay Plc [2005] EWCA Civ 963.

48 In Wall v Rederiaktiebolaget Lugudde [1915] 3 KB 66 it was held that in this circumstance the shipowner was entitled to recover his actual loss and disregard the penalty clause.

49 [1933] AC 20.

effectively rewritten. How a reasonable sum is to be calculated is not expressly indicated, at the very least it may be assumed to be the quantum that would be arrived at applying the relevant legal principles relating to the computation of compensation for breach of contract. On the other hand, it could be a larger sum measured by reference to what it would have been reasonable for the parties to have legitimately agreed in the circumstances. Beyond excessive damages, the DCFR does not address other kinds of abusive consequences which might be agreed to follow from a contractual breach, though these might be policed by reference to the duty of good faith and fair trading.

**37.** The English common law adopts a very different and more comprehensive approach. Under the law of penalties an agreement for the payment of an excessive and unjustified quantum of damages, or any other provision in response to a contractual breach, which has the effect of deterring a breach rather than attempting a genuine pre-estimate of future loss, is struck down as void. This response is justified on grounds of public policy and thereafter damages are assessed as if the agreement had never existed, in other words by reference to applicable legal criteria. But the validity of an agreement is assessed not only on the basis of the measure of the sum stipulated but also by reference to the extent that it may in the circumstances be commercially justified. The development of this two-stage assessment has served to move the law further in the direction of recognising the right of commercial parties to settle their contracts, including remedies for breach, and a corresponding reluctance on the part of courts to undermine such agreements. In the case of commercial contracts, where the parties are in comparable negotiating positions, a court would not be astute to conclude that the agreement is penal and void.[50]

## *4.2. Application to demurrage clauses in voyage charterparties*

**38.** It is of interest to conclude by considering the application of the two contractual regimes examined in this article to the phenomenon of demurrage in voyage charterparties. The universal adoption of the antiquated word "demurrage" has served to conceal the true nature of demurrage which is agreed damages payable when the charterer takes longer to load and/or discharge the chartered vessel than is prescribed by the laytime provisions. Within the industry rarely is demurrage spoken of in these terms and there is even the view that it is to be equated with freight, which could not be further from the truth. Unlike freight, demurrage cannot be freely negotiated and because of its true nature it is subject to the law of penalties when the governing law is English law, and should it one day become the basis of European law, the DCFR will also have a potential relevance. The application of the two systems may be best considered by taking a few examples.

**39.** Let us assume that a chartered ship is operating under a freight rate equivalent of USD20,000 per day, and an agreed demurrage rate of USD250,000 per day. It is clear under the English common law that the provision would be (save in the most exceptional

[50] Cavendish Square Holdings BV and another v Makdessi, *supra* [75] per Christopher Clarke LJ.

circumstances) a penalty and void. The agreed damages are disproportional and anything but a genuine pre-estimate of the loss, the probable true measure of which the equivalent daily freight rate would provide some, possibly a crucial, indication. There following the damages for delay would be assessed as if the demurrage agreement had not existed, by applying the relevant principles of the common law.

**40.** Under the DCFR it would appear clear that the sum stipulated would also be considered "grossly excessive". Thereupon, the demurrage agreement would survive, but the jurisdiction to intervene would be activated and the agreed demurrage rate reduced to a reasonable rate. There is at least the possibility that the owner might fare better under the DCFR because the reasonable rate prescribed might produce greater compensation that the computation of damages for delay under English law, but that possibility would depend on the way in which a 'reasonable sum' was interpreted.

**41.** As a second example, let us assume that the equivalent freight rate is USD20,000 per day and the demurrage rate is USD30,000 per day. Under the DCFR this raises the question whether the agreed payment is "grossly excessive": it may be excessive but that is not of itself sufficient to invoke the jurisdiction to intervene. The agreed payment is set at a rate which is 50% higher than the equivalent freight rate, which may be considered the prima facie loss, though there may be factors in individual cases which would enhance the actual loss and in each case the precise measure of the loss would be assessed at the time it was felt. Nonetheless, under the DFCR there arises a difficult question of degree and there is presently little guidance how it would be judged. It is at least possible that the rate would be considered grossly excessive.

**42.** Under English law there would again be some debate about the agreed demurrage rate and if it was exorbitant and unconscionable, but even if it were that would not be conclusive. The relevant test would apply as at the time the charterparty was entered into, and simply because the rate might be considered high or excessive would not automatically lead to the conclusion that it was a penalty. It would be further enquired into whether the demurrage rate was commercially justified. In the context of a voyage charterparty many commercial factors could come into consideration, such as the risk of cancellation of a future charterparty, the risk of market freight-rate fluctuation, the potential costs that might be incurred to recover valid demurrage and the costs associated with the maintenance of the vessel. These particular heads of commercial risk could be coupled with the wider commercial and shipping practice relating to the setting of demurrage rates, and commercial justification established for the excess. There is not clearly present in the facts the notion of a penalty or oppression: USD10,000 per day is not a significant sum in commercial shipping.

## IUS COMMUNE EUROPAEUM

A peer-reviewed book series in which the common foundations of the legal systems of the Member States of the European Union are the central focus.

The *Ius Commune Europaeum* series includes horizontal comparative legal studies as well as studies on the effect of treaties within the national legal systems. All the classic fields of law are covered. The books are published in various European languages under the auspices of METRO, the Institute for Transnational Legal Research at Maastricht University.



Recently published:
Volume 124: *Inside Policy Custody. Training Framework on the Provisions of Suspects' Rights*, T. Spronken, J. Blackstock, E. Lloyd-Cape, J. Hodgson, A. Ogorodova and M. Vanderhallen
Volume 125: *Coordinating Ombudsmen and the Judiciary. A Comparative View on the Relations between Ombudsmen and the Judiciary in the Netherlands, England and the European Union*, M. Remac
Volume 126: *Legal Evolution and Hybridisation. The Law of Shares Transfer in England*, M. Solinas
Volume 127: *The Role of EU State Aid Law in Promoting a Pro-Innovation Policy. A Review from the Perspective of University-Industry R&D Cooperation*, M. Cisneros
Volume 128: *Tradition, Codification and Unification. Comparative - Historical Essays on Developments in Civil Law*, J.M. Milo, J.H.A. Lokin and J.M. Smits
Volume 129: *Nobody's Perfect. Comparative Essays on Appeals and Other Means of Recourse Against Judicial Decisions in Civil matters*, A. Uzelac and C.H. van Rhee (eds.)
Volume 130: *Legal Aid in the Low Countries*, B. Hubeau and A. Terlouw (eds.)
Volume 131: *State Aid and Public Procurement in the European Union*, S. Schoenmaekers, W. Devroe and N. Philipsen (eds.)
Volume 132: *Property Law Perspectives III*, A. Apers, S. Bouly et al. (eds.)
Volume 133: *Multi-Party Redress Mechanisms in Europe: Squeaking Mice?*, V. Harsági and C.H. van Rhee (eds.)
Volume 134: *Europe at the Edge of Pluralism*, D. Gozdecka, M. Kmak (eds.)
Volume 135: *Cooperative Agreements between Public Authorities. The influence of CJEU case law on national legal systems*, K. Wauters

www.ingramcontent.com/pod-product-compliance
Ingram Content Group UK Ltd.
Pitfield, Milton Keynes, MK11 3LW, UK
UKHW051927100926
8556IPUK00022B/1413

9 781780 683324